AF607871

FROM WORLD RELIGIONS TO AXIAL CIVILIZATIONS AND BEYOND

SUNY series, Pangaea II: Global/Local Studies

Saïd Amir Arjomand and Wolf Schäfer, editors

FROM WORLD RELIGIONS TO AXIAL CIVILIZATIONS AND BEYOND

Edited by

SAÏD AMIR ARJOMAND
AND
STEPHEN KALBERG

Published by State University of New York Press, Albany

Printed in the United States of America

For information, contact State University of New York Press, Albany, NY
www.sunypress.edu

Library of Congress Cataloging-in-Publication Data

Names: Arjomand, Said Amir, editor. | Kalberg, Stephen, editor.
Title: From world religions to axial civilizations and beyond / [editors] Saïd Amir Arjomand, Stephen Kalberg.
Description: Albany : State University of New York Press, [2021] | Series: SUNY series, Pangaea II: global/local studies | Includes bibliographical references and index.
Identifiers: LCCN 2020050107 (print) | LCCN 2020050108 (ebook) | ISBN 9781438483399 (hardcover : alk. paper) | ISBN 9781438483412 (ebook)
Subjects: LCSH: Religion and civilization. | Civilization—Philosophy.
Classification: LCC BL55 .F75 2021 (print) | LCC BL55 (ebook) | DDC 200—dc23
LC record available at https://lccn.loc.gov/2020050107
LC ebook record available at https://lccn.loc.gov/2020050108

10 9 8 7 6 5 4 3 2 1

Contents

About *Pangaea II: Global/Local Studies* vii

Introduction: From World Religions to Axial Civilizations and Beyond 1
Saïd Amir Arjomand and Stephen Kalberg

Chapter 1
World Religions, Civilizations, and the Axial Age 11
Björn Wittrock

Chapter 2
Ideas *and* Interests: From Weber's *Protestant Ethic* to the Later Writings on the Sociology of Religion 49
Stephen Kalberg

Chapter 3
Karl Jaspers on Paradigmatic Individuals: A Complement to His Concept of the Axial Age and a Subtype of Weber's Concept of Charisma 67
Victor Lidz

Chapter 4
Shadows of Forgotten Ancestors: Some Forerunners and Followers of Max Weber's Protestant Ethic Thesis in France and Brazil 95
Roberto Motta

Chapter 5
Images of Natural Order and Rulership by Measure, Number, and Weight, in the Hellenistic-Roman Era: A Study of Intercivilizational Encounters 115
Donald A. Nielsen

Chapter 6
The Pioneers of Islamicate Civilizational Analysis 135
Saïd Amir Arjomand

Chapter 7
More (or Less) than a Civilizational "Formation"? Islam as the "Black Hole" of Comparative Civilizational Analysis 161
Armando Salvatore

Chapter 8
The Reception of Axial Age Legacies: Christianization and the Byzantinization of Russia 183
Yulia Prozorova

Chapter 9
The Forgotten Earth: Nature, World Religions, and Worldlessness in the Legacy of the Axial Age/Moral Revolution 209
Eugene Halton

Conclusion 239
Saïd Amir Arjomand

Contributors 249

Index 253

About *Pangaea II: Global/Local Studies*

This book series of the Stony Brook Institute for Global Studies engages the global challenges confronting humankind with research, analysis, and education. It aims at empowering individuals and communities to enjoy the benefits and avoid the dangers of globalization. Without political partisanship, the Stony Brook Institute for Global Studies will form worldwide partnerships with those who appreciate the vital contribution of academic excellence to achieving these aims. In so doing, it should also contribute to the extension of human rights, security, freedom, and democracy in accord with the diversity of values and cultures throughout the world.

A civilizational project of the global age, Pangaea II is emerging on the scattered geobody that our world maps depict. Pushed forward by globalization and technoscience, Pangaea II is eclipsing the configurations of nature. For the ubiquitous images, sounds, and texts of Pangaea II, earth's current fragmentation into regions, cultures, continents, and islands has vanished. Rapidly branching communication and transportation networks are interweaving widely distributed societies. TV, telephony, and e-mail have escaped from the gravity of the geobody. Pangaea II is pulling the planet together and colonizing near-earth space. Vanquishing the geographic difference between halfway down the corridor and halfway around the globe, Pangaea II is a dense global conglomeration with physical and metaphysical features such as the routers of the internet and the fallacious belief that global communication should be easy because it has become instant.

Pangaea II: Global/Local Studies is committed to interdisciplinary social science and the integration of fact and theory in a global context. As the hegemony of the Western center of the world system wanes, and with it that of metropolitan social theory, pluralistic approaches to research grow and multiple centers of learning around the globe emerge. We believe in opening the social sciences, removing old disciplinary boundaries, and exploring the intricate dialectic of the global and the local in the production of knowledge. This series embraces the epistemic challenge of the global age; it privileges comparative and interdisciplinary approaches to illuminate the simultaneous local generalization of the global and the global constitution of the local. Understanding this dialectic at the core of globalization and globality is the goal of Pangaea II. Accordingly, the global/local studies published under *Pangaea II* combine comparative, universal theorizing with various approaches to local knowledge on national and regional topics.

Saïd Amir Arjomand and Wolf Schäfer

Introduction

From World Religions to Axial Civilizations and Beyond

Saïd Amir Arjomand and Stephen Kalberg

The founding fathers of sociology in its classical period, Émile Durkheim (d. 1917) and Max Weber (d. 1920), have been long proclaimed as theorists of modernization. In truth, however, both abjured a general theory of modern society and were committed to an empirically grounded, comparative-historical sociology as the key toward an explanation of Western modernity. Durkheim (1982[1895], 139) went so far as to declare: "Comparative sociology is not a particular branch of sociology; it is sociology itself!" He further demonstrated his commitment to comparative sociology in a note on civilizations co-authored with his nephew, Marcel Mauss; here, he developed a concept of civilizations in the plural (Durkheim and Mauss 1971[1913]). Durkheim's students in France showed little interest in modern society and instead produced a remarkable set of studies of the Indian and Chinese, as well as ancient Greek and Egyptian, civilizations (Arjomand 2010).

There can be no doubt that Max Weber sought after 1910 or 1911 to understand why the West was the earliest civilization to develop *modern* capitalism and the "rationalization" of "this-worldly" conduct systematically. He sought to do so through a series of highly comparative sociological analyses that placed the "world religions" at the forefront. Major civilizations, he believed, usually developed in reference to them. Interestingly, Weber never used the term *civilization* (as did his brother Alfred). Instead, he viewed regions as civilizational zones (*Kulturkreisen* or *Kulturwelten*), most of which had been strongly influenced by a world religion.

Some four decades later, Weber's younger colleague and friend Karl Jaspers (d. 1969) shifted Weber's pivotal focus on salvation on the one hand and the connection between world religions and sociocultural transformations on the other hand to the nature of the transcendent realm. In doing so, he broadened Weber's civilizational scope to include Greek philosophy. Jaspers then located the radical Greek anthropocentric breakthrough in relation to the theocentric breakthrough of Hebrew prophecy and to major value configurations in Asian religions (Hinduism, Buddhism, and Confucianism). He stressed that these breakthroughs occurred in roughly the same historical period—namely, in the mid-first millennium before the Common Era. He called this epoch the Axial Age.

Durkheimians are rare in the second generation of comparative sociologists. Nonetheless, there are notable exceptions, such as Louis Dumont, who published *Homo Hierarchicus* in 1967, and Joseph Chelhod, whose work in the sociology of Islam is discussed in chapter 6. The Durkheimian mode of studying non-Western societies moved to Britain and mainly assumed the form of Radcliffe-Brown's general—and noncomparative—theory: structural functionalism. Eisenstadt opposed this school's tradition-modernity dichotomy sharply and introduced a "multiple modernities" approach. This depiction of modernity emphasized its *divergent* paths and its formation from the dynamics of—what he eventually would call—axial civilizations (Arjomand 2010).

Eisenstadt modified the primarily philosophical interpretation of the Axial Age by Jaspers by stressing a gradual historical shift in this age—namely, to what he and his colleagues came to call *axiality*. At first, Eisenstadt remained faithful to Jaspers and to the temporal component of the idea of a breakthrough to transcendence in a specific age. However, he and his followers had to resort to the idea of a "secondary breakthrough" in later periods and, at one point, in order to accommodate Islam, as Armando Salvatore contends in chapter 6, even to that of a "tertiary breakthrough." Eisenstadt later abandoned the notion of a secondary breakthrough, together with the idea that the breakthrough to transcendence emerged in a specific epoch in human history. Instead, he constructed a contrasting typological approach to "axial civilizations," one that conceived axiality as a configuration of elements and placed an increasing stress on the intertwining of culture and power in the symbolism and institutional patterns of axial civilizations (Arnason, Eisenstadt, and Wittrock 2005). The most comprehensive statement of the theory of axial civilizations can be found in Arnason's *Civilizations in Dispute* (2003).

Eisenstadt further drew on Jaspers's key idea: transcendence constitutes the regulative principle of the Axial Age *and* it remains effective in the "civilization of modernity" despite skepticism (see Silber 2011, 272). He eventually reached the conclusion that the civilization of modernity is a distinct, albeit composite, axial civilization comprising the *multiple* forms of modernity and the *different* paths to them laid down by varying premodern axial civilizations.

The aim of the present volume is to recover, examine, and expand the seminal Weberian idea that set this long intellectual journey into motion—that is, the fundamental assumption that world religions can be transformative forces in human history and hence can be considered foundational components around which a type of civilization—one we now call *axial*—can expand. Accordingly, we move from the examination of the dynamic features of several world religions to an examination of their corresponding axial civilizations. Thus, each chapter erects an analytical framework for linking a world religion to an axial civilization—either comprehensively (as does Björn Wittrock in chapter 1) or—more typically—partially, through concepts central to one or more components.

In chapter 1, Wittrock provides an intellectual history of the trajectory from Weber's world religions to Jaspers's idea of the Axial Age and to the contemporary theories of axial civilizations by S. N. Eisenstadt (d. 2010) and Robert Bellah (d. 2013). He shows how the idea of the Axial Age was in fact anticipated by Weber, and rightly considers Weber's collected essays on the sociology of the world religions, *Gesammelte Aufsätze zur Religionssoziologie*, the largest sociological oeuvre on the Axial Age.

Moreover, Wittrock places the entire trajectory of the conceptual development from the world religions to axial civilizations in the context of the rise, on the one hand, of the social sciences as the epistemic counterpart to the formation of the modern world and, on the other hand, of the debates since the latter part of the nineteenth century on the study of religion in European and North American universities. In this perspective, Ernst Troeltsch (d. 1923) appears in the first decades of the twentieth century as a significant historical figure beside Weber, and the abject predicament of Germany immediately after World War II provides the historical context for the return of Jaspers to Heidelberg and the publication in 1949 of his book on the Axial Age. Wittrock subsequently analyzes the changes in the axial paradigm from Jaspers's temporal specification in the history of humankind to the configurational conception by Eisenstadt of a set of characteristics found in axial civilizations and to the evolutionary scheme developed by Bellah.

Stephen Kalberg, in chapter 2, seeks to compare the mode of causal analysis in Weber's famous study *The Protestant Ethic and the Spirit of Capitalism* (2011) to the causal procedures in his later sociology of religion writings. Having noted that his causal argument in *Protestant Ethic* rests alone upon ideas and values, and that Weber himself calls for a more far-ranging multicausality in this volume's concluding pages, Kalberg explores whether Weber actually pursued such an agenda. He holds that he indeed sought to formulate and utilize a new causal methodology in his sociology of religion essays, one that recognized "both sides of the causal equation." Weber substituted "ideas *and* interests" causal procedures and strategies, for the *Protestant Ethic*'s "one-sided" and "incomplete" focus upon ideas and values.

Kalberg first notes that Weber's post–*Protestant Ethic* writings in important ways clearly continue this volume's stress upon the causal role of ideas and values; he calls attention to Weber's discussions of worldviews, salvation doctrines, and the "rational thought" of theologians. Nonetheless, his later studies on religion *also* attend to the "other side" of the equation, Kalberg insists. Economic, political, and status *interests* assume a pivotal part in three central analyses found in Weber's post–*Protestant Ethic* writings on religion: the discussion of the ways carrier groups influence the ethical ideals and doctrines of the world religions, the manner in which the routinization of the prophet's charisma occurs, and the different ways in which "lay rationalism" is formed and becomes influential. Kalberg concludes that Weber indeed fulfilled in his sociology of religion writings "both sides" of the multicausal methodology first articulated in *Protestant Ethic*'s concluding paragraphs.

Chapter 3, by Victor Lidz, turns to the works of Karl Jaspers, the author of the term *Axial Age*. The opening section offers, following Jaspers, a general definition of the Axial Age. Indeed, Lidz's brief overview provides a short-form introduction to several of this volume's major themes. However, he quickly moves ahead; Lidz does not seek simply to offer yet a further scrutiny of the Axial Age's major features. Rather, in one of Jaspers's late volumes, *The Great Philosophers*, he discovers a heretofore neglected, though pivotal, construct: "paradigmatic individuals." Lidz sees this concept as central in respect to one of Jaspers's overarching queries: How did the axial civilizations manage to cultivate and sustain a long-range impact?

In a sweeping analysis, he argues that Jaspers defined the Axial Age through his investigation of *these* heroic figures (Socrates, Jesus, Buddha, and Confucius). All are discussed by Jaspers in depth; their personalities, distinctive origins, and messages are examined, as are the social contexts within which they lived. A focus upon these Axial figures, Lidz contends, provides a "more specific" understanding of their features and broad influence than does, following Weber, an exploration of their charisma and its routinization.

Lidz stresses that any exploration of the impact of these paradigmatic figures must acknowledge the importance of their personal relationships with immediate disciples. Moreover, once the "direction" of a civilization has been established by these heroic individuals, it acquires a significant sustaining capacity. A certain "closing off" occurs, Lidz insists, and further leaders, if their message is to be heard, must present a set of related teachings. While Weber, he argues, analyzes moreso the long-range impact of Axial Age values, Jaspers attends to their short-range influence. His notion of paradigmatic individuals constitutes an indispensable aspect of his analysis of the Axial Age and its impact, Lidz concludes.

Chapter 4, by Roberto Motta, returns to Weber's *Protestant Ethic* and traces the "Protestant ethic thesis" of 1904–05 both back in the history of ideas to its forerunners and forward to its influence in contemporary Brazil and France. This informative discussion of the *context* for Weber's pathbreaking study reveals a stark contrast between pre-Weberian, monolithic notions of civilization and modernity on the one hand and, on the other hand, the late-Weberian and post-Weberian conceptions of civilizations in the plural and of modernities as multiple. The contrast clearly reveals the move from the former to the latter as an advance in scholarship. Most of the forerunners of Weber's Protestant ethic thesis discussed by Motta wrote in France and Brazil in the nineteenth century. With the notable exception of Tocqueville, all are now forgotten, even though the *Protestant Ethic* thesis itself still finds echoes in contemporary Brazil and France.

Chapter 5, by Donald Nielsen, offers a case study of intercivilizational encounters in the ancient Mediterranean world. He traces the unique ways in which the images of a natural order, as manifest in debates on "measure, number, and weight," are altered as they travel from early Judaism to Greece and then to Roman jurists, as well as to early Christianity. The distinct setting indigenous to each civilization and its intellectual elites influences significantly the particular adoption of this imagery, according to Nielsen, as well as its expansion in the adopting civilization.

He is convinced that his focus upon images of the natural order offers a research strategy that charts "emerging categories and rationales" in a precise manner, as well as their intercivilizational encounters. Indeed, it does so far more accurately, Nielsen holds, than those approaches that attend alone to large-scale and macrostructural alterations. Finally, Nielsen maintains that the varying ways in which civilizations viewed measure, number, and weight would not be adequately comprehended if the researcher's attention remained focused exclusively upon one cultural setting, for then "the confluence of ideas flowing [across civilizations that] forge new ideas and images" would be missed.

The next three chapters investigate two specific cases of axial civilizations: the Islamicate and the Orthodox Russian heirs to the Byzantine civilization. Arjomand discusses in chapter 6 the forerunners to the sociology of Islam from sociological theory's classical period onward. He argues that limitations of the Durkheimian approach in dealing with the transformative, civilizational impact of Islam as a world religion are due to the fact that it cannot be adequately explained in terms of its birthplace in the Arabian social structure.

He then turns to the work of Weber's student and colleague C. H. Becker, the author of *Islamstudien*, with the hope of in part unveiling Weber's own projected sociology of Islam. Marshall Hodgson's posthumous *Venture of Islam* (1974) is then highlighted as the pioneering second-generation study of Islam as a world religion. Its role in shaping "Islamicate civilization," as Hodgson called it, is emphasized. Arjomand argues that, through the Chicago Comparative Social Anthropology of Civilizations Project, led by the American anthropologist Robert Redfield, the influence of Weber and Jaspers was strong, albeit indirect. Be that as it may, Hodgson did not pay sufficient attention to the military and political importance of nomadic tribes in shaping the Islamicate civilization, Arjomand contends.

Conversely, Ernest Gellner, Hodgson's British contemporary who had worked on the Berber tribes of Mount Atlas, recognized the importance of the tribal component in the social structure of Muslim societies (Gellner 1981). He discovered Abd al-Rahman Ibn Khaldun (d. 1406) as its major theorist. In what he claimed to be his new science of history, Ibn Khaldun considered settled urban dwellers on the one hand and nomads of the desert on the other hand as belonging to two radically different forms of social organization to be found in all civilizations. The major changes under dynasties, in which prophets and religious reformers played pivotal roles, were accordingly explained in terms of two components of this dual social structure distinctive to the Muslim civilization: the interaction between the urban centers and the nomadic periphery (Arjomand 2019, 32–33). Gellner inventively extended Ibn Khaldun's paradigm to explain two forms of Islam: that of the Sufi marabouts in the tribal periphery and the "secularization-resistant" Puritanism of the Muslim bourgeoisie. These groups established the dual social structure of contemporary Muslim societies. In his conclusion, Arjomand turns to Eisenstadt's treatment of Islam as an axial civilization and its multiple modernities. The Jacobin variety, Eisenstadt maintains, is manifest in Islamic fundamentalism.

Marshall Hodgson also occupies the center stage in chapter 7, by Armando Salvatore. Here, Hodgson's notion of "Islamdom" is viewed as a unique phenomenon in world history: a trans-civilizational multiverse rather than a universe. Islam spans entropically over vast distances in the Afro-Asian landmass and, *pace* Weber's idea of a world religion and its core, which Salvatore sees as Euro-Christocentric, was not tied to a fixed origin. Instead, it constantly expanded into a powerful "black hole" endowed with a high capacity for trans-civilizational absorption and processing. Hodgson, Salvatore's argument implies, short-sold the Islam-centered perspective for revisiting the very notions of "civilization" and "civilizational formation" by fitting them into an "Islamicate civilization" straightjacket, as discussed by Arjomand in the previous chapter (6).

Salvatore humorously points out that Islam was only half-heartedly admitted into the civilizational club by Eisenstadt, first, for it represented only a secondary—if not a "tertiary"—breakthrough into axiality. He acknowledged Islam only later as a full member, although even then arguing that Islam/Islamdom remains an awkward member of the club and a misfit. Thus, Salvatore challenges the appropriateness of the very concept of "world religion" to describe Islam and the suitability of using it as the core of an axial civilization comparable to the Western, the Chinese, and the Indian, as is done in the prevailing civilizational analysis paradigm. Salvatore's argument, in a nutshell, is that the intercivilizational properties of Islam should be taken as the benchmark for the comparative analysis of other civilizational formations, including Eisenstadt's Eurogenetic civilization of modernity. This provocative argument should be taken seriously.

In chapter 8, Yulia Prozorova examines the Byzantine axial legacy of Russia. Her account of how the medieval Rus joined what had been called the Byzantine Commonwealth directly focuses on the "religious-political nexus" that led Max Weber to characterize the religio-political structure of the Orthodox Byzantine and Russian empires as "caesaropapist." During the fourth to six centuries of the Common Era, Christianity had become closely associated with Byzantium's Roman imperial culture, which never underwent the so-called Papal Revolution of the late eleventh and twelfth centuries. Nor did Russia, as its heir, experience the Reformation that sundered Western

Christendom apart; instead, the land of the Rus succumbed to the Mongol invasion in the thirteenth century. As Prozorova explains, the Khans of the Mongol Golden Horde, who converted to Islam already in the thirteenth century, became the Tsars of Russia until—and even after—the rise of Muscovy in the sixteenth century. However, the rule of the Golden Horde gradually disintegrated and Muscovy was proclaimed the Third Rome at some point after the fall of Constantinople to the Ottomans.

As Prozorova shows in careful detail, the Orthodox Moscovite Tsars, as emperors of the Third Rome, transformed the *symphonia* between *imperium* and *sacerdotium* in the medieval Rus regime into the caesaropapist model. Russian Canon Law incorporated Roman imperial legislation and rescripts, including the maxim *princeps legibus solutus* (the emperor is above the laws), thereby placing the tsar, as the Roman emperor, above the law. Hence, the Orthodox Church gradually became a subdivision of the imperial bureaucracy. The relevance of this heritage should be evident to anyone aware of Stalin's restoration of the Russian Patriarchate during World War II and the post-1989 reestablishment of Orthodoxy as the official religion of Russia by Putin. Attention to these developments, however, would require a long chapter on Russia's multiple modernities, one beyond our scope here.

Our final chapter 9, by Eugene Halton, offers a critique of the axial civilizations paradigm for what it leaves out—namely, the earth and our rootedness in nature. Halton begins with a summary of his new book on John Stuart-Glennie (Halton 2014), whom he sees as offering a nineteenth-century precursor to Jaspers's idea of the Axial Age. Halton views the former formulation of it as superior owing to its grounding in an intuitive appreciation of nature.

He then provides an extensive discussion of D. H. Lawrence's tragic view of the Axial Age. According to Lawrence, the idealism of the Buddha, Plato, and Jesus (like the intellectualism of Weber and Jaspers) betrays a deep pessimism about life and alienates them from the living earth and the living cosmos. To this posture, Halton adds his own critique in the form of forgotten conversations with nature. Unlike Salvatore, whose critique engages with civilizational analysis constructively, Halton completely rejects the paradigm, owing to its severance of humanity from nature. As such, it offers a more radical critique than that of Salvatore; nevertheless, it too must be taken seriously.

Each chapter in this volume contributes to our understanding of the axial civilizations and to civilizational analysis in general. Distinct to each is a concern with the manner in which the world religions influenced the conduct of believers. They did so in ways that—following Weber—"laid the tracks" for enduring, even millennial, "cultural values." These values not only powerfully influenced the behavior of the faithful over millennia; they also set the *direction* for the development of civilizations for believers and nonbelievers alike. Hence, this volume sets major parameters for a further array of civilizational studies and a further array of cross-civilizational investigations.

References

Arjomand, S. A. 2010. "Three Generations of Comparative Sociologies." *Archives européennes de sociologie/European Journal of Sociology* 51, no. 3: 363–99.

———. 2019. *Revolution: Structure and Meaning in World History*. Chicago: The University of Chicago Press.

Arnason, J. P. 2003. *Civilizations in Dispute: Historical Questions and Theoretical Traditions*. Leiden: Brill.

Arnason, J. P., S. N. Eisenstadt, and B. Wittrock, eds. 2005. *Axial Civilizations and World History*. Leiden: Brill.

Becker, C. H. 1967[1932]. *Islamstudien*. 2 vols. Hildesheim: Georg Olms.

Durkheim, E. 1982[1895]. *The Rules of the Sociological Method*. Edited by Steven Lukes, translated by W. D. Halls. New York: Free Press.

Durkheim, E., and M. Mauss. 1971[1913]. "Note on the Notion of Civilization." English translation by B. Nelson. *Social Research* 38, no. 4: 808–13.

Gellner, E. 1981. *Muslim Society*. Cambridge: Cambridge University Press.

Halton, E. 2014. *From the Axial Age to the Moral Revolution: John Stuart-Glennie, Karl Jaspers, and a New Understanding of the Idea*. New York: Palgrave MacMillan.

Hodgson, M. G. S. 1974. *The Venture of Islam. Conscience and History in a World Civilization*. Chicago: The University of Chicago Press.

Silber, I. F. 2011. "Deciphering Transcendence and the Open Code of Modernity: S. N. Eisenstadt's Comparative Hermeneutics of Civilizations." *Journal of Classical Sociology* 11, no. 3 (2011): 269–80.

Weber, M. 1946. "Religious Rejections of the World." In *From Max Weber*, edited and translated by H. H. Gerth and C. Wright Mills, 323–59. Oxford; Oxford University Press.

———. 2011 [1904–05]. *The Protestant Ethic and the Spirit of Capitalism*. Translated and introduced by Stephen Kalberg. New York: Oxford University Press.

1

World Religions, Civilizations, and the Axial Age

Björn Wittrock

Introduction

Human beings seek to make sense of their existence by locating themselves in relation to other individuals, to societies, to the passing of time, and to possibilities of changing the conditions of their lives, and perhaps also by reflecting on questions of a cosmological nature. Efforts to achieve an orientation and knowledge along such lines seem to be inherent in human existence. In recent centuries some of these types of efforts have been pursued under the label *social science*. This term, and a set of related practices, emerged in response to uncertainties and transformations inherent in distinctly new societies and polities that came into being during the course of the last two and one-half centuries. This shift—some scholars would call it the formation of a modern world—had its origins in some parts of Europe but has come to have repercussions for the entire world. Efforts to grasp these transformations came to manifest themselves in different theoretical and disciplinary guises.[1]

Taking as the point of departure the call of the editors for a consideration of links between world religions and civilizations, I shall discuss the idea of the Axial Age against the background of the last century and a half at three junctures that are crucial both in societal and epistemic terms.[2]

One pivotal time period for the efforts at reconsideration of the nature and pathways of world religions and civilizations occurred in the decades around the turn of the twentieth century. Another critical period is the time around the middle of the twentieth century, and yet a third one occurs in the first decades of the twenty-first century. Each of these periods of change has as its background profound transformations in global patterns of appropriation, trade, and domination but also shifting cultural and academic landscapes. I shall highlight these shifts and contestations as they are reflected in the writings of a few prominent scholars during each of the three transformative periods.[3]

The half-century preceding World War I is an age in which the countries of Europe and North America undergo rapid change on an unprecedented scale. Their contacts with subtropical, tropical, and subarctic areas of the globe change from being largely commercial and colonial into becoming increasingly intrusive and imperialist. It is in this era that some parts of social science become professionalized in terms of associations, academic institutionalization, if on a limited scale, and go through a period in which basic conceptual categories are formulated, contested, and eventually standardized.

One important element in this process is the search for means to make sense of the other, of forms of life, of believing and doing, outside of the North Atlantic region. One focal point in intellectual debates in this period concerns the question whether religions other than Christianity should be addressed within theological faculties at European universities and how such religions should be regarded more generally.[4]

In this discussion, different assumptions about the origins and historical trajectories of world religions have to be clarified but also assumptions about the modern world more generally. Ernst Troeltsch and Max Weber are two important contributors to this debate.

In the middle of the twentieth century, the societal and scholarly terms of this debate were radically reformulated. It was in this changing context that Karl Jaspers's work on the origin and goal of history was published. In some ways, it represented continuities relative to the works of Troeltsch and Weber, in other ways it differed profoundly. I shall then relate the continental European discussion about the Axial Age to the works and views of the leading sociologist and exponent of modernization theory in the American context, namely, Talcott Parsons. I shall highlight the ways in which a natural link between Continental European and American scholars about the study of world religions, civilizations, and the idea of the Axial

Age failed to materialize in these years, and I will end by indicating that this was to occur but decades later.

I shall also analyze some features of current scholarly debates about world religions and civilizations against the background of ruptures in patterns of global economic power and hegemony but also shifts in the intellectual landscape and ensuing conceptual contestations of a new type. I shall finally indicate some features of an emerging scholarly consensus on prerequisites for further efforts to articulate a way of writing a contextually sensitive history and sociology of world religions, civilizations, and their global interconnectedness.

The Study of World Religions: Ernst Troeltsch and Max Weber

The period from the mid-eighteenth to the mid-nineteenth century was one in which Europeans came into ever more frequent contact with the inhabitants of other parts of the world and tried to understand, trade with, and, increasingly, to dominate and subjugate peoples and territories in Africa, Asia, and the Americas. Out of such contacts, disciplines such as anthropology and a variety of linguistic and ethnographic forms of knowledge emerged but also new types of medicine. Gradually, in the second half of the eighteenth century, there was also a shift in the balance of economic, commercial, and political resources that tended to give increasing weight to European powers relative to nations and societies in other parts of the world.

Similarly, there were signs that European cultural and scientific achievements were increasingly being incorporated into an imaginary in which Europe was presented as being no longer one among several civilizations but as epitomizing the characteristics of civilization as such. This imaginary became more prominent relative to an older conception that had depicted other civilizations as different, but not inferior, and sometimes also superior in some respects, as in the views among some Enlightenment thinkers of China as being exemplary in the way in which wisdom and power were linked in the conduct of public affairs.

It is only in the course of the nineteenth century, though, that ever-larger parts of the world became subjected to European territorial expansion and acquisition on a massive scale and that it is possible to characterize the entire age as one of imperialism. In this period, many European scholars and observers took it for granted that a profound divide existed between their own religious faith—most often varieties of Christianity, with a foundation in religious experiences of divine revelation—and other forms of beliefs and practices. Simultaneously, however, the nineteenth century also witnessed a gradually growing interest among European theologians in extra-European religions. In the early twentieth century, this ushered in a debate about the possibility of a sociology of religion and, indeed, about the scholarly study of religion in general. This is a debate, however, that has to be seen in a wider intellectual context.

Thus, this was a period that the intellectual historian H. Stuart Hughes (1958), in a now-classical overview, *Consciousness and Society*, described as one in which an earlier confidence in the universal applicability of a naturalistic and positivistic program to all domains of scholarship was waning despite advances across a range of fields in the natural sciences. At the same time, a variety of programs for the incipient social sciences were competing with each other.

It was also a time when political and social contestations within countries were becoming sharper, a time when deeper international scientific cooperation occurred amid an ever-growing volume of international trade and commerce at the same time as relationships between nations became sharper and more closely tied to armaments. Religion, its study and its roles, was in many ways at the crossroads of this variety of processes. At this juncture in time, programs were outlined for the systematic study of religion. Two of these programs came to be particularly seminal and exemplary for the study of religion in its historical and societal contexts, namely, the historical sociology of the Protestant theologian Ernst Troeltsch and Max Weber's strongly historically orientated sociology of religion.

A sociology of religion in general and of world religions in particular has to articulate a stance toward two sets of problems, namely, the following ones: First, on what grounds can a distinction be drawn between the so-called world religions and other conglomerates of religious practices? Furthermore, if such a dividing line can, indeed, be drawn, what then is the status of the so-called world religions relative to each other and to sets of religious practices of a more local or regional nature?

Second, is it possible to explain how and through which mechanisms world religions influence key societal practices and vice versa? In particular, what are the interconnections between world religions and those wider patterns of exchange, domination, and interpretation that may be labeled civilizations? Furthermore, are there features in some world religions that have been of key significance for the formation of a modern world and for its further efflorescence and radicalization? Is it, for instance, as Weber suggestively proposed, possible to outline mechanisms through which the emergence and growth of modern capitalism depends on a specific type of religious system of beliefs and modes of conduct? Can we, as Weber intimates more than demonstrates, discern tensions that emerge as a result of the unfolding of ever more radical features inherent in both religious practices and other societal and cultural practices?

Both Ernst Troeltsch and Max Weber engage with these problems. They do so in terms that differ in style, temperament, form of exposition, intensity of narration, and theoretical imaginary. Yet, both of them produce versions of answers to these two sets of basic problems for a sociology of religion that, for all their differences, tend to be compatible, complementary, and mutually reinforcing.

However, from its inception in scholarly works and universities in Europe and North America in the course of the nineteenth and twentieth centuries, scholars engaging in any debate about history of religion as an academic subject were confronted with an even more elementary question than the two discerned above, namely the following one: Should the dominant religion in Europe and North America, Christianity, be assigned a special, privileged position as a preeminently universalistic religion of revelation and salvation? Such a stance might be asserted and perhaps even imposed. However, in scholarly terms it required that two intellectual moves be made.

First, Christianity as a religion of revelation would have to be regarded as categorically different from the forms of tribal and clan religions reported by European explorers and administrators as they traveled across or conquered ever larger extra-European areas of the globe. Such a move entailed that religious practices among inhabitants in the subtropical, tropical, and subarctic zones, increasingly subjected to European rule, were assigned to fields of study such as folklore and ethnography and kept separate from those of theology and biblical and religious studies. In practice, most European and North American scholars adhered to a delimitation roughly along these lines. Second, another move had to be performed, namely, one that ensured that a distinction be made between Christianity and other forms of "higher" religion that bore an appearance of being analogous to Christianity in structural, semantic, and even genealogical terms and, possibly, constituting religions of revelation.

In order to perform this second move, some scholars, notably the Leiden Old Testament scholar Abraham Kuenen (1883), argued that a distinction be made between truly universal religions and religions that in fundamental ways were, rather, exponents of various ethnic or national properties. The upshot of this analytical apparatus was that, despite apparent similarities between Christianity and other religions with a vast extension, elaborate rituals, and theologies inscribed in books that had been assigned sacred status, it was in the end only Christianity that might be labeled a truly universal religion rather than merely a cultural and theological expression of a particular nation, a people, or a similarly delimited collective.

Already, at the turn of the nineteenth century, such an assumption about the superiority in terms of universalism of Christianity relative to other world religions was becoming, even though still widely held, increasingly problematic. This problematic position is reflected in the programs for a sociology of religion elaborated by Ernst Troeltsch and Max Weber.

In the German academic world, a group, mainly of theologians, emerged and gained strength within the framework of the so-called religious-historical school. It had taken shape in the 1880s and 1890s at several German universities, including Göttingen, Tübingen, Marburg, Leipzig, and Bonn. Its members argued for a strengthening of the study of the history of extra-European religions also within theological faculties of universities. Ernst Troeltsch was a key member of this intellectual circle. The group met with sympathies in several circles. However, as late as in 1901, Adolf von Harnack, like Troeltsch a Protestant liberal theologian and church historian, but of an older generation, resisted the idea that faculties of theology should create chairs in the history of religion in terms that reveal a deep emotional aversion to the idea of such chairs and of studying the histories of Christianity and other religions on equal terms.

Harnack was not alone in holding such views, but his reputation and position in the German academe was exceptional and he played a prominent role in academic and public life in general. He was also some years later, namely in 1911, to become the first president of the Kaiser Wilhelm Society (KWG), the precursor of today's Max Planck Society (MPG), at the time sometimes ironically described as the emperor's academic guards regiment. Hence, when Troeltsch and Weber addressed the theme of the possibility of a scientific study not only in the form of church history but as a history that treated Christian religion as one among several world religions, this was a theme of interest to many intellectuals, but within theological faculties and also beyond them was still an unorthodox stance, and to some even a scandalous proposition.

In the present context it is possible to indicate Ernst Troeltsch's stance in some of its outlines only by way of pointing to a small posthumous collection of five lectures, which he had been invited in 1920 to deliver in London, Oxford, and Edinburgh, *Der Historismus und seine Überwindung: Fünf Vorträge von Ernst Troeltsch* (Troeltsch 1924). The lecture, first delivered in Oxford, on *Die Stellung des Christentums unter den Weltreligionen*, is particularly fascinating (Troeltsch 1924, 62–83). It contains a strong plea not only for contacts and dialogue between representatives of different world religions; there is also a vision of the elaboration through such contacts of a quest for a deeper understanding of questions of human dignity as they appear from within given traditions, each with its tacit presuppositions and its place within a certain cultural and societal context. Troeltsch articulates a vision that the end result of such communicative interaction might be something much more significant than a vague generalization of values. Rather, Troeltsch holds out the possibility for the emergence of, to use Hans Joas's vocabulary, a new conception of the sacredness of the person, out of the particular conceptions of different forms of universalism inherent in different world religions.

For Troeltsch, this dialogical quest was advocated on the basis of an autobiographical account of the intellectual development of his own views. Thus, he tells how his own research gradually led him to a realization that Christianity as a religion with universalistic claims was nevertheless fundamentally shaped and permeated by the historical experiences of the areas in which it had taken root and grown over centuries in an originally pagan Europe (Troeltsch 1924, in particular pp. 74–83).

However, this sense of a common ground did not extend to forms of Christianity beyond the cultural sphere in which the merger of Latin-Romance and Germanic peoples had taken place. Thus, adherents of Eastern forms of Christianity, such as Jacobites, Nestorians, Armenians, and even the Russian Orthodox Church, fall outside of this image of Christian universalism, Troeltsch maintained, since they had emerged out of a different set of historical experiences and beliefs (Troeltsch 1924, pp. 75–76).

With an even more extended perspective, it had to be admitted, Troeltsch emphasized that a naive belief in something Absolute may be just as genuine a feature in non-Christian religions as among Western Christians, once it was admitted that different historical, geographical, and social conditions and contingencies had given rise to beliefs that were genuine but inevitably had a different appearance from those common in Christians belonging to one of the churches having their origins, whether in the form of adherence or opposition, in some version of Latin Christendom.

In other words, there is, Troeltsch argues, in all the "great and spiritual religions" a sense of "the Absolute." However, this sense takes shape in intimate interaction with the entire cultural system of which it has become an integral part. A sense of the Absolute, which goes beyond the contextual limitations inherent in a religion, may only emerge as the result of a dialogue and a quest that is common to all these religions and which may usher in a common objective that is as yet unknown.

In summary, Troeltsch comes to adopt a position, shared by Weber, according to which world religions were regarded as analogous in categorical terms and should be taken up in scholarly works from both a theological and a sociological vantage point. However, in contrast to Troeltsch, Weber came to develop a program for the comparative study of world religions but also of the cultural worlds, that is, the civilizations, of which these religions formed a significant part, at least in genealogical terms. The most extensive scholarly work, which was prepared for publication by Max Weber himself, are the three volumes, more than 1,400 pages of text, of the "Collected Essays on the Sociology of Religion" (*Gesammelte Aufsätze zur Religionssoziologie*). These volumes constitute a historical and comparative analysis of the early history of the great world religions.

There is an obvious parallelism between the delimitation in terms not only of temporal foci but of the very objects of inquiry between Weber's overview and later works on the Axial Age, in particular works by the two towering late-twentieth-century and early-twenty-first-century scholars who have engaged with this conceptualization within a sociological framework, namely, Robert N. Bellah and Shmuel N. Eisenstadt. In fact, Shmuel Eisenstadt's project in the 1980s and 1990s, in cooperation with Wolfgang Schluchter, on the Axial Age and the great world religions has Weber's collected essays as a key reference point.[5] This project, which I came to join in 1991, was inspired by a vision of probing the continued validity—and the need for a possible rethinking—of Weber's analysis in his collected essays on the sociology of religion.

Furthermore, while the point of departure for Weber's project is the objective of formulating and examining an argument about the causes of a specific form of capitalism in the modern world, a major share of the pages of the three volumes have, as already noted, a focus on the transformations that occurred in the period which many, if not most, historians of world religions have come to label the Axial Age.

This is true for almost all of the third volume, on Ancient Judaism, and for most of the second volume, on Hinduism and Buddhism. As for the first volume, it has, as already indicated, a complex structure with some 20 percent of the 573 pages devoted to four introductory, intermediary, and concluding sections, each with its own tone and emphasis. The remainder is rather equally divided between the two essays on Protestantism and one long section on Confucianism and Daoism, and the latter section has to a significant extent a focus on the Axial Age.

In his new major book *Die Macht des Heiligen* ("The Power of the Sacred"), Hans Joas engages in one of the most thorough and extensive discussions to date of Max Weber's sociology of the world religions.[6] One of the seven chapters of the book is devoted to the relationship between Weber's sociology and the idea of the Axial Age. It builds on earlier works by Hans Joas, including his monograph *Was ist die Achsenzeit?* (What Is the Axial Age?) and the major book edited by him and Robert Bellah, *The Axial Age and Its Consequences.*[7] In several others contexts, Hans Joas has also discussed the meaning and history of the concept. The new volume, however, contains what is arguably the most circumspect and thorough analysis to date of the history of the concept of the Axial Age, including discussions of Ernst von Lasaulx, Abraham Hyacinthe Anquetil-Duperron, John Stuart-Glennie, George Foot Moore, and Rudolf Otto, to name but some of the authors taken up by Joas.[8] I shall return to Hans Joas analysis in another context. However, it might be noted already here that he also refers to Weber's footnote no 1 on page 155 in the second volume of the collected essays on the sociology of religion, with its remark about the temporal simultaneity of the "first blooming of Hellenic and Chinese philosophers" and of the Israelite Prophetic Age. Weber, in contrast to Eduard Meyer, rejects the idea of possible "loans" between these cultures.

In his essay "The Axial Age and Its Interpreters: Reopening a Debate," Johann P. Arnason also discusses this footnote and Weber's interpretation of the Indian case relative to the "first blooming of Hellenic and Chinese philosophy." His conclusion is that Weber has, *in nuce,* formulated an Axial Age hypothesis.[9] However, it would appear to be at least as important for a discussion about the Axial Age to go beyond the footnote and to view it in the context of Weber's oeuvre. In such a context, the most relevant question is that of the overall structure of the three volumes.[10]

Against this background, it might be suggested that Weber's collected essays on the sociology of the world religions constitute the largest sociological oeuvre on the Axial Age to be published before the late-twentieth-century projects of Shmuel N. Eisenstadt with Wolfgang Schluchter and of Robert N. Bellah.[11] The possible exceptions to the validity of this assessment might perhaps be some of the works by, or inspired by, Benjamin Schwartz. Needless to say, nothing of this detracts from the fact that it was Karl Jaspers's book *The Origin and Goal of History* that introduced the term *Axial Age*,[12] even if its empirical part is just an interesting outline.

If this analysis, at least tentatively, is accepted, it entails that it is meaningful in terms of analytical categories to relate different Axial world religions to each other and to explore similarities and differences between them. It is precisely such an exercise that Max Weber undertakes in his collected essays on the sociology of religion.

In an analogous vein, Troeltsch also opens up for such an analysis in his essay on the position of Christianity relative to other world religions. This indicates the structure of a reasonable answer to the first analytical question posed above, about the nature of a demarcation of world religions relative to other types of ritualistic and religious practices. The delineation of the great world religions is not merely conventional. It reflects the status of historical scholarship on some of the major transformations in societal practices that occurred in the centuries around the middle of the first millennium BCE. Both Weber and Troeltsch draw on such scholarship and structure their basic arguments accordingly.

Several later scholars have come to describe these transformations with explicit reference to Karl Jaspers's terminology as constituting an Axial Age. However, what in the last instance is of significance is not whether a particular terminology is employed to describe some of these transformations but whether the transformations themselves are identified and assessed in terms of their causes and consequences (as Weber has an ambition to do in his essays). In Weber's case, this is an explicit ambition; in Troeltsch's case it is only implicitly so, but both arguments are cast in terms that are consistent with each other and follow paths that are to some extent parallel and to some extent complementary.[13]

However, the change of terminology is not merely a matter of convention. It also has consequences for the substance and orientation of an analysis of religions and civilizations. In Hans Joas's words, the shift from a discourse about religions of salvation and redemption to that of an Axial Age entails a sharpening of the focus of scholarly debates.[14] In the next section, I shall, if briefly, outline the conditions and implications of this shift.

Rethinking the World: Karl Jaspers, Talcott Parsons, and the Idea of the Axial Age

Max Weber's three volumes on the sociology of world religions had been published in the wake of what became known as World War I. Although

Weber, contrary to many other German—and American—scholars, long had been cognizant of and interested in the rise of American universities and scientific endeavors in the late nineteenth and early twentieth century, his basic perspective is nonetheless one in which science and economic progress is something that has been uniquely successful and characteristic of Europe and then transposed onto a broadly conceived Western world. In fact, such an assumption forms, as already pointed out, the premise for his argument in the two essays on Protestantism and the spirit of capitalism that, as mentioned, had been reprinted in the collected essays and appeared as the first two chapters of the first volume.

Weber's study of the great world religions is not only a magisterial work on the sociology and history of religion. It is also a global history that presents an overview of the state of the art of knowledge, as it looked in the early twentieth century, about the long-term history of different civilizations. However, as pointed out by Jack Goody,[15] the basic premise of the argument not only affects Weber's assessment of the situation at the turn of the nineteenth century, when Europe's leading position in science, economic innovations, and sheer political dominance, was undeniable, but, if indirectly, exerts an influence on the account of the long-term history of different civilizations; it is difficult to avoid, with this premise and without retreating into a vast compilation of facts, that these civilizations be described, and to some extent assessed, in the light of an eventual European domination. As a consequence, there is an implicit, but inherent, tension in Weber's work between this anticipatory perspective and the spirit of the argument in favor of overcoming a Christocentric perspective in the history of religion, which both Weber and Troeltsch had articulated at some length in academic debates.

The situation in European academia after yet another world war was a different one. Nowhere in Europe was the rupture entailed by this war more undeniable than in the German context. A country that had taken pride in its intellectual achievements and where academics since the mid-eighteenth century often had presented an imaginary of their own position as one analogous to that of the thinkers of ancient Greece now found itself looked upon by the world as a pariah nation, guilty of previously inconceivable crimes.

One reaction to this situation was the one articulated by one of the elderly masters of historiography, Friedrich Meinecke, in a small volume bearing the title "The German Catastrophe" (first edition, 1946). In this book, Meinecke outlines a historical development from the Golden Age of the time of world citizens such as Goethe and Schiller and their circle in Weimar—to which also Wilhelm and, to some extent also his brother Alexander, von Humboldt belonged—via an intellectually eminent but nationally focused Silver Age during the Wilhelmine period, to a stage in which Germany descended into the bestiality and nihilistic horror of the Nazi period.

In this situation, Meinecke and many German scholars saw their task as one of reviving a heritage of classical humanism and of Weimar classicism and also, one may add, the return to a traditional professorial university rather than the centralized university of the Nazi years. In the ensuing decades, this position came to be embraced in a variety of different forms, including also an East German, Marxist variety.

However, a few years later another prominent German scholar, the philosopher Karl Jaspers, who had taken a position in opposition to the Nazi regime, published a small book with the title "The Origin and Goal of History" (1949). Already at the age of twenty-six, Karl Jaspers, then a student of medicine at Heidelberg had met with Max Weber and had come to belong to the circle around the Master until Weber's death on June 14, 1920. Jaspers, who at the time had become professor of psychiatry at Heidelberg, and subsequently of philosophy, gave an oration in memory of Weber in the Great Hall of the university the following month. He also remained in contact with other members of the Weber circle, including Weber's widow Marianne Weber and his brother Alfred. In the following years Jaspers's scholarly fame derived mostly from his work in psychiatry and in philosophy of a phenomenological orientation, although he also wrote, for instance, a much-discussed book about the idea of the university.

In the period after World War II, Jaspers resumed his engagement with questions of higher education and learning. He was active, together with, among others, Alfred Weber, immediately after the end of the war, in efforts to resurrect the University of Heidelberg, which as a relatively liberal university had seen some 30 percent of its faculty, including Jaspers himself, leaving or being forced to leave during Nazi rule.[16] He also published a new version of the book on the idea of the university. However, in the international public sphere he became mostly known for his articles and speeches about the question of the collective guilt of the German people for the crimes committed during the Nazi regime.

Jaspers's book on the origins and goals of history is remarkable in several respect. It is one of the first systematic efforts by a leading European intellectual to outline a notion of history that explicitly rejects a Eurocentric or Christocentric account of world history. Jaspers pointed to the relatively simultaneous emergence in several high cultures of the Old World in the centuries around the middle of the first millennium BCE of the emergence of distinctly new modes of thought. These new modes displayed a greater reflexivity that went decisively beyond those that characterized the mythic thinking that in various forms had dominated earlier societies, whether tribal societies or large-scale Archaic societies. Thereby, they opened up new possibilities for humans to think critically not only about crafts and practical matters but about cosmologies, rituals, and political practices and, indeed, about thoughts themselves and their presuppositions.

Only with this type of second-order thinking, to paraphrase the late historian of science Yehuda Elkana, could humans transcend the limitations of their daily lives and of cosmological assumptions inherent in the rituals of their societies.[17] Societies up until then had been characterized by mythical thinking that was reflected in rituals that were not only designed to provide a sense of cohesion within a tribal or a larger Archaic society. In some of the high cultures, including, China, rituals aimed at securing coherence between the perfection of a celestial domain and the practices of humans in societies by bringing heavenly harmony to bear upon mundane reality. Ultimately, this was a matter of, to paraphrase the subtitle of a book published some years ago, "conforming Earth to Heaven."[18]

Axial thought extended such ideas by making a sharper distinction between a transcendental and a mundane sphere and thereby enabling a more critical stance to mundane reality but also an examination of modes of thinking about this relationship. Benjamin Schwartz has given the sense of transcending and critically reflecting upon the given world that characterized the Axial Age a succinct formulation: "Whether one deals with the Upanishads, Buddhism, or Jainism in India, with the emergence of Greek philosophy or with the emergence of Confucianism, Taoism, and Mohism in China—one finds a kind of standing back and looking beyond, of questioning and reflectivity as well as the emergence of new perspectives and visions."[19]

The term *Axial Age*, which Jaspers erroneously believed he had taken from Hegel, has engendered much discussion, not to say misunderstanding, and has perhaps also invited objections to the effect that the use of this term implies a teleological view, inspired by Hegel, of world history.[20] However, it seems reasonable to argue that Jaspers's argument is more influenced by Weber than by Hegel. This becomes even clearer when attention is shifted from the first section of the book, dealing with the past, to the two following ones with a focus on the present and the future. In fact, the second section, on the present, is not very different in its diagnosis from Weber's accounts of the modern world. However, by virtue of the fact that Jaspers's account carefully avoids exposing itself to an interpretation whereby a reader might come to believe that the author equates recent European history as portrayed as an approximation of what rationality might amount to—something that would have been inconceivable against the background of German history during the twelve years of Nazi rule—the strong affinity between Jaspers's analysis and Weber's may easily be overlooked. A further contributing factor is that Jaspers's book is the work of a philosopher and a public intellectual rather than of a strongly historically orientated economist, legal scholar, and sociologist such as Weber. Thus, there is little of the wealth of historical information contained in Weber's work reflected in Jaspers's account.

Apart from the authors already mentioned above, there are several others who worked on the history of the middle of the first millennium BCE from the point of view of broad traditions of scholarship with some common characteristics, including an interest in the historical dimensions of philosophical analysis, in the existential situation of humankind in historical perspective, and in exploring these fields with a combination of analytical and interpretive procedures.

Hans Joas has, for instance, pointed out that in the second volume (1925) of Ernst Cassirer's magnum opus in three volumes, *The Philosophy of Symbolic Forms*,[21] namely, in the volume that has as its focus "Mythical Thinking," there is a discussion that is not only compatible with what Jaspers writes later but in important respects comes close to investigating precisely what Jaspers describes as a key element of the Axial Age, namely, the transition from *Mythos* to *Logos* (Joas 2006). Similarly, works by Alfred Weber and later by Eric Voegelin touch upon at least partly analogous themes.

All these authors share an interest in exploring linkages between history, philosophy, and religion across regions and across time. However, it still seems reasonable to take the publication of *The Origin and Goal of History* as the starting point for the engagement with the idea of the Axial Age that has become a vital component of modern historiography, humanistic scholarship, and social science. This legacy was taken up by a range of scholars in the course of the decades after its publication.

In this context, it is necessary to mention Talcott Parsons, who since he was promoted to the position of full professor at Harvard University in 1944 and in 1946 saw the establishment of a new department of social relations there, comprising scholars from anthropology, psychology, and sociology, occupied a towering position in American and international social science, and in particular in sociology, at least up until the time when this department was closed down in 1970, and in some respects until his death in 1979, and in others for quite some time thereafter. Thus, Parsons was arguably the most prominent and influential sociologist in the United States for a period of at least a quarter of a century, and possibly for longer than that. During these years, he worked ceaselessly to articulate a comprehensive theoretical system that was meant to be of relevance to all of the social sciences and that also contained a clear focus on the development of human societies across time.

Parsons had studied in Heidelberg, where he obtained a doctorate in 1927. He was well acquainted with the works of Weber as well as with members of the Weber circle and family in Heidelberg. He also translated and introduced into American social science some of Weber's central works, including Weber's essay on the Protestant ethic and the spirit of capitalism. Furthermore, Parsons came from a religious family and maintained a strong interest in the sociology of religion throughout his life. In many ways, Parsons saw himself as both an interpreter of Weber and a guardian of his legacy. Early on, Parsons came to take a clear and uncompromising stand against the Nazi movement and its subsequent rule in Germany, which he saw as a mortal threat not only to Germany but to the world at large. Parsons had also met Karl Jaspers and many years later wrote the entry about Jaspers for the second edition of the International Encyclopedia of the Social Sciences.

Under these conditions, it might seem as if the stage would be set not only for an encounter but perhaps even a fruitful collaborative interaction between two scholars on both sides of the Atlantic whose work had been deeply influenced by Max Weber and his magisterial work on the sociology of world religions. In particular, the further articulation by Karl Jaspers of Weber's legacy in interpreting the long-term history of world religions might perhaps have attracted Parsons's interest.

However, neither Jaspers nor Parsons seems to have been inclined to enter into such a relationship. This may have had to do with differences in scholarly inclinations and interests—Jaspers was first and foremost a philosopher whereas Parsons decidedly was a social scientist, albeit one with strong theoretical and historical interests—but probably also with differences in personality and generally in styles of conduct and interests in life. However, in the early 1960s, Parsons started to prepare what was to become one of his most comparatively and historically oriented books, namely *Societies: Evolutionary and Comparative Perspectives* (1966).

Parsons's discussion of Ancient Israel and Greece as "seedbed societies" in that volume clearly bears the imprint of Jaspers's Axial Age, and yet there is no reference to Jaspers.

As part of this preparation, Parsons was also teaching at Harvard with two younger colleagues, Robert Bellah, sometimes labelled "Parsons's favorite student," and the young Shmuel Eisenstadt, who in 1963 was to publish the large volume that would bring him world fame, namely, *The Political Systems of Empires*, a book whose vocabulary and conceptual apparatus are more clearly influenced by Parsons's sociology than they are, perhaps, in any of his other books. Parsons's interest in these years was focused on cultural innovation in Archaic states, in particular ancient Mesopotamia and Egypt, and the emergence of a divergence between the form of representation of political rulership and the representation of the human condition as such. He believed that this divergence entailed the end of a period when human rulers could be gods.

In other words, Parsons had formulated what the German Egyptologist Jan Assmann was later to call the Mosaic distinction. A distinction of this type, Assmann argued, marked the beginning of the Axial Age. On the other hand, the evolutionary delineation of three stages in the development of states and religions that appears in Parsons's work was later to be used and refined by Robert Bellah, who in this endeavor came to draw on the cognitive scientist Merlin Donald.

Expressed somewhat differently, the core of Parsons's evolutionary schema was preserved and assigned an even more crucial role by Bellah in his work on the Axial Age. This endeavor was to continue for more than a decade and result in the monumental volume *Religion in Human Evolution: From the Paleolithic to the Axial Age* (2011). A core component of this book is a well-researched and elaborate evolutionary account in which Bellah draws upon works by Merlin Donald.

Weber had been hesitant, painfully aware of the inner tensions linked to his basic analytical categories and to a society that for decades had been admired as a world leader in science but was now undergoing a development wherein all its antinomies and tensions came to the forefront. Jaspers and Parsons were writing in a different world from that of Weber and doing so from vantage points that were starkly different from each other. Whereas Parsons might be surprisingly close in epistemic and theoretical views to Weber, Jaspers echoes the tensions and antinomies that make Weber's oeuvre—and his life—intriguing and fascinating. With a gross simplification, which may nonetheless contain an insight, the situation could perhaps be summed up as follows: there are stronger analogies between Jaspers and Parsons than a superficial look reveals.

The Renaissance of Axial Age Theorizing: Robert N. Bellah and Shmuel N. Eisenstadt

It would not be Parsons's sociology, however, that would engender a renewed interest in Weber's and Jaspers's works on the long-term history of world religions and civilizations. Instead, the first strong impetus in this direction would come in 1975 from another Harvard professor, the sinologist Benjamin Schwartz, and a group of prominent scholars, including Peter Brown, Louis Dumont, Eric Weil, and Arnaldo Momigliano. They took up the notion of the Axial Age in a pathbreaking special issue of the journal *Daedalus*, devoted to the theme "Wisdom, Revelation, and Doubt: Perspectives on the first Millennium B.C."[22] Several of them later published major works that further explored these ideas.

Soon afterward the two young colleagues of Parsons already mentioned, namely, Robert Bellah and Shmuel Eisenstadt, embarked on research programs that came to retain their commitment and engagement for the rest of their lives. These two scholars are rightly said to have "done more than anyone to make the Axial Age significant for comparative historical sociology."[23] As to the substantive core of Axial thought, Jaspers and, even more so, later interpreters such as Bellah and Eisenstadt and their collaborators and colleagues have recognized the complexity and sophistication found in the long history of narrative accounts in the form of myths and the rituals associated with such myths, and also the multiple forms of Axial thought. It is largely due to the dual commitment of Eisenstadt and Bellah to focus both on detailed empirical scholarship and on theorizing opening wide theoretical perspectives that the idea of the Axial Age in later years has come to occupy center stage in social science debates and theorizing.

Bellah and Eisenstadt represent different intellectual styles, but both have been crucial in transmitting to the scholarly community at large a strong sense of the intellectual urgency of the debates around the idea of the Axial Age. This idea has been the subject of an increasingly intense but also increasingly well-informed debate, involving ancient historians, historians of religion and philosophy, and linguists.[24] Scholars not only in the humanities and social sciences but also in fields such as cognitive science have explored ideas of the Axial Age. Most notably perhaps, a range of theoretically orientated scholars such as Johann P. Arnason, José Casanova, Merlin Donald, Jürgen Habermas, Hans Joas, Charles Taylor, and Roberto Mangabeira Unger have come to deeply engage in the dialogue about the Axial Age. As a result, the Axial Age debate has now emerged as one of the great scholarly discussions of the late twentieth and early twenty-first century.[25]

Robert N. Bellah: The Axial Age in Human Evolution

In his late magnum opus *Religion as Human Evolution: From the Paleolithic to the Axial Age* (2011), as well as in the parallel volume, edited together with Hans Joas, *The Axial Age and Its Consequences* (2012), Robert Bellah explores in detail the different paths that led up to Axial breakthroughs in different cultural parts of the Old World, namely in Ancient Greece, Ancient Israel, and Ancient China, and plausibly also in the case of India. (As for Iran, Bellah refrains, with reference to the paucity and uncertainty of source materials, from analyzing this fifth "classical" case of an original Axial transformation.)

In Bellah's account, the Axial Age heralds the emergence of a new cultural stage in human evolution, namely, that of so-called theoretic culture. In this characterization, Bellah is inspired by the evolutionary and cognitive perspective of Merlin Donald. Bellah emphasizes that the Axial Age is expressive of the possibilities that opened up to humankind at the time of the emergence of a fourth evolutionary stage in the development of human culture.[26] Thus, from the earliest forms of human interaction in so-called episodic culture, over mimetic culture and the development of language and the possibility of constructing "a unified, collectively held system of explanatory and regulatory metaphors," a "comprehensive modeling of the entire human universe" made so-called mythic culture possible.

In this evolutionary scheme, the Axial Age represents a relatively early phase of the fourth fundamental stage, the so-called theoretic age that allows for a new type of critically reflexive activities. These activities complement those of bodily reactions and mimetic imitation and gesturing, as well as those of mythical narratives. Bellah also argues that this perspective serves as a means toward avoiding teleological reasoning. This is a convincing argument as far as the four, or possibly five, original cases of Axial breakthroughs are concerned. In this perspective there is no need to privilege any one of the five cases as being the precursor. Nor is there a need to construe a genealogy and to establish streams of influence and of borrowing. However, it seems less clear how an evolutionary perspective can help explain developments once the original Axial qualitative changes have taken place.

Jaspers had argued that a distinctive feature of the Axial Age was the emergence of forms of thought that did involve not only transpositions and variations of mythical narratives but new forms of thinking that clearly transcended the limits of existing practices of human society. This feature figures prominently as a key characteristic in the analyses of many scholars, including Shmuel Eisenstadt and Hans Joas, but also in the works of Robert Bellah. Bellah, however, also tries to construe the preconditions for the possibility of expressing a distinction between a transcendental and a mundane sphere.

One element in this line of argument is to emphasize that the Axial Age involved the emergence of a distinction between narrative and analytical accounts. Thereby, humans are not only able to give expression to visions and ideas of the world beyond the constraints of existence at a specific time and place, but the distinction also enables a critical and analytically orientated stance toward both material and intellectual practices and beliefs. Already for Jaspers this marked the transition from mythos to logos, a breakthrough in critical reflection and indeed the emergence of history in the sense of an epoch in human existence characterized by a reflexive, historical consciousness.

Bellah also devotes much attention to the question of the form of religious practices in two main types of pre-Axial societies, namely, tribal societies and large so-called Archaic societies. Thus, in earlier tribal societies, the invocation and articulation of mythical beliefs in ritualistic practices would normally serve the social and cultural coherence of a collective. They would, of course, involve practices outside of the bounds of day-to-day practices of production and reproduction. They might also involve or usher in changes in the collective life of a community. In this way, myths could be reinterpreted but also, more or less extensively, supplanted by additional myths, as could imaginations about the primacy of different forces or divinities associated with the different forms of myths. In large-scale Archaic societies with rituals performed by emperors or other centrally placed rulers, occasional and irregular, but inevitable, catastrophic external events involving, for instance, droughts, famines, pandemics, and flooding, might lead to questioning and reinterpretation but rarely, if ever, to a fundamental challenge to notions of an ideal cosmological or societal order.

In other words, in both types of pre-Axial societies, there might be, Bellah argues, instances of disruption, but which rarely ushered in more than a partial adaptation and not a critical reflection and rejection of some myth by way of questioning its premises or engaging in a comparative exposition of its merits and shortcomings in, say, a Platonic or Aristotelian dialogical form. This started only in some societies in the Old World around the middle of the first millennium BCE. This change was profound enough to justify the designation Axial Age and the identification of those civilizations where this first occurred.

In many ways, Bellah's argument is similar to Jaspers's. However, it is less philosophical and involves an incomparably more extensive and careful reconstruction of historical scholarship. It is also, contrary to Jaspers's and Eisenstadt's inquiries, grounded in—the expression "inspired by" seems too weak—an evolutionary perspective represented, as already mentioned, not least by the works of Merlin Donald. Interestingly enough, this link between evolutionary theorizing and psychology has also come to exert an influence on discussions in the field of cognitive science. Bellah's project on religion in human evolution was meant to be carried on beyond the original Axial Age. Alas, Robert Bellah's death in July 2013 meant that this project has not been finalized. Whether manuscripts covering later periods exist and may come to be published remains an open question.

Shmuel Noah Eisenstadt: From Comparative Historical Sociology to World History and the Dynamics of Civilizations

Shmuel Eisenstadt's early studies involved a focus on the study of cultural and religious practices and traditions. Already in these early works there was also one important feature that came to pervade virtually all of Eisenstadt's works, namely an emphasis on antinomies, inherent tensions and processes that have opposing consequences, and on a dialogical view of human action and of society. In 1963, as already mentioned, his early magnum opus appeared, namely, *The Political System of Empires*.

The new direction of Eisenstadt's research program gradually took form during the second half of the 1970s and the first half of the 1980s. These were, as analyzed above, the years when there occurred what might perhaps best be termed a rediscovery of both Max Weber's collected essays on the sociology of religion and Karl Jaspers's book *Vom Ursprung und Ziel der Geschichte.* For Eisenstadt, the hypothesis of the Axial Age held out a triple promise. Firstly, it might broaden and complement the institutional analysis of the political systems of empires. Secondly, it might provide, or at least suggest, an understanding of the emergence in some societies, as well as the nonemergence in others, of distinctly imperial political forms of rulership in some parts of the world at a, broadly speaking, similar period in time. It might also, however, and thirdly, provide an analytical account that would be less constricted by the somewhat rigid taxonomic categories of structural-functional analysis of Parsons.

Together with a prominent Weberian scholar, Wolfgang Schluchter, Eisenstadt made the idea of the Axial Age the focus of a sustained research program. He extended the analysis considerably and involved humanistic scholars in fields such as Egyptology, Assyriology, Sanskrit studies, history of religion, Sinology, and many others with an interest in an overall analysis of societies and cultures in their historical contexts and in exploring linkages between history, philosophy, and religion across regions and across time.

The idea of the Axial Age suggested a research focus that was related to Eisenstadt's earlier works and to his interest in Weber's sociology. It also provided an analytical framework that gave prominence to both institutional and cultural phenomena. Furthermore, it went beyond a North Atlantic perspective, given that the key sites of the axial breakthroughs were located in the Eastern Mediterranean, the Middle East, and in South and East Asia. In a sense, it was a form of analysis that had affinities with a cultural and intellectual cosmopolitanism that recognized the achievements of different sites across the world. Eisenstadt published a large number of monographs, edited volumes and articles in the 1980s and 1990s on the idea of the Axial Age. A succinct presentation of the early part of his project together with Wolfgang Schluchter is given in the edited volume *The Origins and Diversity of Axial Age Civilizations* (1986).

Eisenstadt's interest in the Axial Age was never that of an antiquarian. Rather, it reflected his sense that the momentous upheavals of the Axial Age provided an echo for the most deeply transformative events of our own age as well. There is a deep connectivity between his interests in antiquity and in modernity. In both areas, his original Buberian influences became gradually more pronounced and both his theorizing and scholarly style came to differ ever more from those of his former colleague Talcott Parsons. More precisely, for Eisenstadt, modernity was never mainly the successful end result of a process of differentiation and modernization. Even if those elements are relevant, modernity for him is rather a situation characterized by a lack of markers of certainty. As such it entails great potentials but also great threats of the use of violence.

In practical terms, Eisenstadt elaborated the ideas of multiple modernities in Jerusalem from the early 1990s but also in the context of a joint research program with Wolfgang Schluchter (at Heidelberg and Erfurt) and myself (in Uppsala). Some of these ideas involved exploring societal transformations in the course of the second millennium CE, what was sometimes called "early modernities" or, to use a term coined by the Sanskrit scholar Sheldon Pollock, the "vernacular millennium." In this context, Shmuel Eisenstadt and some of his colleagues elaborated what became an alternative to both classical modernization theory and to ideas about an inevitable clash of civilizations, namely, the paradigm of so-called multiple modernities.

In many ways, the age of modernity was for Eisenstadt an age of pervasive institutional and cultural transformation of a significance equal to that of the Axial Age. In fact, he sometimes described it as a second Axial Age, that is to say, an age in which new notions of temporality, of the construction of social bonds, and of cosmology ushered in institutional transformations previously unimaginable. However, in this respect modernity represented an intensification of features of the Axial Age to such an extent that it threatened to undermine its own conditions.

Moreover, and more systematically than perhaps any other social scientist, Eisenstadt argued against the identification of modernity solely with a Western tradition. Even if the contemporary world is one characterized by a belief in the potential of human action to change social and political conditions, there are many different sets of such beliefs and many different institutional paths. In works on India, China, Japan—in particular, the great study *Japanese Civilization: A Comparative View* (1996)—and on Islamic societies, Eisenstadt was able to demonstrate that these societies in fact exhibited both cultural and institutional features, typical of modern societies, at a much earlier stage and in much more widespread form, than scholars had assumed.

In works such as *Fundamentalism, Sectarianism and Revolutions* (1999) he consistently argued that fundamentalism is not a traditional but a distinctly modern phenomenon. Specifically, it is modern not only by the fact that its adherents tend to use modern technologies to the limits of their capacity. It is also profoundly antitraditional in its rejection of practices of continuous textual contestation and reinterpretation. Instead of such practices, the different varieties of fundamentalism assert the absolute and unchangeable validity of their own decontextualized interpretations of textual passages in those scriptures about sociality, cosmology, and temporality that they elevate to an ontological status of self-referential and eternal validity.

In practice, this tends to entail a social and political stance characterized by efforts to violently impose upon society at large a combination of political voluntarism, institutional enforcement, technological pragmatism, and intellectual curtailment and inflexibility. In other words, it means the emergence of cultural and institutional practices that are completely at odds with those of traditional institutions, be they classical empires, traditional religious orders, or the legal and political organs of preindustrial societies.

In parallel to his interests in the contemporary age, he extended and deepened his engagement with research on the Axial Age. In dialogue with a variety of historical experts he explored the emergence of axial forms of cultural and institutional phenomena in the first millennium BCE. Perhaps the most extensive demonstration of this from later years of his career is the volume *Axial Civilizations and World History* (2005), edited together with Johann P. Arnason and Björn Wittrock. In these historical contexts, Eisenstadt always pressed for a close inquiry into precisely those cases that might constitute the strongest and most convincing counterinstances to the hypothesis of the emergence of the Axial Age in those civilizations that had been highlighted by Jaspers, Bellah, and Eisenstadt himself. In the volume just mentioned those instance were the ones of Pharaonic Egypt and of Mesopotamia. The authors of these chapters, Jan Assmann and Piotr Michalowski, explored them in depth as possible examples of axial-analogous breakthroughs prior to the Axial Age proper—but came out strengthening rather than weakening the original hypothesis about the location of the axial breakthroughs.

Furthermore, Eisenstadt argued that many previous forms of ritualistic practice were, if in a different guise, continued in religious practices after the axial breakthroughs, and thereby contributed to the tensions and antinomies inherent in all highly articulated civilizations. Besides that, in the core epoch of the axial transformation, the fact that the most important proponents of the transformations had a peripheral and heterodox position vis-à-vis mainstream cultural and political order led to an opening of horizons and the emergence of a variety of critical voices. Eventually, however, the axial ruptures were, in Eisenstadt's view, given a standardized form and became more or less closely tied to new political centers and to new cultural/religious orthodoxies. However, they still retained a potential for the emergence of new heterodox interpretations that might take the form of a serious threat to central political power, no matter how closely linked the clerical and religious interpreters had become to that center.

This served as yet one more source of inspiration for Eisenstadt's fascination with possible parallels between the ruptures in some civilizations in antiquity and the revolutionary transformations of the modern age. It is not coincidental that while working on the large volume about the Axial Age, he also wrote a monograph with the title *The Great Revolutions and the Civilizations of Modernity* (2006). In both periods there was a crisis in terms of the, at least temporary, absence of markers of certainty. In both there was also an emphasis on the role of human agency to shape mundane reality so as to better conform to a visionary imagination of human amelioration.

This emphasis on parallels between transformative sequences of events had important epistemic consequences. It meant that Eisenstadt, while fascinated with the ruptures both in the middle of the first millennium BCE and in the middle of the first millennium CE (with the rise of Christendom and later Islam) as well at the end of the second millennium CE (with the Great Revolutions of Modernity) needed analytical categories capable of grasping the similarities and differences between transformations in distant and different historical landscapes.

Two strategies immediately presented themselves. Occasionally, Eisenstadt tended to deal with this problem in terms of temporal notions. Thus, one possibility was to recognize the similarity of later developments to those that had occurred in the middle of the first millennium by describing later developments, for example the emergence of Islam, as constituting a "secondary" breakthrough. This might appear as a convenient stratagem; however, with an increasing distance in time and space, the case for suggesting a reasonable genealogy tends to become weaker. As a consequence, it became rarer for Eisenstadt to use such terminology.

An alternative stance might be to distinguish between the temporal notion of an Axial Age and an analytical one of axial civilizations or features characteristic of axiality. This was an epistemic stance that was reflected in Eisenstadt's famous book about Japan as an example of a modern but nonaxial civilization. Even though possible, this is perhaps always an analytically satisfactory solution. An alternative way to proceed might be to recognize that at the core of Jasper,'s, Bellah's, and Eisenstadt's analysis there is an assumption that human beings, once they have acquired access to the means to record and store their memories and have recognized their capacity to change states of affairs in the world, cannot avoid the possibility of reflecting on their own existence relative to the passage of time, to their relationship to others, to their own finite existence, and to their potential to intervene into the world. These dimensions of human existence may, however, be given vastly different interpretations in different contexts, some of which might enable, while others obfuscate, different types of institutional practices.

Major institutional restructurings will tend to occur in conjunction with the articulation of different positions along such dimensions and, if deep-seated enough, to constitute something of a cultural crystallization that might create paths of developments of some endurance. In this perspective, both the original transformations of the Axial Age and those of the modern era—and, for that matter, those that occurred in the eleventh to thirteenth centuries at the Western and Eastern seaboards of the Old World—constitute such periods of cultural crystallization. Furthermore, in recent decades, historical social science seems to have arrived at a set of relatively well-documented hypotheses about conditions for the occurrence of such crystallizations.

Shmuel Eisenstadt, perhaps more than any contemporary scholar, explored these types of conditions for deep-seated change in human societies. In particular, few scholars of equal prominence in his generation maintained such a keen interest in the great variety of societies and cultures across time and space. These interests did not subside but became greater with the passage of time. Eisenstadt became ever more deeply engaged with the study of the world beyond the Atlantic seaboard. This engagement was also reflected in a dialogical form of curiosity-driven research that ensured him of friends, readers, and colleagues far outside of the areas along the North Atlantic where most historical social science at that time was being pursued. It is difficult to imagine a scholar more driven by intellectual curiosity than Eisenstadt, or anyone more interested in exploring the antinomies of human life and more prepared to expose his own favorite ideas to being probed in dialogue with others.

Contemporary Crossroads: Jürgen Habermas and Hans Joas

At the beginning of the twenty-first century it became increasingly evident that questions about the history and future of humankind could not be limited to accounts of the achievements of a relatively small number of North Atlantic societies in the course of the last two or three centuries. Shmuel Eisenstadt's proposal that the implications of a notion of multiple modernities be spelled out and that ancient history might profit from exploring the hypothesis of an axial breakthrough in human self-reflectivity, emerging at different global locations, reflected such concerns. So did calls for a renewed reflection on the nature of grounded knowledge vis-à-vis different forms of Faith and religious belief and about the possibilities of human beings using reason and creativity to overcome societal constraints and impositions. Toward the end of the second decade of the century, two prominent sociologists, Jürgen Habermas and Hans Joas, have each written a magnum opus that addresses these themes from a vantage point in which an analysis of an Axial Age is of constitutive significance.

Jürgen Habermas: Constellations of Faith and Knowledge and the Occidental Genealogy of Reason and Liberty

In his late magnum opus *This Too a History of Philosophy*, to quote the title of the not yet published English translation (first German edition, 2019), Jürgen Habermas explores the complex and rich genealogy of a philosophical and ethical tradition that embraces efforts to establish and articulate a conception of philosophy entailing the closest possible link between notions of reason and liberty.

This involves tracing a genealogy that takes as its starting point the period of the Axial Age. In fact, the idea of the Axial Age has been introduced by Habermas already in the preface to the first of the two volumes, the one with a focus on *The Occidental Constellation of Faith and Knowledge*, and is then pursued throughout this volume, being the main theme of the analysis for some three hundred pages, as well as recurring in many instances also in the following volume, *Rational Liberty: Traces of the Discourse on Faith and Knowledge*.[27] In this analysis, Habermas is elaborating an account that in many ways is situated in close proximity to Weber's account of the ethics of world religions.

In both volumes of Habermas's oeuvre there is a sustained engagement with the question about the relationship between an "occidental constellation" and the gradual emergence of a political philosophy with a focus on exploring inextricable links between notions of reason and liberty. However, Habermas's analysis also takes up ideas among some social theorists, including John Meyer and Johann Arnason, about properties of a world society or of a global, if diverse, modernity constituting a form of civilization *sui generis*. Thus, while Habermas's analysis has a focus on a broadly defined occidental genealogy, this does not entail negligence of or indifference to analogous developments on a global scale either in antiquity or in the modern world.

In fact, there is a near-book-length-long section in the first volume devoted to "a tentative comparison of axial-age world imaginations." In this section, Habermas has a focus on the same cultural worlds that Weber analyzed in his study of the economic ethics of the world religions. Thus, Habermas discusses ancient Judaism, Buddhism, Confucianism, and Daoism, and philosophical developments in Ancient Greece, but leaves the Iranian case to the side, as did both Weber, although not entirely so, and Bellah.

Habermas's inquiry is focused on ideational phenomena. It includes reflections on societal and contextual elements of these developments. However, an analysis of societal, economic, and even geographical aspects of the type that Weber, and to a considerable extent also Eisenstadt, engaged in, is not pursued unless there is an immediate relationship to the formation of different constellations of Faith, philosophy, and knowledge.

Habermas points to the fact that Jaspers had been stimulated in his effort by Max Weber's studies on the sociology of religion. However, Habermas emphasizes that despite these efforts of Jaspers, it is only with Shmuel Noah Eisenstadt that the historical philosophical concept of the Axial Age becomes the focus of an interdisciplinary research program. Furthermore, he stresses that it is only through embedding the concept in this research context, with social scientists playing a key role, that its seminal nature has become apparent; religions are, Habermas continues, not only reflected in the cognitive dimension of imaginations of the world but are also constitutive for the structuring of early forms of sociocultural forms of life in their entirety.

Habermas argues that through religious transmutations in antiquity, in particular the emergence of a Christian version of Platonic thought in the Roman Empire, an important point is marked in the development of elements: a genealogy that will eventually usher in the emergence of, to use Habermas's term, of a postmetaphysical strand of thought that in the course of the nineteenth century will become a linguistically interpretable embodiment of an idea of liberty grounded in reason.

From its early traces in late antiquity, he explores this genealogy into the medieval period and then analyzes further its articulations in the early modern and modern periods, with Hume and Kant eventually outlining two main philosophical paths. Thus, in this account the spelling out of a conjoined idea of reason and liberty is a phenomenon of postmetaphysical thought, drawing on Kant but, in Habermas's account, with a critically significant step taken with the emergence toward the end of the eighteenth century and the beginning of the nineteenth century of philosophical and linguistic notions, formulated by Herder, Schleiermacher, and Wilhelm von Humboldt. It is this step that allows notions of reason and liberty to be extended from conceptual formulations into ideas about how they might take societal form via language and communicative processes, with knowing and acting human beings at the core of the analysis rather than ideas about an objective spirit.

In this genealogy, Ludwig Feuerbach, Karl Marx, and Sören Kirkegaard but also American pragmatism, in particular Charles Sanders Peirce, are some of the significant participants in an exploration of the possibilities of formulating a postmetaphysical idea of reason and liberty. Needless to say, Jürgen Habermas himself has, arguably, contributed more than any other social scientist or social philosopher to the articulation of these types of ideas in the present age. Throughout the two volumes, Habermas also returns to and expounds themes that he has made pioneering contributions to earlier, including the theme of the legitimacy of rulership, incidentally, another instance where the research interests of Habermas and Eisenstadt meet.

Finally, Habermas himself has ventured outside of the occidental constellation to which he refers. But it is in the case of this constellation that his analysis has ushered in a rich genealogy that is pursued by way of a detailed argument at every step. However, it will engender an interest on a global scale. Hopefully, this may entice scholars to explore analogous genealogies in the history of philosophy and political thought of other cultural worlds. If so, the potential will be greatly enhanced for an understanding both of features of the contemporary world and of the emergence and grounding of these features in a history that has some of its anchoring points traceable to axial developments in different parts of the world in antiquity and earlier—and sometimes, if in transmuted forms, echoing down to the contemporary age.

Hans Joas: The Power of the Sacred and the Critique of the Narrative of Disenchantment

Hans Joas elaborated his ideas in a series of works with his book on *The Creativity of Action* (1992, 1996), outlining a comprehensive theory of action. In particular, this book refused to reduce the problem of action to a problem of the nature of means-ends-rationality. Instead, he also proposed that other types of action also be included, be they norm-guided or forms of transformative action that Hans Joas has analyzed in terms of the creativity of action. In a further step, Joas extended his inquiry to include studies of processes of the constitution and emergence of values and of commitments that come to identify the core of a human being. This is a main theme of his book on *The Genesis of Values* (2001).[28] Through this move he was also able to open up a realm of research that both the neo-analytical and the linguistic-interpretive scholars had tended to place outside of their concern and as external to analysis of action proper.

Joas then pursued an analysis of ways in which value commitments are consolidated and contested on a collective level as well as an analysis of norm-guided actions. His major study of this type had a focus on the emergence and the articulation of basic human rights over long periods of time and in different contexts. This work was presented in a major volume on *The Sacredness of the Person: A New Genealogy of Human Rights* (2011, 2013). The book stimulated a dialogue between scholars in social theory and those with a focus on legal theory. It also provided an example of how universalistic claims, inherent in notions of human rights, are not specific to a particular, occidental, tradition but might be arrived at from a starting point in different cultural, societal, and religious traditions. With this project, Hans Joas approached issues that had preoccupied Ernst Troeltsch in his efforts to discern pathways whereby human agents from different societal and religious backgrounds might, through human interaction and interpretation, articulate a commitment, expressed in universalistic terms.

This research program also had links to Joas's publications on the cultural values of Europe and on world religions and on the possibilities of extending an action-based analysis to processes of global change. With this step, Joas once again touched upon themes taken up by Troeltsch, Weber, and other scholars in the period of a reconstruction of European social thought in the late nineteenth and early twentieth centuries.

Joas's contributions in this field extend and deepen a historical understanding of the role of human action in the constitution of human institutions. They also highlight links between human action and experiences of a transcendental nature.[29] Thus, we arrive at the core of what was at stake, at the time of a reconstruction of social thought, in debates a hundred years ago about world religions and world history. In his already mentioned book, *Die Macht des Heiligen* (*The Power of the Sacred: An Alternative to the Narrative of Disenchantment*), Joas has chosen to focus on these themes and to outline an alternative to Max Weber's writings on disenchantment. However, there is an almost equally extensive and intensive engagement with the concepts of secularization, rationalization, and modernization. There is also a treatment of a range of other concepts, not least those of differentiation, sacralization, and ritual, as well as a discussion of the thesis of the Axial Age and of other historical, theological, and sociological categories, including, if more briefly than the ones just mentioned, the concept of power that also appears in the title of his book.

The inquiry into the uses and validity of the concept of disenchantment serves as a pivot for a scholarly engagement that reexamines the history of the social and human sciences, the role of contemporary social theory, and the interweaving of sociology, theology, and the history of religion. In effect, Hans Joas outlines a conception of the sociology of religion that draws on classic works by Ernst Troeltsch and Max Weber but that also goes beyond these works. In particular, Joas proposes a new interpretation of Max Weber's conception of a sociology of religion.

This interpretation is profoundly critical and argues that, through Weber's use of concepts that assign magical properties to religious categories, not least to the sacraments of the Catholic Church, a meaningful dialogue about religion and society between believers and nonbelievers tends to become preempted. Furthermore, Joas argues that Weber's concept of Disenchantment entails that there is no other way to a modern capitalist economy than that of an inner-worldly asceticism. This, Joas implies, is an unwarranted simplification. Inherent in Weber's notion of Disenchantment is also a tendency to exclude reversibility and processes whereby antinomies are actualized.

The first chapters of the book constitute inquiries into ways in which three (or rather more) disciplines have addressed the history of religion and the existence of religious practices. Thus, the first has David Hume's *The Natural History of Religion* (1757) as its focus. It highlights the way in which a moral philosopher writes about religion as a natural phenomenon with a historical progression. An important chapter has the title "The Ritual and the Sacred" and is a broad review of notions in classical and contemporary sociology and anthropology. The key protagonist is Émile Durkheim. It is a learned and carefully argued text that leads up to a conclusion that is significant throughout the rest of the book, namely, the definition that a ritual creates a controlled environment in which the mechanisms of everyday life are temporarily bracketed. This provides a setting in which ideal conditions may be experienced and after the return to everyday life remain in memory as an intense experience.

This definition appears reasonable. It also turns out to be useful in the further analysis. Two observations may be immediately suggested. First, the chosen definition is by no means limited to Christian religious practices. It would, for instance, be equally applicable to early Chinese religious practices.[30] Second, the definition is only applicable to the practices of so-called axial religions, that is, religions that are premised on the existence of a chasm between a mundane and a transcendental sphere and on the assumption that Gods do not inhabit a blurred zone, partially mundane, partially transcendental, nor that they appear in embodied form as kings, pharaohs, or emperors.

These exploratory chapters provide the background for an inquiry into the possibilities, as they appeared to be in the early twentieth century, for a sociology of religion and, indeed, for a scholarly study of religion. Joas highlights, as already discussed, two programs as being particularly seminal and as exemplary for the study of religion in its historical and societal contexts, namely, the historical sociology of the Protestant theologian Ernst Troeltsch and Max Weber's strongly historically oriented sociology of religion. This chapter is followed by one in which sacredness is interpreted reflexively and related to the concept of transcendence. The discussion of this theme has as its focus the idea of the Axial Age that is subjected to an extensive inquiry involving conceptual history, historical sociological arguments, and an examination of contemporary social theory in the light of recent research on the Axial Age.

Hans Joas has outlined some key requirements of a sociology of religion and, to some extent, also of world history in which the Axial Age marks a crucial juncture. However, it is in his analyses, as in those of Bellah and of Merlin Donald, not merely a temporal category. Instead, axiality also denotes an analytical category that may characterize tendencies in the contemporary world as well as in antiquity. In this sense, it forms one element in a vocabulary that also contains a rich conceptual variety of forms of human action and human institutions and in which both wars and catastrophic events may occur, but where there is also a potential, despite all differences, for human beings to jointly articulate values that may be characterized as universalistic and that may be respectful of the sacredness of the person.

Notes

1. I have addressed some of these questions in Wittrock et al. 1991a; 1991b; 1998; and 2017.

2. For a relatively recent overview see Wittrock 2015, Joas 2014, Bellah 2011, Bellah and Joas 2012, Arnason, Eisenstadt and Wittrock 2005, Arnason 2005,

Wittrock 2005, Joas 2012, Wittrock 2012. Bellah 2005 is a succinct statement of his basic position and attests to his lasting contribution to the Axial Age debate. See also Torpey 2017 and Strathern 2019.

3. In that context, I have in other contexts also discussed the philosophical background to the discussions about world religions and civilizations. For the period of the 1950s, for instance, two of the key protagonists are Carl Gustav Hempel and Peter Winch (Wittrock 2010).

4. The situation of European and American Universities in this period is discussed in Rothblatt and Wittrock 1993. See also Marchand 2009.

5. See Eisenstadt 1986; 1987; 1992. See also Schluchter 1996; 1998, and Schluchter and Graf 2005.

6. Joas 2017.

7. Joas 2014 and Bellah and Joas 2012.

8. See also Stroumsa 2018, 161–74.

9. Arnason 2005.

10. See also Arnason 2003 as well as Arnason 2010.

11. For Eisenstadt see footnote xxiv but also Eisenstadt 2010 and 2019 as well as Benjamin Kedar et al. 2017.

12. Jaspers 1949.

13. Some years after Max Weber's essays on the Protestant ethic and the Protestant sects were published for the first time, his friend Ernst Troeltsch undertook an extremely careful analysis of the emergence of and divergence between Lutheran and Calvinist forms of Protestantism in his magnum opus *Die Soziallehren der kristlichen Kirchen und Gruppen*, 1912, 3. Auflage, 1923, III Kapitel, in particular Section 3, Der Calvinismus, 605–794. Even if Troeltsch was a theologian, his writing is sociological and underpinned by a keen historical sense. The Protestantism part of his book takes up more than half of the nearly one thousand pages of the volume and the first section has the characteristic title "Das soziologische Problem des Protestantismus." What Troeltsch writes is compatible with the thrust of Weber's analysis but formed by a deep and detailed understanding of every stage in the early history of Protestantism. For an understanding of Weber's interest in China, the "Studienausgabe" to the volume of the collected works of Max Weber, Band I/19, provides interesting materials about the context in which Weber was writing and revising his study of the ethics of economy of the world religions as well as of its reception. See Max Weber, *Die Wirtschaftsethik der Weltreligionen. Konfuzianismus und Taoismus, Schriften 1915–1920, Studienausgabe der Max Weber Gesamtausgabe*, Band I/19, herausgegeben von Helwig Schmidt-Glintzer in Zusammenarbeit mit Petra Kolonko. Tübingen: J. C. B. Mohr (Paul Siebeck), 1991.

14. Joas 2017, 290 f.

15. Goody 2007, 225–40, in particular 239.

16. For an interesting analysis of West German universities in the first years after World War II, see Defrance 2000. For a meticulous account of university developments in the 1940s and 1950s in East Germany, see Jessen1999.

17. Yehuda Elkana, 1986.

18. Pankenier 2013.

19. Schwartz 1985, 3.

20. Hans Kohn (1951) wrote a short, appreciative review of the first German edition of Jaspers's book in *American Historical Review*. In this review Kohn translates "*Achsenzeit*" as "axis-period."

21. Ernst Cassirer 1925; English translation 1955.

22. *Daedalus* 104, no. 2 (Spring 1975).

23. The quotation is from an article wherein he generously acknowledges the significance of Shmuel Eisenstadt's contribution, a recognition that any fair observer should extend to include Bellah himself. See also Bellah 2005, 68–69.

24. This fact is most evident in the following publications, all edited by Shmuel N. Eisenstadt (Eisenstadt 1986, 1987, 1992) as well as in Arnason et al. 2005. See also Robert N. Bellah's magisterial works in this field in recent years: his monograph *Religion in Human Evolution: From the Paleolithic to the Axial Age* (2010) and his already mentioned co-edited volume from 2012 *The Axial Age and Its Consequences*.

25. One example of the relevance of the Axial Age for efforts to reach an understanding of our contemporary age is Charles Taylor's magisterial work, *A Secular Age* (2007).

26. Donald 1991, 214.

27. I have hesitated to use the expression "rational liberty" to denote the German term "*vernünftige Freiheit*." Instead, I have, tentatively, settled on using a circumscription in the form of a conjoined concept of reason and liberty. This is linguistically clumsy but avoids some of the infelicitous misunderstanding that might otherwise occur.

28. The German original, *Die Entstehung der Werte* was published in 1997 by Suhrkamp.

29. Joas 2004.

30. See, e.g., Puett 2001 and 2002. See also Loewe and Shaughnessy 1999 and Pankenier 2013.

References

Arnason, Johann P. 2003. *Civilizations in Dispute: Historical Questions and Theoretical Traditions*. Leiden: Brill.

———. 2005. "The Axial Age and Its Interpreters: Reopening a Debate." In *Axial Civilizations and World History*, edited by Johann P. Arnason, S. N. Eisenstadt, and Björn Wittrock, 19–49. Leiden: Brill.

———. 2010. "Interpreting History and Understanding Civilizations." In *The Benefit of Broad Horizons: Intellectual and Institutional Preconditions for a Global Social Science*, edited by Hans Joas and Barbro Klein, 167–84. Leiden: Brill.

———, Shmuel N. Eisenstadt, and Björn Wittrock, eds. 2005. *Axial Civilizations and World History*. Leiden: Brill. Jerusalem Studies in Religion and Culture, Vol. 4.

Bellah, Robert N. 2005. "What Is Axial about the Axial Age?" *European Journal of Sociology* 46 (2005): 69–89.

———. 2011. *Religion in Human Evolution: From the Paleolithic to the Axial Age*. Cambridge: The Belknap Press of Harvard University Press.

———, and Hans Joas, eds. 2012. *The Axial Age and Its Consequences*. Cambridge: The Belknap Press of Harvard University Press.

Cassirer, Ernst. 1925. *Philosophie der symbolischen Formen. Zweiter Teil: Das mythische Denken*. Berlin: Bruno Cassirer. In English: 1955. *The Philosophy of Symbolic Forms. Volume Two: Mythical Thought*. New Haven: Yale University Press.

Defrance, Corine. 2000. *Les allies occidentaux et les universités allemandes, 1945–1949*. Paris: CNRS Éditions.

Donald, Merlin. 1991. *Origins of the Modern Mind: Three Stages in the Evolution of Culture and Cognition*. Cambridge: Harvard University.

Eisenstadt, Shmuel N. 1993. *The Political Systems of Empires*. New York: Free Press of Glencoe, 1963. New edition with new Introduction 1993. New Brunswick: Transaction.

———. 1996. *Japanese Civilization: A Comparative View*. Chicago: University of Chicago Press.

———. 1999. *Fundamentalism, Sectarianism, and Revolution*. Cambridge: Cambridge University Press.

———. 2006. *The Great Revolutions and the Civilizations of Modernity*. Leiden: Brill.

———. 2010. "The Reconstitution of the Realm of the Political and the Problematique of Modern Regimes." In *The Benefit of Broad Horizons: Intellectual and Institutional Preconditions for a Global Social Science*, edited by Hans Joas and Barbro Klein, 3–14. Leiden: Brill.

———. 2019. "From Local Universalism to Global Contextualism." In *Sociology at the Crossroads*. Annals of the International Institute of Sociology, Vol. 13. In honour and memory of Shmuel N. Eisenstadt and Yehuda Elkana, edited by Shalini Randeria and Björn Wittrock, 153–64. Leiden: Brill.

———, ed. 1986. *The Origins and Diversity of Axial Age Civilizations*. Albany: State University of New York Press.

———, Hg. *Kulturen der Achsenzeit I: Ihre Ursprünge und ihre Vielfalt*, Teil 1, *Griechenland, Israel, Mesopotamien*. Teil 2: *Spätantike, Indien, China, Islam*. Frankfurt am Main: Suhrkamp, 1987; *Kulturen der Achsenzeit II: Ihre institutionelle und kulturelle Dynamik*, Teil 1: *China, Japan*. Teil 2: *Indien*. Teil 3: *Buddhismus, Islam, Altägypten, westliche Kultur*. Frankfurt am Main: Suhrkamp, 1992.

Elkana, Yehuda. 1986. "The Emergence of Second-order Thinking in Classical Greece." In *The Origins and Diversity of Axial Age Civilizations*, edited by Shmuel N. Eisenstad, 40–64. Albany: State University of New York Press.

Goody, Jack. 2007. "Weber, Braudel, and Objectivity." In *Max Weber's 'Objectivity' Reconsidered*, edited by Laurence McFalls, 225–40. Toronto: University of Toronto Press.

Habermas, Jürgen. 2019. *Auch eine Geschichte der Philosophie* [*This Too a History of Philosophy*]. Band 1: *Die okzidentale Konstellation von Glauben und Wissen*. Band 2: *Vernünftige Freiheit. Spuren des Diskurses über Glauben und Wissen*. Berlin: Suhrkamp.

Hughes, H. Stuart. 1958. *Consciousness and Society: The Reorientation of European Social Thought, 1890–1930*. New York: Alfred A. Knopf.

Jaspers, Karl. 1949. *Vom Ursprung und Ziel der Geschichte*. München: R. Piper. English edition, *The Origin and Goal of History*. New Haven: Yale University Press, 1953.

Jessen, Ralph. 1999. *Akademische Elite und kommunistische Diktatur. Die ostdeutsche Hochschullehrerschaft in der Ulbricht-Ära*. Göttingen: Vandenhoeck und Ruprecht.

Joas, Hans. 1997. *Die Entstehung der Werte*. Frankfurt am Main: Suhrkamp Verlag. English translation: *The Genesis of Values*. Chicago: University of Chicago Press, 2001.

———. 2004. *Braucht der Mensch Religion? Über Erfahrungen der Selbsttranszendenz*. Freiburg im Breisgau: Herder.

———. 2006. *A German Idea of Freedom? Cassirer and Troeltsch between Germany and the West*, Occasional Papers of the Swedish Ernst Cassirer Society, vol. 2. Malmö.

———. 2010. "The Contingency of Secularization in the Work of Reinhart Koselleck." In *The Benefit of Broad Horizons: Intellectual and Institutional Preconditions for a Global Social Science*, edited by Hans Joas and Barbro Klein, 87–104. Leiden: Brill.

———. 2012. "The Axial Age Debate as Religious Discourse." In *The Axial Age and Its Consequences*, edited by Robert N. Bellah and Hans Joas, 9–29. Cambridge: The Belknap Press of Harvard University Press.

———. 2014. *Was ist die Achsenzeit? Eine wissenschaftliche Debatte als Diskurs über Transzendenz*. Basel: Schwalbe.

———. 2017. *Die Macht des Heiligen: Eine Alternative zur Geschichte von der Entzauberung. Berlin*: Suhrkamp Verlag, 2017. An English edition will be published by Oxford University Press with the title *The Power of the Sacred: An Alternative to the Narrative of Disenchantment*.

———, and Barbro Klein, eds. 2010. *The Benefit of Broad Horizons: Intellectual and Institutional Preconditions for a Global Social Science*. Leiden: Brill.

Kedar, Benjamin Z., Ilana Friedrich Silber, and Adam Klin-Oron, eds. 2017. *Dynamics of Continuity, Patterns of Change: Between World History and Comparative Historical Sociology*. In memory of Shmuel Noah Eisenstadt. Jerusalem: The Israel Academy of Sciences and Humanities.

Kohn, Hans. 1951. Review of the first German edition of Jaspers's book. *American Historical Review* 56, no. 2 (January 1951): 327–28.

Kuenen, Abraham. 1883. *Volksreligion und Weltreligion: Fünf Hibbert-Vorlesungen.* Berlin: Reimer.

Loewe, Michael, and Edward L. Shaughnessy, eds. 1999. *The Cambridge History of Ancient China: From the Origins of Civilization to 221 B.C.* Cambridge: Cambridge University Press.

Marchand Suzanne L. 2009. *German Orientalism in the Age of Empire: Religion, Race, and Scholarship*. Cambridge: Cambridge University Press.

Meinecke, Friedrich. 1946. *Die deutsche Katastrophe: Betrachtungen und Erinnerungen.* Zürich: Aero. First English edition: *The German Catastrophe: Contemplations and Recollections.* Cambridge: Harvard University Press, 1950.

Pankenier, David W. 2013. *Astrology and Cosmology in Early China: Conforming Earth to Heaven.* Cambridge: Cambridge University Press.

Parsons, Talcott. 1966. *Societies: Evolutionary and Comparative Perspectives.* Englewood Cliffs, NJ, Prentice–Hall.

Puett, Michael J. 2001. *The Ambivalence of Creation: Debates Concerning Innovation and Artifice in Ancient China.* Stanford: Stanford University Press.

———. 2002. *To Become a God: Cosmology, Sacrifice, and Self-Divination in Early China.* Cambridge: Harvard University Asia Center for the Harvard-Yenching Institute.

Randeria, Shalini, and Björn Wittrock, eds. 2019. *Sociology at the Crossroads.* Annals of the International Institute of Sociology, Vol. 13. In honour and memory of Shmuel N. Eisenstadt and Yehuda Elkana. Leiden: Brill.

Rothblatt, Sheldon, and Björn Wittrock, eds. 1993. *The European and American University Since 1800: Historical and Sociological Essays.* Cambridge: Cambridge University Press.

Schluchter, Wolfgang. 1996. *Paradoxes of Modernity: Culture and Conduct in the Theory of Max Weber.* Stanford: Stanford University Press.

———. 1998. *Die Entstehung des modernen Rationalismus: Eine Analyse von Max Webers Entwicklungsgeschichte des Okzidents.* Frankfurt am Main: Suhrkamp.

———, und Friedrich Wilhelm Graf, Hrsg. 2005. *Asketischer Protestantismus und der ‚Geist' des modernen Kapitalismus.* Tübingen: Moor Siebeck.

Schwartz, Benjamin I. 1985. *The World of Thought in Ancient China.* Cambridge: The Belknap Press of Harvard University Press.

Strathern, Alan. 2019. *Unearthly Powers: Religious and Political Change in World History.* Cambridge: Cambridge University Press.

Stroumsa, Guy G. 2018. "Anquetil Duperron et les origines de la philologie orientale: l'orientalisme est un humanisme." *ASDIWAL: Revue genevoise d'anthropologie et d'histoire des religions* 13: 161–74.

Taylor, Charles. 2007. *A Secular Age.* Cambridge: The Belknap Press of Harvard University Press.

Torpey, John. 2017. *The Three Axial Ages: Moral, Material, Mental.* New Brunswick, NJ: Rutgers University Press.

Troeltsch, Ernst. 1912/1923. *Die Soziallehren der kristlichen Kirchen und Gruppen.* Tübingen: Verlag von J. C. B. Mohr (Paul Siebeck), 3. Auflage 1923, III Kapitel, in particular, Section 3, Der Calvinismus, 605–794.

———. 1924. *Der Historismus und seine Überwindung: Fünf Vorträge von Ernst Troeltsch.* Berlin: Pan Verlag Rolf Heise.

Weber, Max. 1991. *Die Wirtschaftsethik der Weltreligionen. Konfuzianismus, und Taoismus, Schriften 1915–1920, Studienausgabe der Max Weber Gesamtausgabe,* Band I/19, herausgegeben von Helwig Schmidt-Glintzer in Zusammenarbeit mit Petra Kolonko. Tübingen: J. C. B. Mohr (Paul Siebeck).

Wittrock, Björn. 2005. "The Meaning of the Axial Age." In *Axial Civilizations and World History,* edited by Johan P. Arnason, Shmuel N. Eisenstadt, and Björn Wittrock, 51–85. Leiden: Brill. Jerusalem Studies in Religion and Culture, Vol. 4.

———. 2010. "Menschliches Handeln, Geschichte und Sozialer Wandel: Rekonstruktion der Sozialtheorie in drei Kontexten." In *Handlung und Erfahrung: Das Erbe von Historismus und Pragmatismus und die Zukunft der Sozialtheorie,* edited by Bettina Hollstein, Matthias Jung, and Wolfgang Knöbl, 343–76. Frankfurt am Main: Campus Verlag.

———. 2012. "The Axial Age in Global History: Cultural Crystallizations and Societal Transformations." In *The Axial Age and Its Consequences,* edited by Robert N. Bellah and Hans Joas, 102–25. Cambridge: The Belknap Press of Harvard University Press.

———. 2015. "The Axial Age in World History." In *The Cambridge World History, Vol. IV, A World with States, Empires and Networks, 1200 BCE–900 CE,* edited by Craig Benjamin, 101–19. Cambridge: Cambridge University Press.

Wittrock, Björn, and Peter Wagner. 2017. "Social Science and the Building of the Early Welfare State." In *States, Knowledge, and the Origins of Modern Social Policies,* edited by Dietrich Rueschemeyer and Theda Skocpol, 90–13. Princeton: Princeton University Press.

Wittrock, Björn, Peter Wagner, and Richard Whitley, eds. 1991. *Discourses on Society: The Shaping of the Social Science Disciplines.* Dordrecht: Kluwer.

Wittrock, Björn, Peter Wagner, Carol H. Weiss, and Hellmut Wollmann, eds. 1991. *Social Sciences and Modern States: National Experiences and Theoretical Crossroads.* Cambridge: Cambridge University Press.

Wittrock, Björn, Johan Heilbron, and Lars Magnusson, eds. 1998. *The Rise of the Social Sciences and the Formation of Modernity: Conceptual Change in Context, 1750–1850.* Dordrecht: Kluwer.

2

Ideas *and* Interests

From Weber's *Protestant Ethic* to the Later Writings on the Sociology of Religion

Stephen Kalberg

Max Weber acknowledges at the end of *The Protestant Ethic and the Spirit of Capitalism* (hereafter *PE*) that he has addressed only "one side of the causal question." This volume has provided a "religion-oriented analysis" of the "spirit of capitalism's" origins, he holds. Its roots are traced back to the ideas and values that constitute "a Protestant ethic" (2011, 178–79).

Weber insists that his "case study" must be viewed as simply the "beginning stage" of a larger causal investigation focused upon the spirit of capitalism's sources. An *adequate* research methodology must stress *both* the "material and ideal sides of the equation" (2011, 178–79).[1] One of his most famous passages captures this aim:

> Not ideas, but material and ideal interests, directly govern men's conduct. Yet very frequently the "world views" that have been created by "ideas" have, like switchmen, determined the tracks (*Gleise*) along which action has been pushed by the dynamic of interests. (1946c, 280)

Weber never lost sight of his goal to investigate "both sides." Hence, a serious query must be formulated: Did he actually pursue an "ideas *and* interests" agenda distinct from *PE*'s presuppositions in his post-*PE* sociology of religion?

This question assumes great urgency once we recognize that several of Weber's discussions in his post-*PE* writings attend closely to ideas and values: they offer analyses of the causal capacity of worldviews (*Weltbilder*), salvation doctrines, and "rational thought." These discussions capture our attention in Part I below. They would seem to separate him further from the multicausal—ideas *and* interests—research procedures so abundantly praised in *PE*'s concluding pages. Our query remains: Did Weber abandon the multicausal goal pronounced in *PE* (2011, 178–79)?

His post-*PE* sociology of religion presents a complex picture: albeit not easily visible, it places at its core *both* ideal and material analyses (Part II). Three concepts in Weber's writings demonstrate the importance for him of *interests*—namely, "carrier groups," the "routinization of charisma," and "lay rationalism."[2] The conclusion of this chapter maintains that Weber's post-*PE* sociology of religion emphatically supports an "ideas *and* interests" causal methodology.[3]

Part I. Worldviews, "Rational Thought," Salvation Doctrines, and Weber's Post–*Protestant Ethic* Attention to Ideas and Values

Worldviews and Rational Thought

Worldviews imply a coherent set of values, Weber argues. Although they span a wide spectrum in terms of their content and internal cohesiveness, these "ethical orders" always address ultimate questions. What is the meaning of life? What purpose does our existence serve? How do we best live our lives?

Hence, rooted in shared cultural presuppositions, worldviews demarcate a moral universe and a cosmological vision. Both offer instructions regarding the meaningfulness—or lack thereof—of mundane activity. Meaning constellations in strict opposition to diffuse and random action, traditional action, and the practical-rational, utilitarian "flow of life" are articulated. Weber especially attends to whether religion-based worldviews direct the devout to "adapt to" the world (China) or to orient their social action "toward" (as in the West) or "away from" (as in India) the world. And does a worldview imply modes of social action that can be realistically pursued and fulfilled by the laity as well as by elites?

Both the *world and religion realms* may ground a worldview's expansive value constellation, Weber maintains. Secularized intellectual, social, and political groups may define broad-ranging sets of values. In other words, wherever worldviews congeal and become influential, social action becomes concerted and directed—perhaps even toward ethical values.

Thus, a disjunction is apparent: although varying in intensity depending upon the worldview's values and the forcefulness of their articulation, this "meaningful order" always sets standards in reference to which pragmatic action is evaluated. Adherents now query: Is my social action consistent with the unified ethical purpose expressed by the worldview's value constellation? Indeed, the *discrepancy* between an "ordered totality" and "irrational" earthly events itself places an *ideal thrust* into motion, Weber holds. To the extent that persons *cognitively* evaluate the degree to which their social action logically conforms to their perception of a worldview's values, a thrust is placed into motion toward patterned, value-oriented social action. For example:

> To the prophet, both life and the world, both social and cosmic events, have a certain systematic and coherent "meaning" to which man's conduct must be oriented if it is to bring salvation and after which it must be patterned in an integrally meaningful manner. . . . [This meaning] always contains the important religious conception of the "world" as a "cosmos" which is challenged to produce somehow a "meaningful," ordered totality, the particular manifestations of which are to be measured and evaluated according to this postulate. (1968, 450–51)[4]

In sum, Weber stresses that the integrated values of a worldview provide a deep cultural legitimation and ideational thrust for values-based patterned action—even for a comprehensively organized, "methodical-rational" directing of life (*methodisch-rationale Lebensführung*). Group formation, significant events, and history's development arise not only from the economic, legal, political, and status interests of daily life, he contends, nor alone from traditions, mundane values, organizations, power considerations, and rational choices. The transformation, for example, of Christian religious doctrine throughout the Middle Ages and from medieval Catholicism to Lutheranism, and then to seventeenth-century ascetic Protestant sects and churches, cannot be comprehended by reference alone to worldly action oriented to the rulership, law, economy, family, clan, and social status domains (see Kalberg 2012, 43–72).

Christianity's worldview, for example, offers a set of below-the-surface values that justify innumerable historical developments, Weber insists. The birth of the notion of universal citizenship in the West's medieval cities took Christianity's rejection of all dualistic, insider-outsider ethics as its deep cultural point of legitimation (see 1968, 1226–50). The ethos of radical equality and "brotherhood" in the congregation is scarcely conceivable, Weber argues, without the emphasis in Christian doctrine upon an "equality before God" and the *shared* status—as His children—of all. And the development of individualism in the West finds its ideational point of reference in Christianity's commanding and awesome God who proclaimed His children as "tools" for His Will and *demanded* ethical behavior of *each* person (see 1927, 315–37; 1968, 1236–62).

Similarly, the impetus for the unfolding of modern science becomes comprehensible only if the attempt by sixteenth- and seventeenth-century scientists to prove the existence of God through the discovery of the laws of the universe is included in the multicausal explanation; however hidden, their presence would offer proof of a superior intelligence, it was believed (see 1946b, 142). In China, the respect for ancestors and authority cultivated in the family mirrored the call for such respect and deference in Confucian values. And in India, the aim of the Buddhist monk to withdraw from the world in order to silence the inner being through meditation, and then to merge into the Deity, can be comprehended only in light of this figure's particular perception of the supernatural realm, namely, as constituted from a cosmic and immanent All-One Entity (see Kalberg 2012, 77–78).

In these ways, worldviews as moral universes stand "behind" surface-level occurrences and justify particular patterns of social action. If cultivated by powerful carrier groups, they cast broad shadows across millennia and across civilizations. They contribute coherence to history's unfolding. As well, they oppose all schools oriented exclusively to, for example, secular traditions, sheer power, and utilitarian axioms (see Kalberg 1990, 61–63). Constituted from configurations of values, worldviews directly extend *PE*'s "idealism."[5]

Attention to values and ideas is manifest in Weber's post-*PE* sociology of religion in another manner: in some worldviews severe tension exists across their values. A "dynamic autonomy" arises as a consequence and arguments rooted in logical deduction become overt as "theoretical rationalization processes."[6]

Weber addresses in this regard the problem of theodicy. To the extent that the universe is conceptualized as rationally ordered, unified, and a totality of "universal meaning," continuing misery becomes increasingly difficult to explain. "Undeserved" woe is now recognized as frequent (1946c, 275). If the universe has been created as a meaningful and unified cosmos by an omniscient ethical Force,[7] how can all forms of internal and external suffering continue to exist (1968, 519)?

This conundrum became the concern above all of prophets, priests, theologians, and monks. Solutions were formulated on a regular basis and believers altered their behavior to conform to new admonitions. Nonetheless, because hardship and injustice persisted, *rational thought* led repeatedly to one conclusion: the nature and wishes of the supernatural Being had been misunderstood. Further scrutiny of the worldview's values led to new definitions and new proposals for *ethical* action—yet distress endured (1946a, 353; 1968, 519).

In this manner, a dynamic was placed into motion, one that sought repeatedly to order and unify a worldview's constellation of values through logical deduction. Cognitive thought—a rational "theodicy of misfortune"—again and again came to the fore to seek "rationally satisfactory answers to the questioning [regarding] the basis of the incongruity between destiny and merit" (1946c, 275). Rather than involving simply a varying response to "the social conditions of existence" or fluctuating economic and political forces, this dynamic followed an "imperative of consistency," Weber insists:

> Religious interpretations of the world and ethics of religions created by [religion-oriented] intellectuals and meant to be rational have been strongly exposed to the imperative of consistency (*Gebot der Konsequenz*). The effect of the *ratio,* especially of a teleological deduction of practical postulates, is in some way, and often very strongly, noticeable among all religious ethics. This holds however little the religious interpretations of the world in the individual case have complied with the demand for consistency and however much they might integrate points of view into their ethical postulates which could *not* be rationally deduced. (1946a, 324; emphasis in original; see also 1946c, 286)

The development of ideas regarding the supernatural realm's features and contours was pushed by just this *religious* question as articulated by those in search of salvation: Given the unity of the cosmos, why does suffering continue? As Weber stressed: "The rational need for a theodicy of suffering and of dying has had extremely strong effects" (1946c, 275) and "this problem belongs everywhere among the deciding forces determining religious development and the need for salvation" (1968, 519; translation altered). It also served as an impetus for the *constitution* of social groups: The dilemma presented by the problem of theodicy itself has the effect of drawing together persons concerned about this puzzle, Weber argues. Group formation arises not only from the economic, political, and status interests of daily life, nor from traditions alone, utilitarian action, or mundane values. Confrontations with the transcendent sphere also play a causal part.

In sum, Weber's post-*PE* attention to values and ideas is manifest in his discussion of worldviews. Driven by an "imperative of consistency," prophets, priests, monks, and theologians, as well as secular thinkers, search for clues to explain distress and to unveil hints that offer strategies to alleviate terrestrial misery and injustice, he maintains.[8]

Salvation Doctrines and Rational Thought[9]

The effect of salvation doctrines upon the social action of the devout differs distinctly in *intensity* from the influence of the ideal thrusts of worldviews, all of which involve cognitive assessments of whether action stands in a relationship of teleological consistency with the ideal thrusts. An entirely new dimension comes into play with salvation religions, Weber insists: namely, psychological rewards.[10]

As mediated generally by doctrines, these incentives are placed directly upon action that, if properly executed, promises salvation to the believer. In his analysis, the capacity of these rewards to convince the faithful of their redemption from this-worldly suffering and evil endows them with a *far greater* influence upon action than does a cognitive pondering of the consistency between mundane action and the values of a worldview (see 2011, 114–15; 1927, 364; Kalberg 1990, 64).

All salvation religions involve, as a means of specifying their promises of a release from suffering and responding to the discrepancy between the "rational" supernatural realm and a terrestrial sphere saturated by unexplained misery, at least a minimum of religious doctrine (1968, 563). As "rational religious systems of thought," doctrines generally originate from the theoretical rationalization processes undertaken by priests, monks, and theologians in reference to the problem of theodicy (see Kalberg 2012, 18–25, 43–72; 1990; Levine 1985). They constitute ethical claims, according to Weber, rooted in a stable body of related teachings that are accepted as "revealed" knowledge. Doctrines, as constellations of values, prescriptions, laws, and norms internally consistent with one another to a greater or lesser extent, endow all thinking regarding God and sin with a further "rational element" (1968, 426). In doing so, they fulfill the demand that Weber sees as the "core of religious rationalism":

> Behind [the great varieties of doctrines] always lies a stand towards something in the actual world which is experienced as specifically "senseless." Thus, the demand has been implied: that the world view in its totality is, could, and should somehow be a meaningful "cosmos." This quest [is] the core of genuine religious rationalism. . . . The avenues, the results, and the efficacy of this metaphysical need for a "meaningful" cosmos have varied widely. (1946c, 281; see also 1946a, 325, 351; 1968, 427, 450–51, 458, 540, 563)

> The rational religious pragmatism of salvation, flowing from the nature of the images of God and of the world, [such as the Indian doctrine of Karma, the Calvinist belief in predestination, the Lutheran justification through faith, and the Catholic doctrine of sacrament], have under certain conditions had far-reaching results for the fashioning of a practical way of life. (1946c, 286)

Owing to their capacity to bestow psychological rewards upon action, salvation doctrines became endowed under certain circumstances with the potential to combine, on a *continuous basis*, the comprehensive ideal thrusts of worldviews, the quest for salvation, and the daily action of the devout, Weber maintains. In these cases, a methodical-rational organization of life congeals (see Kalberg 1990).[11] The devout and the sincere, as well as the much smaller group of "true believers," will continue to orient their action to religious doctrines even when their interests oppose doing so.[12] For him, a dynamic autonomy originating from ideas placed a "religious developmental process" into motion.[13]

In this manner Weber's religion-oriented analysis answers a question pivotal to him: How, and to what extent, do worldviews, salvation doctrines, and rational thought regarding suffering and the problem of theodicy assist the development of salvation religions? However, as evident from *PE*'s last pages, he wished to offer not only an "ideas" and "values" answer to this query; rather, he sought to provide a multicausal analysis. We are now prepared to evaluate whether his analysis of the development of salvation religions includes sustained consideration of *both* ideas *and* interests.

Our orienting query should now be restated: Did Weber, in his post-*PE* sociology of religion, fulfill his goal of offering causal analyses that investigated "both sides of the equation"? Or did he remain focused on ideas, values, a "systematization of thought," and an "imperative of consistency"?

Part II: Max Weber's Attention to Material Factors

The above discussions on worldviews, salvation doctrines, and "rational thought" have charted an *expansion* of *PE*'s orientation to ideas and values. Indeed, these sections appear to lead to a clear conclusion: Weber downplayed material factors in his later sociology of religion and awarded priority to ideas and values. With the above queries in mind and now searching for the "other side," a turn to Weber's post-*PE* sociology of religion is again necessary. Does he in fact investigate *both* an "autonomous religious development" *and* the "materialist side of the causal equation"?

Weber stresses in chapter 6 of *Economy and Society*, as well as throughout the Economic Ethics of the World Religions volumes, that the influence of worldviews upon social action remains extremely fragile. Although the impact of salvation doctrines is greater, a series of facilitating, intermediate patterns of action by followers in groups is indispensable if worldviews and salvation doctrines are to call forth an internally unified, methodical-rational organization of the believer's life. They are also necessary if this action is to circumscribe sheer utilitarian patterns of action (2012a, 315).

A central lesson from Weber's post-*PE* sociology of religion is already evident: the thrusts set into motion by worldviews and the psychological premiums of salvation doctrines may both be drastically weakened by *interest*-oriented actions emanating from, for example, the economy, political, law, and status spheres. This might even occur in a widely pluralistic manner. Weber's far-reaching multicausality will become apparent.

This "other side"—the "material side"—of his post-*PE* writings on religion is visible throughout the "Religious Rejections" (1946a) and "Social Psychology" (1946c) essays as well as *Economy and Society*'s chapter on the sociology of religion. Multiple examples could be offered. Particularly illustrative, in light of this chapter's sociology of religion focus, are his multicausal analyses that chart the origins of carrier strata, the routinization of charisma, and lay rationalism. We now turn to these analyses and explore Weber's *mode of procedure*; it calls attention to "both sides of the causal nexus." Indeed, these later writings seek to implement the goal articulated at *PE*'s conclusion: researchers must integrate "ideas and interests" if causality is to be adequately established (2011, 178–79). Perhaps our attention to *PE*'s ideas and values has neglected the full array of research strategies utilized in Weber's sociology of religion.

SOCIAL CARRIERS

Weber attends repeatedly in his post-*PE* sociology of religion to the groups, strata, and organizations that "carry" the values of worldviews and the values and doctrines of salvation religions. This orientation constitutes a significant turn away from *PE*'s presuppositions.

To influence conduct, worldviews and salvation doctrines must possess cohesive and powerful social carriers. Their contours must not only be articulated by charismatic figures and their immediate disciples, Weber holds; in addition, powerful and demarcated groups with amenable interests and values must cultivate and carry them. Followers must congeal into lay circles and these groups must expand in size and internal organization into churches, mosques, synagogues, temples, and sects. Only then can the prophet's basic ideas and values be consistently defended; only then can a religion endure and remain viable (1968, 439–67, 500–503).

Indeed, the values and interests of powerful social strata significantly influence the formation and definition of a religion's belief configuration and teachings (see 1946c, 270). The impact of an intellectual stratum was particularly strong in the world religions of the East, Weber maintains. Confucian teachings in China were influenced significantly by the status ethic of a cultured stratum of intellectuals (see 1951, 107–70; 1946c, 268). In India, the formation of Hinduism's salvation doctrine was strongly imprinted by an hereditary caste educated in Vedic ritual, and the teachings of early Buddhism were influenced significantly by contemplative, itinerant, and mendicant monks (1958, 215; 1946c, 268–69). The religions of China, India, and ancient Greece involved "representations appropriate to any cultivated intellectual stratum," as did ancient Judaism (1952, 352, n. 5). The transformation and rationalization in ancient Israel of old oracles and promises, and the introduction of the "characteristically different and independent conceptions" that formulated the intellectual traditions of this religion, could not have occurred if an "independent cultured stratum" had been absent (1952, 205). The situation has been entirely different wherever strata practically active in life influenced the development of a religion: "Where they were chivalrous warrior heroes, political officials, economically acquisitive classes, or, finally, where an organized hierocracy dominated religion, the results were different than where genteel intellectuals were decisive" (1946c, 282).

To Weber, the interests and values of itinerant artisans, journeymen, petty-bourgeois merchants, and, more generally, urban civic strata shaped significantly Christianity's belief system in antiquity. And the fact that functionaries held bureaucratic offices in the later church itself influenced the character of its ecclesiastical lawmaking. The impact, Weber further contends, upon ascetic Protestantism's doctrines of the typical patterns of action, interests, and ways of directing life found in the middle and lower bourgeoisie is generally clear (see 1946c, 268–69; 1968, 479–80, 828, 1180).

The influence of a carrier stratum's ethic and interests upon religious belief is also readily visible whenever a world religion changes its carrier stratum. As Weber notes, "[A] change in the socially decisive strata has usually been of profound importance" (1946c, 270). Carried in its classical period by Brahmins educated in the Vedas, Hinduism, for example, became a sacramental religion of ritual, belief in saviors, magic, and even orgiasticism in India's Middle Age, when its carriers became plebeian mystagogues and the lower strata (1946c, 269; see 1958, 176). Weber succinctly indicates the importance of carriers for religious ways of life in general:

> The various great ways of leading a rational and methodical life have been characterized by irrational presuppositions, which have been accepted simply as "given" and which have been incorporated into such ways of life. What these presuppositions have been is historically and socially determined, at least to a very large extent, through the uniqueness of those strata that have been the carriers of the ways of leading a life during its formative and decisive period. (1946c, 281; translation altered; see 279–85)

Throughout his post-*PE* sociology of religion Weber attends to the interests and values of the strata that influenced the formation of various salvation religions and served as their major carriers. This orientation constitutes a strong break from the focus in *PE* upon values in a worldview, salvation doctrines, and "rational thought."

The Routinization of Charisma: Interests and Values[14]

The attribution of charisma to leaders plays only a minor role in *PE*. However, charismatic personalities—above all, exemplary and emissary prophets—play a large role in Weber's sociology of religion generally, especially in respect to the origins of salvation religions. Disciples uphold and cultivate the prophet's original message. Nonetheless, also prominent in his post-*PE* considerations of the world religions are opposing groups pushing toward a "routinization of charisma." Absent from *PE*, this concept breaks decisively from its analysis. Just as does Weber's discussion of social carriers, the routinization of charisma analysis moves distinctly away from *PE*'s procedures. Interests—"the other side of the causal equation"—assume a pivotal part in this ideas *and* interests imbroglio.

Weber insists that the faithful experience the transcendent realm in different ways. Charismatic figures, all of whom are believed to possess unusual qualifications, do so in a direct manner. An intense "relationship to the supernatural"[15] infuses these "virtuosi" (*Virtuosen*). Conversely, the lay devout are endowed with "religious qualifications" of lesser intensity. Also oriented to the supernatural realm's ideas and values, they operate in a manner less compelling than occurs for the virtuosi (1968, 468–517; see Kalberg, 1990, 67–70). Conflicts rooted in ideas *and* interests become regular.

As non-elites, members of churches, mosques, synagogues, temples, and sects regularly demand from elites *revisions* of the prophet's extemporaneous and imprecise pronouncements involving routes to salvation. His inspirational sayings and speeches must be clearly comprehensible and rendered in systematic form. The devotion of the laity must be awakened and, if it is to be influential, their conduct must be directed; salvation paths must be demarcated and, not least, "adjusted" to meet religious qualifications of the laity (1968, 439–67). Disciples, followers, priests, ministers, and theologians all undertake the task of interpreting the prophet's worldview and original ideas. The growth of religious organizations follows in part this conflictual pathway, Weber insists.

However, these interpreters perform their tasks not only in reference to variations in respect to ideas and qualifications. Owing to frequent competition with other religious groups and sheer survival issues, salient also are economic, status, and political *interests*. They become in some cases central. Religious groups wish to ensure a livelihood in *this life as well as* salvation in the next, Weber maintains (1968, 452–67, 486–88).

He designates this conflict-ridden process the "routinization of charisma" (1968, 246–54, 1121–25; see Kalberg 1994, 124–27). As religious groups and organizations become cohesive and firm, charisma becomes more and more cultivated not only in order to rejuvenate and sustain the founder's message but also to strengthen the capacity of organizations and groups to "institutionalize" charisma. "Office charisma" (*Amtscharisma*) comes into existence. Simultaneously, a *dynamic interaction* of interests, beliefs, values, ideas, power, and authority congeals among both elite and lay groups (see 1968, 1121–23, 1139–41; Kalberg 1994, 126). Status groups, each defending its own social, economic, and political agenda, as well as values-based aims, also crystallize. Charisma's "creative aspect" now becomes absorbed—to varying degrees—into the permanent institutions of everyday life (see 1968, 1131–33, 1156; "EK," 470).

The interest of followers in legitimizing positions of prestige and rulership, as well as to secure economic resources, plays a central role, Weber argues. Indeed, especially important at each stage of charisma's routinization has been the search for economic advantage (see 1968, 148, 262, 1120, 1146, 1156). Those holding economic and social power seek, with the aim of legitimating positions of privilege, to "capture" the charismatic movement and to utilize its ideas, energy, and aura for their own ends (see 1968, 252, 1121–23). Concomitantly, now impersonal and transformed into routinized forms, firm hierarchies appear within the religious organizations. These developments further influence the charismatic founder's pronouncements and enable persons in possession of authority to view their superior positions as legitimate (1968, 1122–23, 1126–27).

Weber's analysis of charisma's routinization pathway is central to his post-*PE* sociology of religion. Absent from *PE*, it qualitatively diverges from this classic study's framework. Weber has here expanded his sociology of religion to include "the other side" of the causal equation, namely, a "materialist" analysis that takes the role of economic, status, and political interests directly into account.

Lay Rationalism

Weber's post-*PE* sociology of religion moves distinctly beyond *PE*'s attention to ideals and values in a further overt manner: his later writings include discussions of the ways in which interests become intertwined with "lay rationalism."

The founders of salvation religions interacted with lay believers "located" in varying social contexts, he insists. This population, locked within encompassing magic, ritual, and age-old traditions and ethnic dualisms, was in some regions highly insulated from, and resistant to, new beliefs and utilitarian conduct. In other regions, a lay rationalism was widespread: the devout here were urban dwellers less rooted in magic and tradition and more anchored in guilds, as well as in production and exchange activities.

This rationalism implied a significant break from magic, ritual, traditions, and ethnic dualisms, Weber holds. A more mobile population could arise. Moreover, a more active posture vis-à-vis religious doctrines, rituals, and sacred traditions could now crystallize. In this context, the laity's corresponding rationalism was endowed with a greater capacity to evaluate and challenge a worldview's values, as well as salvation doctrines, on a regular basis (see 1968, 452–57, 464–67). Pressure for their alteration also arose externally, namely, from transformations of action patterns oriented to the economy, social status tensions and conflicts, and political struggles.

Interests might more frequently become manifest in this milieu. Indeed, this elevation of diverse interests in Weber's post-*PE* sociology of religion relocates his mode of analysis distinctly away from *PE*'s orientation to values and ideas and toward multicausal research procedures—ones that acknowledge a range of political, economic, and status interests.

Conclusion: Ideas *and* Interests

Where does Weber stand? He instructs his readers in a concerted manner that, even when understood as strongly interactive, the economic, political, and status interests of daily life, as well as traditions and mundane values, fail to constitute for his sociology of religion the *full spectrum* of potentially causal patterns of action. The directed action of the devout toward religious values and ideas, albeit at times without consistency despite orientations to worldviews and salvation doctrines, must not be neglected. This social action at times even stands firm against the utilitarian "flow of life." To Weber, confrontations with the transcendent sphere also imply causality.

Moreover, he stresses that an "imperative of consistency" influences the patterned social action of the faithful and particularly of religion-oriented elites: prophets, priests, monks, and theologians. The problem of theodicy in the end *can* burden their souls, in certain contexts, to such an extent that an alteration of their social action occurs in consistent ways. *Nonetheless*, and although the capacity for "rational thought" must never be omitted from "the causal equation," Weber's sociology of religion *also* charts the impact of mundane interests.

Thus, despite his attention to ideas and values in *PE* and in many of his post-*PE* writings, as noted above. Weber cannot be categorized as a theorist oriented exclusively to these factors. Rather, he must be viewed as attending to *both* ideal and material forces. He seeks perpetually to combine "ideas *and* interests" throughout his sociology of religion and unrelentingly attempts to do so in spite of his repeated acknowledgment of the complexity of this task.

Perhaps Weber's unending struggle to interlock tightly, if causality is to be established, "*both sides* of the causal equation" accounts in part for the well-known difficulty of his texts. This unfortunate feature of his mode of analysis and research procedures seems invariably to render "a Weberian analysis" multicausal and nonlinear. To him:

> Neither religions nor men are open books. They have been historical rather than logical or even psychological constructions without contradiction. Often they have borne within themselves a series of motives, each of which, if separately and consistently followed through, would have stood in the way of the others or run against them head-on. In religious matters "consistency" has been the exception and not the rule. The ways and means of salvation are also psychologically ambiguous. (1946c, 291)

Notes

1. The full passage deserves attention: "This study has attempted, of course, merely to trace ascetic Protestantism's influence, and the particular *nature* of this influence back to ascetic Protestantism's motives in regard to one—however important—point. The way in which Protestant asceticism was in turn influenced in its development and characteristic uniqueness by the entirety of societal cultural conditions, and especially *economic* conditions, must also have its day. . . . Of course it cannot be the intention here to set a one-sided religion-oriented analysis of the causes of culture and history in place of an equally one-sided "materialistic" analysis. *Both are equally possible.* Historical truth, however, is served equally little if either of these analyses claims to be the conclusion of an investigation rather than its beginning stage" (2011, 178–79; translation altered; emphasis original).

2. It is evident from the quotation above (n. 1) that Weber's reference to "materialistic analysis" implies a strong rejection of the Marxian understanding of this term, especially its broad usage and reductionist features. Hence, any reference to "materialism" and "interests" as synonyms is precluded (see also Weber, e.g., 1968, 341; 2012b, 113; 1988, 456). Although Weber never offers a systematic discussion of "interests" (see the abbreviated treatment at 1968, 29–32), his usage is clear: the *varying* interests of people in diverse groups are emphasized (whether, for example, economic, status, or political groups), as is the capacity of interests to become causally significant in a specific context (as opposed to Marx's clear elevation of material factors to epistemological status). Weber's passage at the end of *PE* follows this pattern (see again note 1). This usage is compatible with the "ideas and interests" pluralism he calls for—that is, a multicausal framework anchored in a variety of societal domains (the economy, law, rulership, religion, status groups, and family spheres; see Kalberg, 2012, 97–112, 129–40) that legitimize values and ideas on the one hand and interests on the other hand.

3. Unfortunately, this chapter cannot undertake the enormous task of exploring the major aspects of "the material side" as discussed in *Economy and Society* (1968), *General Economic History* (1927), and the Economic Ethics of the World Religions series on China (1951), India (1958), and ancient Judaism (1952). However, it should be noted that these writings address the theoretical issue of concern here in an irregular manner. The *analytic* sources for Weber's post-*PE* sociology of religion provide a more suitable terrain for an analysis of the "ideas and interests" relationship: "The Social Psychology of the World Religions" (1946c) essay, the "Religious Rejections of the World" (1946a) essay, and chapter 6 (The Sociology of Religion) in *Economy and Society*. Our focus will be upon the *concepts and modes of analysis* prominent in these texts. Nonetheless, the omission of an analysis rooted also in Weber's investigations on China, India, and ancient Judaism, it must be stressed, render this study a *preliminary* investigation only.

4. The "correctness" or "superiority" of a worldview can never be scientifically proven, Weber argues (see 2005, 331). The subjective meaningfulness of beliefs to a group of people alone establishes its legitimacy.

5. For a more detailed discussion of world views, see Kalberg, 2012, 73–92.

6. "Dynamic autonomy" is the author's term. See ibid., 79–81.

7. That is, monotheism on the one hand and the immanent, impersonal All-One of Buddhism and classical Hinduism on the other hand.

8. For more detail on this "religious development" to ethical salvation religions, and then to ethical salvation religions that devalue the world, see Kalberg, 2012, 43–72.

9. The following four paragraphs are indebted to ibid., 81–83.

10. On the critical distinction between the influence of cognitive consistency as opposed to the effect of psychological rewards (*Prämien)* on action, see Weber, 2011, 114–15, 230 (note 37), 327–29 (notes 39, 40); 1946c, 267; 1946a, 338;

Kalberg, 2012, 67 (note 31). Weber employs the terms *psychological impulse* [*Antrieb*] and *psychological strength* [*Kraft*] synonymously.

11. This very complex process, which relates to the salvation goals and salvation paths articulated by the doctrine, is examined in detail at Kalberg, 2012, 47–62; see also 73–92.

12. For example: "The power of [a fully developed ecclesiastic hierarchy] rests upon the principle that 'God must be obeyed more than men,' for the sake of spiritual welfare both in the here and the hereafter. This has been the most ancient check on all political power, the most effective one up to the great Puritan Revolution and the declarations of the Rights of Man" (1968, 1175).

13. Weber stresses that a clear difference remains between worldly interests and religious values in regard to his "autonomy" theme: owing to the omnipresent and enduring question of salvation, religious development retains a *highly consistent* focus—the supernatural and the problem of suffering—quite separate from the flux and flow of mundane reality, all the more whenever religion-oriented groups crystallize into cohesive organizations and even social strata. Interests, however, whenever unencumbered and hence able to "follow their own laws," do so alone on the basis of power coalitions. Thus, while an *internal* consistency and continuity of development in reference to the problem of suffering characterizes the dynamic autonomy of religious ideas and their accompanying values, interests follow a different course: they remain subject to the push and pull of power configurations. They follow various routes simply as a consequence of history's perpetually shifting alliances and antagonisms across groups (see Tenbruck, 1980).

14. A more detailed discussion can be found in Kalberg, 1994, 124–26.

15. This is Weber's definition of religion. See 1968, 424; see also 399–400.

References

Kalberg, Stephen. 1990. "The Rationalization of Action in Max Weber's Sociology of Religion." *Sociological Theory* 8, no. 1 (Spring): 58–85.

———. 1994. *Max Weber's Comparative-Historical Sociology*. Chicago: The University of Chicago Press.

———. 2012. *Max Weber's Comparative-Historical Sociology Today*. London: Routledge.

———. 2014. *Searching for the Spirit of American Democracy: Max Weber's Analysis of a Unique Political Culture, Past, Present, and Future*. London: Routledge.

———. 2016. *The Social Thought of Max Weber*. Twin Oaks, CA: Sage.

———. 2021. *Max Weber's Sociology of Civilizations: A Reconstruction*. London: Routledge.

Levine, Donald. 1985. "Rationality and Freedom." In *Flight from Ambiguity*, 142–78. Chicago: The University of Chicago Press.

Tenbruck, F. H. 1980 (1975). "The Problem of Thematic Unity in the Works of Max Weber." Translated by Sam Whimster. *British Journal of Sociology* 31, no. 3: 13–51.

Weber, Max. 1927. *General Economic History*. Translated by Frank H. Knight. Glencoe, IL: The Free Press.

———. 1946a. "Religious Rejections of the World." In *From Max Weber (FMW)*, edited and translated by H. H. Gerth and C. Wright Mills, 323–59. New York: Oxford University Press.

———. 1946b. "Science as a Vocation." In *FMW*, 129–56.

———. 1946c. "The Social Psychology of the World Religions." In *FMW*, 267–301.

———. 1951. *The Religion of China*. Edited and translated by Hans H. Gerth. New York: The Free Press.

———. 1952. *Ancient Judaism*. Edited and translated by Hans H. Gerth and Donald Martindale. New York: The Free Press.

———. 1958. *The Religion of India*. Edited and translated by Hans H. Gerth and Donald Martindale. New York: The Free Press.

———. 1968. *Economy and Society*. Edited by Guenther Roth and Claus Wittich. Berkeley: The University of California Press.

———. 1973. "Über einige Kategorien der verstehenden Soziologie." In *Gesammelte Aufsätze zur Wissenschaftslehre*, edited by Johannes Winckelmann, 427–74. Tübingen: Mohr.

———. 1988. "Diskussionsrede zu W. Sombarts Vortrag über Technik und Kultur." In *Gesammelte Aufsätze zur Soziologie und Sozialpolitik*, 449–56. Tübingen: Mohr.

———. 2005. *Max Weber: Readings and Commentary on Modernity*. Edited by Stephen Kalberg. New York: Wiley-Blackwell.

———. 2011. *The Protestant Ethic and the Spirit of Capitalism*. Translated by Stephen Kalberg. New York: Oxford University Press.

———. 2012a. "The Meaning of 'Value-Freedom.'" In *Max Weber: Collected Methodological Writings*, edited by Hans Henrik Bruun and Sam Whimster; translated by Hans Henrik Bruun, 304–34. London: Routledge.

———. 2012b. "'Objectivity' in Social Science and Social Policy." In *Max Weber: Collected Methodological Writings*, edited by Hans Henrik Bruun and Sam Whimster; translated by Hans Henrik Bruun, 100–38. London: Routledge.

3

Karl Jaspers on Paradigmatic Individuals

A Complement to His Concept of the Axial Age and a Subtype of Weber's Concept of Charisma

Victor Lidz

> In their transhistorical character, they (great philosophies) are like eternal contemporaries.
>
> (T)his book is not conceived as a loose list of some of the author's favorite thinkers. The selection has not been made by a single historian of philosophy. This selection has already been made in history through history.
>
> —Ruth Burch, Florian Hild, and Helmut Wautischer, foreword to Karl Jaspers, *The Great Philosophers*

In *The Origin and Goal of History*, where he developed the concept of the Axial Age, Jaspers cited, as his key source for the idea, Hegel's discussion of Jesus's life and teachings as the axis of history (Jaspers 1953, 1). However, Jaspers continued, Jesus's life can define the axis of history only for believing Christians. For a universal history, valid for all people and for all cultures, a broad empirical investigation comparing major civilizations is necessary. Thus, Jasper's extends Hegel's idea of the axis to other civilizations and finds the period centering on 500 BCE, including 800 to 200 BCE, to have been a time of extraordinary religio-philosophic creativity in civilizations across Asia and the Eastern Mediterranean.

Jaspers designated that era as the Axial Age, a period "with the most deepcut dividing line in history" during which several world religions and related great civilizations created and clarified their basic orientations (Jaspers 1953, 1). He also noted that the Axial Age should be viewed not as "a universal stage of human evolution, but a singular ramified historical process" (Jaspers 1953, 17). That is, the axial cultures emerged through different processes and developed significantly different histories across the various civilizations. The profound differences in developmental paths and institutional forms among several major civilizations in Asia and Europe, extending from ancient times down to our own era, gained their respective religio-philosophic frames during the Axial Age.

In characterizing the Axial Age, Jaspers emphasized the broad effervescence of ideas in China, India, Persia, Greece, and ancient Israel, highlighting in each case, except Persia, for which he mentions only Zoroaster, a variety of important thinkers. In each case, he observed, "man becomes conscious of Being as a whole . . . experiences the terror of the world . . . asks radical questions . . . and experiences absoluteness in the depths of selfhood and in the lucidity of transcendence" (Jaspers, 1953, 2). *Logos* struggles against *mythos,* religious belief becomes radically ethicized, rationality is embraced, and philosophy comes into existence (ibid., 3). Other scholars have since emphasized that the radical changes in prior cultures due to the struggles of *Logos* all involved the development of conceptions of transcendental orders standing above and beyond the world of human experience and serving as ultimate sources of value. Yet, the conceptions of transcendental orders were radically different across civilizations, and thus became sources of profound differences among cultures and patterns of social institutions (Bellah 1970). It is this broad understanding that has made the Axial Age a basic starting point for a large body of scholarship in the comparative historical sociology of civilizations in recent decades.

Complementing Hegel's idea of an axis of history, Max Weber's broad multicivilizational body of research, methodological writings, and comparative studies in the sociology of religion helped to shape Jaspers's understanding of axial civilizations. Weber's effort to develop a universal perspective in his investigations in the sociology of religion, his emphasis on the diverse and complex processes of rationalization in the development of each of the world religions, his analysis of the unique path of rationalization that has given rise to Western modernity, and his refusal to project any closed formulation on the future of mankind were cited with approval in Jaspers's writings (Jaspers 1964), including *The Origin and Goal of History*.[1] They appear to have provided important elements of the scholarly framing that underpins the idea of the Axial Age. This is not surprising, even though Jaspers's citations of Weber's specific comparative studies are thin as compared with the empirically more specialized monographs of scholars who wrote during the several decades after Weber's death.

We should recognize that Jaspers was something of a polymath. He is now known principally as an Existential philosopher, but there were earlier phases of his intellectual career. After a couple of years of study in the law, he gained professional training in medicine and then, at the University of Heidelberg, psychiatry. Due in part to health problems and in part to a wish to treat only selected patients of particular interest to himself, Jaspers had relatively little clinical experience as a psychiatrist. Yet, his first professional reputation was based on the very methodical *Allgemeine Psychopathologie* (Jaspers 1997 [1913]), now regarded by some as an early model for recent editions of the *Diagnostic and Statistical Manual of Psychiatry*. The publication of this first major volume initiated a process that led to his transfer to the faculty of psychology. Some years later he transferred to the faculty of philosophy, having recognized that discipline as his basic interest. Throughout his career, he retained wide-ranging interests in the sciences as well as the humanities. He corresponded with some of the leading physicists, poets, novelists, and historians as well as psychiatrists of the early and middle twentieth century (Jaspers 2016). As his interest in philosophy matured from a sideline to the focus of his work, Jaspers developed a close relation to Weber.

Jaspers admired Weber greatly, apparently viewed him as one of his mentors, and gained a thorough knowledge of his writings.[2] The relation to Weber was personally close, but it was also sufficiently recognized within the academic community of Heidelberg that Jaspers was invited to speak at Weber's memorial service. He viewed Weber's methodological writings as standing among the outstanding contributions to twentieth-century philosophy (Jaspers 1964). He also discussed Weber's conception of charisma and charismatic authority in more than one treatment of modern political institutions (Jaspers 1964 and 1951, 87ff and 149–55).[3]

In *The Origin and Goal of History*, Jaspers wrote remarkably little about the key figures who gave rise to the axial religio-cultural movements. The chapter in which the concept of the Axial Age was introduced is only twenty-one pages. Most of its analysis is sociological and focuses on establishing three main points. First, civilizations around the world have continued down to modern times to rely on the religio-philosophic orientations established during the Axial Age. Second, each of the civilizational areas that gave rise to Axial Age movements had been divided into many small and competing states in ways that fostered ferment over the constitutive elements of their cultures. Third, in the wake of the Axial Age, each of the same civilizational areas experienced a political efflorescence resulting in consolidation and, for substantial periods, stabilization of much larger empires.[4]

Although the larger empires eventually fragmented, the resulting cultures have, in each case, experienced episodes of renewed ferment and creativity, episodes that have recurred down to our own times. Jaspers's treatment of the Axial Age and its consequences leaves many ambiguities in its wake, only some of which are addressed in the next chapter on the "Schema of World History," which is only five pages of text plus an accompanying chart. Among the ambiguities is a lack of clarity about the details of how each of the Axial Age religio-philosophic breakthroughs[5] occurred.

In the first section of the first volume of *The Great Philosophers*, written approximately half a decade after *The Origin and Goal of History*, Jaspers discusses the lives of Socrates, Buddha, Confucius, and Jesus as figures who "have exerted a historical influence of incomparable scope and depth" (Jaspers 1962, 3). In the introduction to *The Great Philosophers*, he says that these figures, "through their existence and character define humankind historically as no other men did. Their lasting influence is witnessed through the millennia to the present day" (Jaspers 2017, 22).[6]

In this later work, Jaspers curiously does not use the term *Axial Age*. The section of the text discussing Socrates, Buddha, Confucius, and Jesus never refers to that conception, although in the introduction he makes an indirect reference to it, mentioning "that there are eras of great personalities, such as the sixth to the fourth century in Greece, India, or China" (Jaspers 1962, 33) when addressing the foundations of later philosophies. Notably, this statement and his subsequent treatment pass over the Old Testament prophets, whose religio-ethical innovations had been so important to Max Weber and many of whose lives fell into the sixth to fourth century BCE that Jaspers had noted (Weber 1952). Yet, he later concentrates on Jesus as a Jewish prophet and acknowledges the unsettled religious and ethical situation—Roman rule, Hellenistic culture, and Hebraic traditions, complexly mixed together—in which Jesus lived, to be sure in a later era than the Axial Age. Yet, Jaspers makes clear that the cultural frameworks of great civilizations were shaped by the legacies of his four key figures in respects that can be claimed for few, if any, other historical persons. In this context, his discussion seems in substantial degree to parallel and, more importantly, to complement his earlier claims about the Axial Age.

For Weber, these key historical figures were charismatics, an understanding that carries over to the social science of our times. For Jaspers, they were "paradigmatic individuals." Why, however, did Jaspers, who knew, admired, and was deeply influenced by Weber and his writings, eschew the term *charismatic* and instead develop the concept of paradigmatic individuals? I will now explore, first, the apparent reasons for this interesting terminological change, and second, how the concept of paradigmatic individuals might affect our conceptions of the Axial Age and axiality, and, third, the implications for our contemporary understanding of charisma.

Charisma

For Weber, charisma is a very general concept. Charismatic figures have existed in every type of society, from the tribal to the archaic to the axial and post-axial to the modern (Weber 1968, vol. 1, 212–301). Charismatic leaders have emerged in a vast variety of situations: the chief of tribal warriors, the shaman, the prophet, the mystagogue, the popular king or emperor, the Crusader, the buccaneer, the head of an urban proletariat uprising, eighteenth-century revolutionaries, the leaders of sects, innovative entrepreneurs, perpetrators of financial frauds, and democratically elected prime ministers and presidents. In modern times, we may think of Churchill or Roosevelt, but also Mussolini, Hitler, or Lenin. Weber says we should not use moral judgment to restrict our sense of who is an authentic charismatic. Anyone who presents himself to followers as having a special "gift," often but not always a sacred or God-ordained gift, and finds his claim accepted by followers who will break with traditional or rational forms of conduct to follow him, should be regarded as a charismatic (ibid., 124). Yes, to his ardent base, Donald J. Trump is a charismatic leader in this sense, just as many other mountebanks, political or economic,[7] have been. Indeed, it is his charisma and his self-confidence in exercising it that creates such a deep threat to the American legal and constitutional order.

Much of what Weber wrote about charisma concerned the forms and paths of its routinization, especially the routinization of forms of authority first established in personal relationships between leader and followers. Charisma in its pure form is unstable. A leader may lose his charisma, as when a warrior chief is defeated in battle, the charismatic entrepreneur goes bankrupt, or the religious charismatic is revealed to have behaved scandalously or his predictions of future outcomes, for example, the End of Days, are falsified by events. In all cases of initially sustained charisma, the leader eventually dies, precipitating a number of questions: Who will succeed him? How will his "gift" be sustained? How will the relationships he established be continued over time? How will his teachings be maintained, upheld, and transmitted to others?

Weber identified the first order concern among the lieutenants of former charismatics as one of how authority relations could be maintained. Famously, he suggested that charismatic authority can over the long run be continued through the routes of either traditionalization or rationalization, or, more typically, some combination of tradition and rationality (Weber 1968, vol. 1, 212–301; vol. 3, 1111–1357). The path of tradition tends to result in patriarchal or, in larger-scale systems, patrimonial authority. The path of rationality, when sustained over the very long run, may develop into formal law, even constitutions, bureaucratic administration, and elective and formally appointive offices. Rational forms of authority often involve highly complex divisions of specialized powers among large numbers of offices. Some forms of routinization, as in the British monarchy, are subtle mixtures of the traditional and rational.

Weber, in his *Religionssoziologie* (1988), sections of which are translated as *Religion of China* (1951), *Religion of India* (1958), *Ancient Judaism* (1952) *The Protestant Ethic and the Spirit of Capitalism* (1930), and "Religious Rejections of the World and their Directions" (1946), discussed a different dimension of the long-term fates of charismas.[8] In this context, Weber was concerned with charismatic movements that addressed and unsettled the spiritual and moral grounds of institutional orders. In some cases, they gave rise to new religious ethics that over time established new foundations for social institutions. But to do so, they had to meet the religious needs of followers in order to sustain and stabilize their social movements on the basis of continuing religious commitments. How religious needs were met in the very long run, through substantial rationalization in the case of the world religions, tended to differ from the ways they were met among the original followers and lieutenants of the founding charismatics. For example, a new *mythos* was prominent among the disciples of Jesus, even though the religious ethics they formulated, with emphasis on faith and love, provided a basis for later rationalization.

Among the religious needs of followers—both immediate followers and those who came centuries later—would be a core body of sustaining beliefs, legitimating both the commitments of individual followers and the solidarity of the charisma-based movements. Another need would be for a soteriology, a conception of salvation and doctrine of how followers could attain salvation. Similarly, there would be a need for a theodicy (Weber 1968, vol. 2, 439–51, 518–76), a set of beliefs about the ultimate grounds of justice and ways of understanding experiences of justice and perhaps particularly injustice, in the lives of the followers. Resolving these "spiritual" problems, which are complexly personal, psychosocial, and institutional, typically involved modification of the original revelations of the founding charismatic leader. The result might be more complex and fully realized doctrines, typically some mix of rational and traditional elements (Weber 1968, vol. 3, 1111–57).

Weber's core interest was in the ways in which the routinization of religious movements shaped civilizations and their major institutional complexes over long periods of time, indeed, millennia. He noted that the lieutenants or fairly immediate followers of the original charismatics played key roles in the early stages of these developmental processes. They sustained aspects of the relations of fellowship, communality, and ethical ties that they had experienced in their relationships with the original charismatic figures. The protégés of Confucius, the followers of Old Testament prophets, the mendicant monks who lived communally with the Buddha, or the Apostles of Jesus all played roles of this type, and in doing so sustained the original charismas to later generations. But in doing so, they also initiated processes of rationalizing, and in varying degrees also traditionalizing, the religious ethics, soteriologies, and theodicies introduced by the original charismatic figures.

Yet, Weber's analyses tended to concentrate less on the immediate followers of the great charismatics than on the figures who carried out major rationalizing changes in doctrines over hundreds of years and gave shape to the particular patterns of social institutions of each civilization. Often these processes involved repeated outbreaks of charismatic figures and movements. Thus, the many Hebrew prophets created, over generations, more universalistic and powerful understandings of Jahweh; the figures who formulated the increasing dominance of Brahmin ethics shaped the development of Hinduism; reformers in China strengthened the commitments to the ancient classics and, hence, the social status of classically educated mandarins, eventually instituting the system of qualification for office through formal examinations in the classics; and, in Western Christianity, figures such as St. Dominic, St. Francis, Savonarola, Luther, Calvin, and Jonathan Edwards developed conceptions of religious asceticism in a variety of different forms.

Routinization over the Long Run

Weber also emphasized that the patterns of routinization involved in the world religions were in each case shaped by the interests of a core social stratum. The Brahman priestly *jati* that shaped Hindu religious ethics and the gentleman *literati* of Confucian China are perhaps the clearest cases. But the warrior groups that initiated the spread of Islam and the institutionalization of *Koran* and *Sharia* are another, as are the predominantly urban *bourgeois* who have been especially influential in shaping the modern forms of Western Christianity (Weber 1968, vol. 3, 1236–65).

Weber's subtle analysis of the relations between key social strata and the resulting religious ethics underscored the radical differences in the *directions* of rationalization embodied in the basic religious orientations to the "world" among the resulting civilizations. The West has developed in the direction of asceticism, often with "other-worldly" emphases, as in the early anchorites and then more methodical medieval monasticism, but eventually "inner-worldly" emphases after the rise of Lutheranism and Calvinism. Premodern Chinese civilization developed in the direction of "rational adjustment to the world," as contrasted with ascetic efforts to master the "world." Hindu India and Buddhist civilizations produced complicated combinations of "other-worldly mysticism and/or asceticism." Weber argued that the radical differences across these major civilizations in economic, political, community, familial, educational, and other institutions were due fundamentally to the differences, religiously rooted, in their respective orientations to the "world," that is, in terminology introduced by Robert Bellah, to the forms of their philosophic breakthroughs—or their forms of axiality.

In the broadest perspective, Weber argued that the movements that started with the charismas of figures such as the Old Testament prophets, Jesus, Mohammad, Confucius, and Buddha have played out through repeated processes of outbreak of new charismas followed by new routinizations, some more rationalistic, some more traditionalistic, to shape the religious ethics at the foundations of entire civilizations. The charismatic teachings of Confucius were routinized into the main framework of the complex institutional order of premodern China. They are now being revived again in contemporary China, with emphasis on an authoritarian conception of social harmony and in a complex relation to Mao thought, with its more ascetic frame. Buddha's charismatic teachings affected Chinese, Japanese, Thai, Vietnamese, and other Asian civilizations.

The teachings of Jesus, modified by many subsequent thinkers, some of them charismatics, from Saint Paul to Augustine to Saint Thomas to Luther to Calvin and a number of Calvinist New England "Divines," among others, have provided the religio-ethical core of "Western" civilization. Differently routinized, Christianity has also shaped civilizations in the Orthodox areas of Southeastern Europe and Russia.

Weber's analysis of the religio-ethical grounds of civilizations as they developed over centuries and millennia out of ancient charismas is, again, the outstanding classic source for comparative sociology of today. A major emphasis of Weber's, well known to and understood by Jaspers, was the different paths of civilizational development associated with the different *directions* of rationalization of religious ethics, soteriologies, and theodicies. Much of the resonance of Jaspers's conception of the Axial Age has been due to the respects in which more recent scholarship on comparative civilizations, especially that of Parsons, Eisenstadt, Bellah, Geertz, Schluchter, and Joas, had built on Weber's scholarship prior to the revival of Jaspers's idea.

Paradigmatic Individuals

Jaspers presents his conception of paradigmatic individuals in the first section of *The Great Philosophers*, following the "Introduction." He discusses each of the four paradigmatic figures in a chapter of just over twenty pages and then concludes with a generalizing comparative chapter of ten pages. The total is just under one hundred pages, quite brief, but substantially more than the presentation of the Axial Age in *The Origin and Goal of History*. The treatment is still short, given the broad range and importance of the materials in religio-philosophic history that it discusses.[9]

It is important to keep in mind that Jaspers's topic was the ancient foundations of schools of philosophy, not, as in Weber's writings, comparative analysis of whole civilizations and their courses of development. However, his very comprehensive conception of philosophy is also in play, and his attention to figures in Oriental traditions of philosophy as well as the conventional origins of Western philosophy reflects the influence of Weber.

By contrast with Weber's comprehensive concept of charisma, Jaspers's notion of paradigmatic figures is very specific. He discusses only the four figures of Socrates, Buddha, Confucius, and Jesus. He notes that there are a number of other great and highly influential figures in history, but that only

Mohammad might properly be added to the list of paradigmatic figures as a comparable founder of a world religion, major form of civilization, and orientation in philosophy (Jaspers 1962, 87). Jaspers acknowledged that there were great figures in the history of philosophy, including many successors in the philosophic traditions of Buddha, Confucius, and Mohammad, whom he did not know well enough to discuss. Yet, he insisted on the distinctive importance of the four figures he discussed, plus Mohammad. Socrates was included as a founder of schools of Western philosophy and thought, including later theology, even though he was not a founder of a world religion.

Jaspers observed that each of his four cases of paradigmatic individuals arose from backgrounds in which there were somewhat similar figures before them: the Old Testament prophets as well as a number of prophets and seekers of truth in Jesus's own time in areas of the Middle East affected by Hebraic culture; pre-Socratic philosophers and the Sophists, with whom Socrates was often confused during his life; the authors of the Upanishads as well as Brahmin ascetics; perhaps the philosopher Lao-Tse and certainly the many political advisors to kings of the small states into which China was divided who filled roles similar to that of Confucius.[10] However, these predecessors and contemporaries did not set the frames for later world religions and philosophies, even if, as in the case of Lao-Tse and the prophet Deutero-Isaiah, they were major creative thinkers of the Axial Age. In particular, such predecessors and contemporaries did not affect groups of followers in similarly compelling ways, nor did their thought, as amplified by followers, generally appeal to individuals beyond their own ethno-cultural backgrounds.

Comparable paradigmatic figures have not emerged since Confucius, Buddha, and Jesus,[11] again with the exception of Mohammad. A crucial element of the idea of paradigmatic individuals is that they carried extraordinarily rare charismas. Comparable charismas were not embodied by any contemporary figures who competed with the paradigmatics in their own times and in their respective civilizations. Nor have comparable charismas been embodied or emulated over the last 1,400 years anywhere in the world. It is a striking quality of the paradigmatic figures that their modes of thought and modeling of ways of life have proved so persuasive that no subsequent paradigmatic figures have emerged within the traditions they established. Each of them has in this respect come, largely through the works of followers, to monopolize the religio-ethical-philosophical foundation for a civilization or group of civilizations. To be sure, Lenin and Mao, with Marx in their backgrounds, were charismatics and might be considered paradigmatic figures, but we may doubt that they will prove to have established enduringly broad philosophic ethical orientations to the world or to have founded durable civilizations in the manner of Jesus, Buddha, or Confucius.

Jaspers's focus was on the development of philosophy, but his sense of philosophy encompassed, as well as modern academic works, the creation of a broad range of the central ideas of the world civilizations. In this respect, his treatment of the paradigmatic individuals was close to, and likely derivative of, Weber's writings on charisma and the origins of world religions. Although Jaspers did not follow Weber in emphasizing the various status groups that have been central to the institutionalization of world religions, he did note the historical backgrounds and social roles of the paradigmatic figures and major philosophers. He noted that figures who have contributed to recognized schools of philosophy have filled many different roles under various historical conditions: poets, monks, priests and bishops, prophets, theologians, court officials or advisers, lawyers, physicians, scientists, political critics, historians, private scholars, and so forth, as well as academic philosophers (Jaspers 2017, 23–24).

Jaspers took care in his chapters on the paradigmatic figures to characterize the manner of living each of them pursued and its relation to the type of social role each could fill in his particular sociocultural setting. Buddha was born into a well-to-do, high status family, married and had children early in life, then devoted himself to solitary meditation, then became a wandering mendicant who attracted many followers, and, finally, founded and led at least one monastic community. Jesus was born into a commoner social status, little is known about his upbringing and early years, but he became a prophet who wandered much of ancient Israel with a group of disciples. Socrates was an active citizen who served as hoplite in famous battles, filled official roles in the manner of dutiful citizen but refused to take up a political career, and gained popularity, and notoriety, as an active critic encountering others in philosophic give and take in the public area of Athens. Confucius, like Buddha, married early and had children, but served as an official of a small state, advanced to become a close advisor to a king, became a traveling advisor to rulers of other states, and then retired to become a philosophic educator, teaching the traditional classics as the grounds of civilization, to an expanding circle of student-followers.

Jaspers emphasized that a basis of the extraordinary influence developed by each of the paradigmatic individuals was their mixing with common people of their times and civilizations. Jesus traveled through the land and encountered people of many stations in life, apparently making deep impressions on them, and over time collecting his group of disciples. Socrates encountered all citizens who would engage in, or at least observe with interest, his dialogues with others in public. Over time, he gathered a group of devoted students, some of them, including Plato, talented and creative thinkers on their own. Buddha, after his period of solitude, meditated and taught meditation among his followers, wandered the land, and made a point of taking his begging bowl out every day to whomever he might encounter. Confucius filled public roles, but perhaps most importantly, retired to a circle of students whom he engaged actively.

In each case, the paradigmatic figure developed a group of dedicated followers who became the initial audience to his teachings and his crystallization of a creative philosophy or religious ethic. In each case, the immediate followers or disciples became the figures who, according to legends, reduced the teachings of the paradigmatic individuals to first versions of their doctrines. Thus, the immediate and powerful impact of the personalities of the paradigmatic individuals on their followers played a key historical role. Jaspers's analysis of each of the paradigmatic figures focused on the especially intense relationship between the paradigmatic individual and his close adherents or followers. Jaspers also emphasized that in each case the paradigmatic figure served as a religio-ethical model for his immediate followers. However, a key point underlying Jaspers's use of the term *paradigmatic figures* is that emulation of these axial figures has remained central to the ethics of the world religions. Even in our day, followers seek to adhere to the models of paradigmatic figures. In Christian preaching, individuals are often encouraged to "do as Jesus would do" or are admonished for failing to emulate Jesus. In Buddhist mendicancy, the daily practice of placing a begging bowl before others is an emulation of Buddha's otherworldliness. Following the model of Confucius in respecting senior figures in patrilineal kinship groups, in villages, in neighborhoods, and in politics, of submerging the self to maintain the harmony of social groups and of society, and in study of the classics remains central to Confucian thought and life-practice. Philosophers identify with Socrates in commitment to critical examination and persistent questioning of previously accepted thoughts and beliefs—as well as often teaching through the Socratic method of questioning students.

The deaths of the paradigmatic individuals had, Jaspers observed, important symbolic and ethical importance in relation to the meanings of their lives. Socrates accepted his death sentence with equanimity, calmed the reactions of his followers with the observation that he was seventy years of age and near the end of a natural life, and drank the hemlock poison voluntarily, even as he continued to protest the injustice of his sentence. Jesus was painfully crucified after suffering earlier tortures and, on the cross, cried out his concern that God had forsaken him. His suffering came to have important symbolic significance for Christianity, apparent in the cross as symbol of belief and adherence, and preserved in all of the varieties of that religion. Buddha lay down to die as he felt his last days approaching, but having attained Enlightenment, anticipated escape from the suffering of the world. Confucius also lay down to die as he felt his life forces waning, but did so in full acceptance that death is itself a natural part of life, for humans as for all living beings. In each case, the meaning of the particular death was to become an important element in the accruing mythology about, and formal theology attributed to, the paradigmatic figure.

The Importance of Jesus

For Jaspers, the central paradigmatic figure was Jesus, and the central problem for his treatment of Jesus concerned the respects in which Jesus's life and message set foundational issues for Western philosophy. He emphasized that Jesus's own teachings were greatly amplified, modified, and rationalized by followers over long periods of time. Some of the followers presented themselves as immediate disciples, although, like other scholars of his time and more recently, Jaspers knew that the Gospels were written several decades or longer after Jesus's death. They introduced ideas important to later Christianity, not least the claim of Resurrection. They also claimed that Jesus was the Messiah, even the Son of God, and would participate with God in a Last Judgment, beliefs absent from Jesus's own thought and self-presentation. Only centuries after Jesus did theologians introduce ideas now regarded as central to Christianity, such as the Trinity, a concept so complex that it required more than a century of theological proposals, critiques, and revised proposals to refine.[12]

Of particular note in Jaspers's discussion is the important observation that the individualism of the West has emphasized the personalities of thinkers in a way much less characteristic of Chinese and especially Indian culture. Thus, Socrates and especially Jesus—and, we might add, several of the Old Testament prophets—are vivid personalities in a sense not true of Buddha or Confucius. The same vivid quality applies to many later Western philosophers: Machiavelli, Hobbes, Locke, Hume, Kant, Rousseau, Tocqueville, Simmel, and Weber come to mind, while we know very little by comparison of the personalities of Indian and even Chinese philosophers. Perhaps Islamic figures such as Ibn Khaldun have an intermediate type of presence for modern scholarship. More broadly, as *The Origin and Goal of History* and the pre-Nazi-era work *Man in the Modern Age* make clear, Jaspers was deeply interested in the special developmental path of Western thought and civilization, and the emphasis on the vivid personality of creative thinkers is part of this broader concern. Jaspers's interest in the religio-philosophic foundations of Western rationalism and, in the modern age, its global consequences was likely central to his personal engagement with Weber and Weber's writings.

Setting aside the question of Jesus's teachings and their ultimate relation to modernity, Jaspers emphasized that there were parallel situations in the connections between the life of Confucius and the complex development of philosophy and civilizational traditions in China and between the life of Buddha and philosophy and civilization in a number of Asian societies, not least China and Japan. Socrates's life of intense and focused questioning of the arguments and beliefs of others in the public spaces of Athens also influenced, largely through Plato's writings about him, long traditions of thought in the West, not least dialectics, logic, and the more technical aspects of philosophy as well as many of its substantive concerns, notably, understandings of right and wrong, worthy and unworthy life pursuits, and proper forms of political institutions and political action.

The Paradigmatic Heritages

In Jaspers's treatment, the paradigmatic figures were not themselves philosophers. They could not be philosophers because they did not write. None of paradigmatic figures, he argues, left a written legacy of his own, not Jesus, not Buddha, not Socrates. The *Analects* may be a partial exception to this generalization, but Jaspers argues that "we do not possess a line which in its present form can definitely be attributed to" Confucius (Jaspers 1962, 41). The *Analects* was most likely not written by Confucius himself, but by followers, perhaps compiling actual sayings and/or brief notes written by Confucius. At any rate, Jaspers's chapter on Confucius quotes the *Analects* extensively and presents the series of quoted ethical maxims as likely representing Confucius's thought authentically. Yet, Jaspers maintains that, however wise, the maxims of the *Analects* are too unsystematic to establish a philosophy. Philosophic Confucianism emerged only with the more methodical works of followers, from Mencius on, writing centuries after Confucius. Jaspers treats Confucian thought after the Sung period as increasingly narrow and rigid, even to the point of losing an authentic representation of Confucius. Jaspers viewed the formal examinations in classic writings that mandarins generally had to pass in order to gain their special social status and access to office as an element of such rigidity. Others, including Weber, have treated the examinations as a crucial mode of the routinization of Confucius's thought.

Jaspers noted that Hinayana Buddhism was deeply stereotyped and remained uncreative down to modern times, in sharp contrast to Mahayana Buddhism, which sustained important elements of Buddha's thought and charisma while it also developed interesting adaptations to various cultures and epochs across Asia. Yet, despite the history of Hinayana Buddhism, he treats only later Confucianism as having a comparable rigidity among the axial religions.

The importance of the paradigmatic figures derives from the model lives that they led and the impact of their lives and thought on groups of immediate followers. In using the term *paradigmatic figures,* Jaspers may seem to be echoing Weber's term, exemplary prophets, as distinct from the missionary prophets, ones who attempt, like some of the Old Testament prophets, to carry out a mission God has burdened them with. Jesus, following in the tradition of Old Testament prophecy, is a clear case of missionary prophecy. However, Jaspers was emphasizing that, even in the cases that fit the Weberian type of missionary prophecy, especially Jesus and Mohammad, the essential quality of the paradigmatic individuals was that their *lives* provided ethical models for their followers, who amplified and extended their teachings. Their paradigmatic qualities also affected later theologians and philosophers who, over long periods, sought to emulate their special characteristics and capture those characteristics in new systematizations of their religious ethics.

For example, Saint Francis and the ethics he promulgated cannot be understood outside of his effort to relive what he understood to be key elements of Jesus's life and mission, including his suffering as graphically symbolized by the stigmata. Given that each of paradigmatic figures lived in civilizations that included "craft literacy," that is, literacy largely confined to priestly, accounting, and administrative officials, it is notable that they, with the partial exception of Confucius, did not themselves write, but that literate individuals among their followers, immediate or not so immediate, created their written legacies.[13] In all of the "historic" civilizations created on the basis of the teachings of paradigmatic figures, literacy became more widespread and more central to the continuity and development of the cultures, not least the religio-philosophic cultures.

In the "Introduction" to *The Great Philosophers,* Jaspers echoes a basic Weberian theme in saying that of all figures in the major philosophic traditions, "[i]t is not irrelevant whether the sociological condition of the philosophers' existence is that of independent aristocrats, allowance recipients, priests, itinerant teachers, academic professors, independent literary figures, patronage-supported ones, vagrants, or monks" (Jaspers 2017, 33). Yet, in the section of the volume dealing with the paradigmatic individuals, Jaspers does not follow Weber by emphasizing the social strata of the immediate followers of paradigmatic figures in sketching the long-run development of the religio-philosophic frameworks of the world religions. Rather, Jaspers emphasized the directly personal relations between the paradigmatic figures and their immediate followers who promulgated the initial formulations of the various traditions. Even in discussing the theologians and philosophers who later sought to systematize the earlier formulations, Jaspers underscores their individual contributions rather than their social roles and statuses, although broad historical conditions receive some attention.

In highlighting the roles of immediate followers, Jaspers argues that the paradigmatic figures are essentially unknowable through the mythologies created by their followers. The mythologies include stories of magical powers, extraordinary wisdom, and exceptionally virtuous acts that modern scholarship no longer regards as fully credible. These complex legacies and sets of traditional beliefs mask aspects and elements of the actual lives and actions of the paradigmatic figures. Yet, it is through the mythic formulations that we know these world-historical figures and their imputed messages that have had such profound appeal over millennia. Jaspers argues that even tools of modern historical criticism cannot penetrate through the mythologies to the actualities, aside from the extraordinary impacts that the paradigmatic individuals had upon their followers. In Jaspers's understanding, it was these exceptional effects on followers that selected them out, rather than numerous other somewhat similar figures active in their own times, as founders of great civilizations.

Paradigmatic Lives

Jaspers gives several examples of this masking of the actualities of the paradigmatic lives. He observes that there is agreement among those who knew

Socrates and wrote about him that his physical appearance was unattractive, but very little agreement about his thought and direct influence on others. Socrates is familiar to modern readers mainly through Plato's *Dialogues*. But the dialogues use the figure of Socrates to advance Plato's thought, not simply Socrates's thought and manner of persistent questioning. Other early Greek sources present quite different understandings of Socrates's teachings. It was Jesus's followers who, after the presumed Resurrection, presented him as most certainly the Messiah, a status that Jesus only occasionally and at most ambiguously claimed for himself. Through belief in the Resurrection, Jesus was later acclaimed an aspect of God or figure of the Godhead. Centuries later, Jesus was understood to be the second personage of the Trinity. These claims were ones that Jesus never made of himself (Jaspers 1962, 83). The conception of the Trinity was not fully formulated until more than three centuries after Jesus, yet has become a core element of Christian belief, one affirmed by nearly all churches, denominations, and sects (ibid., 84ff.).

Jaspers emphasizes that it was only after the proclamation of the Resurrection that Jesus became Christ. In historical fact, Jesus was never Christian, but merely a late Jewish prophet, following in a tradition of prophecy that asserted the need for cleansing and reform of corrupt institutions in the Jewish community. His prophecy was that the end of time was near and that faith in God was a requisite of salvation. Only individuals who had faith in God and were able to demonstrate it through love for their fellow men would be saved. Others would soon be condemned when time ended and the Day of Judgment arrived. Early Christians, who knew of Jesus's suffering and death on the cross and believed in his resurrection, yet experienced the continuation of time, had to relativize Jesus's message of the impending end of the world. Indeed, the various documents of the New Testament show that the belief in the impending end of time had to be revised several times in the course of the first century CE.[14] The belief in Jesus's divine being and as Christ followed, marking, Jaspers argues, the true beginning of Christianity.

The advocacy attributed to Confucius that kingdoms should return to ancient traditions on the grounds that they most closely emulate permanent truths and ideals is apparently a systematization of his personal maxims. But it is far from the institutionalization of patriarchal ethics in all hierarchical relations, a genteel lifestyle of emulating classical ritualism, patrimonial administration through a Mandarinate literate in classic documents, and a ritualist-ceremonial manner of settling legal cases in terms of social proprieties (Jaspers 1962, 60ff; cf. Weber 1951). In these respects, the classical

Confucianism of the later Chinese dynasties emerged only through a series of philosophic extensions and refinements of early Confucian thought, many of them originating in the Tang and Sung dynasties a millennium or so after Confucius.

Buddha's wandering mendicancy was basically individual action, even though in his later years he attracted a group of followers and assumed the role of teacher. But the stories of his miracles, his founding of monastic groups, and the later institutionalization of orders of monks and monasteries were all the creations of followers (Jaspers 1962, 29ff). Buddhism, as Weber noted, was extruded from India early in its history due to its opposition to the Brahmin-led institutionalization of the hierarchical "caste" order, grounded in a wide range of daily rituals and ritual relationships. Buddhism's influence has thus been mainly in a number of other Asian societies.

As we have seen, Jaspers emphasized repeatedly the importance of transformations of the teachings of the paradigmatic figures through the written legacies of followers. The initial phases of the transformations derived from the works of immediate followers, whose own lives were profoundly changed by their relationships with the paradigmatic figures. They exalted their leaders and teachers to paradigmatic status, based on the effects that model lives had on them personally. However, Jaspers also underscores that philosophies created by immediate followers could lead others over generations, centuries, and millennia to make further additions and revisions to the philosophic traditions. Key examples are the relative suppression of Jesus's emphasis on the end of time being imminent in his own days and, later, the belief that Jesus was Christ, and then the development of the idea of the Trinity. The founding of the Catholic and Orthodox Churches and even the emergence of Protestantism are further examples of revision with institutional consequences. It is an important consideration that neither Luther nor Calvin, to cite key figures, influenced followers as paradigmatic figures, but rather as presenting doctrines that renewed the understanding and personal experience of Jesus as a paradigmatic figure. They were themselves in important respects charismatic, but not paradigmatic. However, their thought included an important element of seeking to live in ways that revived the love and faith modeled by Jesus.

Jaspers and Weber

Jaspers gives less emphasis than Weber to the problems of soteriology and theodicy, but more to philosophic systematization of thought (Jaspers

1957), his parallel to Weber's rationalization, in treating the development of religio-philosophic belief systems. Jaspers's principal interest was in the foundations of philosophies, much less in the sociological or social psychological processes shaping interests in the ethical emphases of the philosophies.

Yet, Jaspers followed Weber in emphasizing that a crucial outcome of the Axial Age is that the resulting civilizations diverged from one another both in philosophies and in institutional forms. Jaspers fully understood that Western Judeo-Greek-Christian, Buddhist, and Confucian religious ethics developed in radically different ways and formed the bases of radically different institutional orders (Jaspers 1962, 87–96; 1953, chs. I, V, VI, and VII). In this respect, his conceptions of both the Axial Age and the founding paradigmatic individuals is importantly different from such claimed predecessors in the discovery of the Axial Age as John Stuart-Glennie, who believed that the "Moral Revolution" of approximately the sixth century BCE had essentially the same outcome across Asia and represented a unitary stage of human history (Stuart-Glennie 2015, 1880, 2017; also Halton 2014). For Jaspers, only the West, with its foundations in Greek philosophy and Hebraic prophecy, united through the paradigmatic figure of Jesus and the doctrines developed by his followers, has developed modernity and its philosophical, cultural, and institutional complexes with their "universal" importance, an understanding that again was likely derived in large part from Weber. In *The Origin and Goal of History*, in *The Great Philosophers*, and in other works, Jaspers fully acknowledges the originality and complexity of later works in theology, philosophy, and political theory that created modern thought and ethics. Yet, he also understood that these developments took place within the frame of civilization that derives from teachings established by the followers of Jesus.

The Axial Age and Axiality

The paradigmatic figures discussed in *The Great Philosophers* overlap the Axial Age. Jaspers's treatments of Socrates, Buddha, and Confucius in the later volume read as if they were amplifications of the slim discussions of their lives and works in *The Origin and Goal of History*. But Jesus was not a figure of the Axial Age, nor was Mohammad, whom, as noted, Jaspers acknowledged also to have been a paradigmatic individual. Buddha, Confucius, Jesus, and Mohammad were all, through the revisions of their life messages by numerous followers, inspiring figures for world religions. Socrates was not a founder of a great religion, even if one considers the amplification of his thought by Plato. But he was in crucial respects a paradigmatic founder of the questioning, critical, rationalizing tradition of Western philosophy, which in the form of theology has also rationalized Christian thought and ethics, notably in the works of Augustine, Aquinas, and Calvin.

Jesus and Mohammad, in addition to living centuries after the Axial Age, derived the manner of their lives and thought largely from the Hebraic prophets and Greek philosophers who were Axial Age figures. The portions of the New Testament that present themselves as historical accounts of Jesus's life, mission, and death follow the model of Old Testament accounts of prophets, with added emphasis on Jesus's miraculous works. The Koran presents in part a reframed mythology of Abraham, the Hebraic prophets, and Jesus. In both cases, the religio-philosophic messages returned to themes of the Axial Age. In that respect, the paradigmatic statuses of Jesus and Mohammad derive from distinctive integrations of elements of Axial Age developments. Thus, like Buddha and Confucius, they were axial in the sense that they addressed transcendental issues opened up by predecessors as well as in the sense that they founded world religions and great civilizations. By contrast, the Greek philosophers, including Socrates, and the Hebraic prophets were axial with respect to the era of their lives and their thought and teaching. But in terms of founding world religions and great civilizations, they were axial only through their later influences on Christianity, Islam, and, one might argue, philosophic thought from the fourth-century theologians to the groundings of modern intellectual disciplines and ideologies.

If one considers the full scope of what we mean by axial figures, that is, both in terms of their creativity and as founders of world civilizations, only Buddha and Confucius fully qualify. Jesus and Mohammad, although not part of the Axial Age and derivative of Axial Age predecessors, were axial in the sense of the civilizational consequences of their paradigmatic lives. Thus, Jaspers's later focus on the lives and messages of paradigmatic figures helps us to understand the consequences of axial thought for later religion and philosophy in a sense only indirectly addressed in his earlier treatment of the Axial Age. This is especially true for his discussion of Jesus and the importance of Christianity for the civilization and philosophy of the modern West, the central concern of *The Great Philosophers*.

In one place or another, Weber discussed all of Jaspers's paradigmatic figures, and all except Socrates were treated as charismatic authorities. Weber saw the routinization of the charismas of Confucius, Jesus, and Buddha as centuries-long processes that shaped the religious ethics of entire civilizations. He emphasized the respects in which the differences among their respective religious ethics led the resulting civilizations to diverge from one another and their major social institutions to take very different forms. Economic institutions, political institutions, institutions of community life, institutions of family life and kinship, educational institutions, and the forms of religious action have differed—and still differ—by the "directions" in which the original charismas were routinized. Weber's complex analysis of the routinization of charismas still forms a principal basis for comparative historical sociology, despite the contributions of many other scholars. Indeed, this is true in large part because the contributions of more recent scholars have been built directly and substantially upon Weber's scholarship.

In this perspective, it is essential to understand that Jaspers's paradigmatic figures were charismatics. His analyses of the paradigmatic figures add to our understanding of religio-philosophic charisma and should not be viewed as standing off from it, however interesting his introduction of a new term and concept. Paradigmatic figures should be treated as a subtype of charismatic leadership, one that, viewed retrospectively, leads us to understand the origins of the axiality at the foundations of world civilizations.

Yet, there is another interesting and fundamental aspect of Jaspers's treatment of the paradigmatic figures. There have been only a small number of such personages throughout human history: only Socrates, Buddha, Confucius, Jesus, and Mohammad. It stands as a striking fact that there were none before the Axial Age, a phenomenon we understand in terms of civilizational developments in the more highly developed "archaic" civilizations, including craft literacy and social supports for complexly speculative, if predominantly mythological, thought, as in traditional Egyptian, Mesopotamian, or Greek mythologies. But there have also been no paradigmatic figures since Mohammad. Jaspers's treatment suggests that the opportunity to assume the role of a paradigmatic individual has been closed off for a millennium and a half. It seems that, once a paradigmatic figure is recognized and a sophisticated, transcendentally grounded civilization develops around the religio-philosophic thought attributed to him, no successor can attain the role and status of a paradigmatic. Through the contributions of the paradigmatic figures themselves, and through the roles of their followers and the rationalizers of their ethics, the role of the paradigmatic has been monopolized for the resulting civilization. The opportunity for any figure to become a comparable paradigmatic founder has apparently been closed off, perhaps permanently.

Why, in terms of civilizational dynamics, this fact should be so deserves further investigation through comparative research. However, the complement to the closing off of paradigmatic roles has been an opening up of opportunities in civilizations based on world religions for individuals to become *charismatic* leaders. Charismatic leaders have proliferated, but with the limitation that, insofar as they claim to be propounding ethical beliefs or ideologies, they must present their teachings as deriving from or relating to the teachings of founding paradigmatic figures. The relations between charismatic successors and paradigmatic predecessors, although certainly a theme explored in some histories of philosophy, seem also to be important phenomena for further sociological investigation.

Conclusion

Jaspers's concept of paradigmatic figures is an important complement to his conception of the Axial Age. Although the Axial Age has become a major focus of recent comparative research, the concept of paradigmatic individuals introduced in *The Great Philosophers* has not. This is true even though, while relatively brief, the chapters on the paradigmatic figures are more intensive than Jaspers's earlier discussion of the Axial Age.[15]

The concept of paradigmatic individuals is far more specific than Weber's comprehensive notion of charisma and charismatic figures. The paradigmatic individuals emerged against backgrounds of essentially archaic civilizations with craft literacy, although in the case of the Hellenized and Romanized Israel/Palestine of Jesus's time, literacy was likely more widespread. In their extraordinary lives, the paradigmatic individuals affected groups of followers who sought to capture their personal essences in new religious or philosophic doctrines. As Jaspers emphasizes, given that the paradigmatic individuals lived long before the development of historical criticism, their actual lives are so profoundly covered over by myth that they remain unrecoverable. He deemed Buddha to be the figure most completely hidden from us, but Jesus, Confucius, and even Socrates are essentially unknown in their actualities.[16]

What we do know is that each of the paradigmatic figures had such powerful effects on followers that they stimulated the creation of new religio-philosophic doctrines, each highly distinctive from the others. Engagement with the resulting frames of theology and philosophy has been sustained in each of the traditions from the times of the paradigmatic figures to the present. In each case, theologies and philosophies have continued to be elaborated, systematized, and revised for many centuries. Part of the paradigmatic role has been that the figures have represented models for subsequent thinkers over millennia, such that innovations have often been presented as new efforts to embody the life experience and teachings of the guiding paradigmatic figures. Moreover, as the thought and teachings of each of the paradigmatic persons has been distinctive, so each of the resulting civilizations and traditions of philosophic thought has become distinctive as compared with the others.

Jaspers's insight in emphasizing the conception of paradigmatic figures provides deeper understanding of the distinctive *origins* of such millennia-long processes than Weber's conceptions of charisma and its routinization by themselves. Jaspers emphasized that the followers of the paradigmatic figures, not the paradigmatic figures themselves, created the axial religio-philosophic belief systems. Confucius was not a Confucian in the sense of later Chinese civilization, Buddhism in its various forms rests on the systematized thought of Buddha's followers, what we understand by Socratic philosophy is largely the doing of Plato, and Jesus was not a Christian. Jaspers emphasizes the impacts of the personal models of paradigmatic individuals on their immediate followers as the sparks of cultural reformulation, but also emphasizes the creativity of the reformulations of the followers in establishing the subsequent, long-lived frames of belief. His difference from Weber's treatment of charisma lies in the analysis of the relationships between paradigmatic individuals and their followers, initially immediate followers, but also later followers over centuries and millenia. He acknowledges the long historical developments that followed the initial written doctrines of followers, but does not subject them to intensive analysis. In that respect, his treatment of axial developments is far short of Weber's. Yet, he follows Weber in underscoring the different directions of development of the world religions, an insight largely obscured in Stuart-Glennie's earlier treatment of the Moral Revolution.[17]

Finally, Jaspers's treatment of the paradigmatic individuals leads us to relativize the conception of the Axial Age. Not all axial figures became founders of world religions and two of the founders of world religions were post–Axial Age paradigmatic figures. Moreover, Jaspers leaves us with important questions for the comparative sociology of religions and civilizations: Why have there been so few paradigmatic figures in all of human experience? Why have there been no paradigmatic figures since Mohammad? How do the messages of ethical charismatic figures who have emerged in the history of each of the axial civilizations relate to the teachings of the founding paradigmatic figures? That is, how have the paradigmatic axial teachings both stimulated and constrained the creativity of all subsequent religio-ethical charismatic thinkers?

Notes

Both epigraphs are from the new, and first complete, translation of the Foreword to Karl Jaspers's *The Great Philosophers* by Ruth Burch, Florian Hild, and Helmut Wautischer, in *Existenz; An International Journal of Philosophy, Religion, Politics, and the Arts*, 12, no. 1 (Spring 2017): 9–12.

1. Jaspers acknowledged Weber's perspective: "[Sociology] is represented by Max Weber and his works, with his clear and multi-dimensional conceptuality in this widest of all horizons of historical interpretation, which he has kept free from fiction in a total conception" (Jaspers 1953, 266–67). Weber's work is also cited as a basic contribution to the understanding of modern times and civilization in Jaspers 1951.

2. See Jaspers 1964. The essay includes an elegant summary of Weber's Protestant ethic thesis, one of the best in the very large literature. Jaspers's personal relation to Weber was the basis of his selection to speak at Weber's memorial service. That selection is notable in that Jaspers was a generation younger than Weber and thus not one of his lifelong colleagues.

3. There is a sense in which *The Origin and Goal of History* is a recasting of the prewar *Man in the Modern Age* in light of the horrors of the Nazi era. The grounding of the work in the Axial Age breakthroughs and especially in the civilizational tradition then established for the West was an effort to clarify the religious and ethical foundations of modernity that had been so deeply disrupted by the Nazis, especially for individuals in the tradition of German philosophy. See also Jaspers's brief forewords to both the 1951 and 1953 volumes.

4. The distinction between what recent scholars, including Bellah (1970), Parsons (1966), and Eisenstadt (1963) and in various other works, have termed "archaic civilizations" and the larger, better consolidated "historic civilizations" is now well established in comparative sociology. It coincides directly with Jaspers's distinction between the pre–Axial Age kingdoms and the larger empires that were consolidated on the basis of Axial Age religio-philosophic movements. It is notable that neither Bellah in making the distinction between mythological and philosophic religions, nor Parsons in generalizing the distinction to many aspects of the institutional structures of ancient societies, cited Jaspers. Nor did they cite Jaspers in conceptualizing the "philosophic breakthroughs" on which the world religions and thus the early historic, as distinct from archaic, civilizations were based. Parsons's lack of knowledge of Jaspers's conception of the Axial Age is notable in that he

had been Jaspers's student in Heidelberg in the 1920s. Later, it was Eisenstadt who, with various collaborators, including Bellah, revived Jaspers's concept of the Axial Age for sociology.

5. *Philosophic breakthrough* is a term Bellah (1970) introduced.

6. In a short introduction to the new translation of Jaspers's introduction to *The Great Philosophers*, Florian Hild explains that the introduction to the original English edition had been substantially expurgated from the German text due to a belief that American readers would be impatient with its length and detail. The new translation was undertaken to make the content of the full *Einleitung* available to readers in English.

7. The extent to which Trump's self-presentation, widely accepted among his followers, as a self-made billionaire is substantially a hoax was revealed by *The New York Times* on October 3, 2018, in a lengthy feature article exposing both his financial dependence on his father and his ethically and perhaps legally dubious tax filings over many years. The *Times* article admitted that it and other mass media had for years given little attention to several major bankruptcies of his businesses and failed to examine critically Trump's personal boasts about his business successes and wealth, even during the presidential campaign of 2016. One devastating response to Trump's claims of being a business "genius" is the observation that if he had invested the funds he received from his father in a Standard and Poor's 500 index fund, he would now be even wealthier than he claims to be. The capacity to avoid critical examination is also a quality of some forms of charisma.

8. The present discussion of Weber's sociology of comparative civilizations is influenced, among many other secondary works, principally by Talcott Parsons (1937), Wolfgang Schluchter (1989), and Stephen Kalberg (2012).

9. The Introduction to *The Great Philosophers* (Jaspers 2017) indicates that there are figures of substantial significance in the world history of philosophy whom Jaspers will not discuss due to the limitations of his personal knowledge. See Section VIII: "The Functions of the Exposition." The outline presented for the projected three volumes makes clear that the treatment of non-European philosophies was to be highly selective. Volume Two includes treatments of just one Chinese philosopher, Lao-Tse, and one Buddhist philosopher, Nagarjuna. Volume One discusses, after the four paradigmatic figures, only Plato, Augustine, and Kant, with brief treatments of their later heritages and followers, which gives us a sense of Jaspers's high standard for inclusion as a great philosopher. Volume Two discusses from the Western traditions of philosophy Anaximander, Heraclitus, Parmenides, Plotinus, Anselm, Nicholas of Cusa, and Spinoza. The planned Volume Three was never published. Notable in the published volumes is a lack of attention to the German academic philosophers of Jaspers's own times, for example, Dilthey, Windelband, Rickert, Husserl, and Heidigger, with little said about Hegel or Marx. Similarly, there is little about such important English philosophers as Hobbes, Locke, and Hume or the major figures of the French Enlightenment, such as, Voltaire, Condorcet, and Rousseau.

10. Suzanne Kirkbright (2004, 173–74) reports that it was the distinguished Heidelberg scholar of Indian philosophy Heinrich Zimmer (e.g., Zimmer 1956), who persuaded Jaspers to study Eastern philosophies.

11. Socrates represents a somewhat different case. Jaspers presumably included him as a charismatic who established the critical dialogue, and the rational thought realized through it, as the foundation of Western philosophy. Important as his charisma was for philosophy, it must be viewed as of a different order than the charismas of Confucius, Buddha, and Jesus, which founded civilizations in a more comprehensive sense.

12. Compare Diarmaid MacCulloch (2009). See also Paula Fredriksen (2018) on the writing of the Gospels over several generations.

13. How immediate were the followers who wrote down the "original" teachings of the paradigmatic figures is open to question in light of more recent scholarship. For example, Diarmaid MacCulloch (2009) estimates that the core Gospels were written some fifty to one hundred years after the death of Jesus. Whether immediate disciples wrote any of the Gospels seems open to question, given the discussion in Fredriksen (2018).

14. Fredriksen (2018) is especially clear when reviewing the various circumstances in which the end of times seemed again to be immanent to followers of Jesus and then failed to occur.

15. In order to focus on the different perspectives that Jaspers presented in *The Origin and Goal of History* and *The Great Philosophers*, I have not tried to address the relation of the growing recent scholarship on the Axial Age to Jaspers's writings and conceptions. However, I do wish to acknowledge the following key works: Robert N. Bellah (2011), S. N. Eisenstadt (1986), and Robert N. Bellah and Hans Joas (2012).

16. Interestingly, this is a point on which Stuart-Glennie did anticipate Jaspers. He, too, held that all of the sixth-century BCE central figures of the Moral Revolution had been so covered over by mythology as to have long become unknowable. He wrote of Jesus, "From narratives so meager as that of Matthew, so fragmentary as that of Mark, so mythological as that of Luke, so mystical as that of John, so late and unsupported by external evidence as them all, it was now probably impossible to reconstruct the life of Jesus. And though . . . Renan has, with admirable genius and learning, made the attempt, that conclusion does not seem to require any material modification." John Stuart-Glennie (1880, 392).

17. As noted above, Jaspers considered the Axial Age to be a time of interesting *processes* of religio-philosophic innovation, processes that in each case developed in an highly distinctive manner. Stuart-Glennie, as a positivist attempting to construct a universal history that could lawfully forecast the future, regarded the Moral Revolution of the sixth century BCE as a *stage* of human history, one of great importance due to the essentially similar changes it had brought to peoples across the continents of Asian and Europe.

References

Bellah, Robert N. 1970. "Religious Evolution." In *Beyond Belief; Essays on Religion in a Post-Traditional World.* New York: Harper and Row.

———. 2011. *Religion in Human Evolution; From the Paleolithic to the Axial Age.* Cambridge: Harvard University Press.

———, and Hans Joas, eds. 2012. T*he Axial Age and Its Consequences.* Cambridge: Harvard University Press.

Eisenstadt, S. N. 1963. *The Political Systems of Empires.* New York: Free Press.

———, ed. 1986. *The Origins and Diversity of Axial Age Civilizations.* Albany: State University of New York Press.

Fredriksen, Paula. 2018. *When Christians Were Jews; The First Generation.* New Haven: Yale University Press.

Halton, Eugene. 2014. *From the Axial Age to the Moral Revolution; John Stuart-Glennie, Karl Jaspers, and a New Understanding of the Idea.* New York: Palgrave Macmillan.

Hild, Florian. 2017. "Introduction" to new translation of the "Introduction" to Karl Jaspers, *The Great Philosophers*, Existenz; *An International Journal of Philosophy, Religion, and the Arts* 12, no. 1: 50–52.

Jaspers, Karl. 1951 [1931]. *Man in the Modern Age.* London: Routledge and Kegan Paul.

———. 1953. *The Origin and Goal of History.* Oxford: Routledge and Kegan Paul; reprinted 2010.

———. 1957. *The Great Philosophers.* New York: Harcourt, Brace and World.

———. 1962. *Socrates, Buddha, Confucius, Jesus.* New York: Harcourt, Brace; separate printing of "Part One" of *The Great Philosophers.*

———. 1964. "Max Weber." In *Three Essays: Leonardo, Descartes, Max Weber.* New York: Harcourt, Brace and World.

———. 1997 [1913]. *General Psychopathology.* Baltimore: Johns Hopkins University Press.

———. 2016. *Korrespondenten*, 3 volumes. Goettingen: Wilhelm Verlag.

———. 2017. "Foreword" and "Introduction" to *The Great Philosophers*, a new translation by Ruth Burch, Florian Hild, and Helmut Wautischer. *Existenz; An International Journal of Philosophy, Religion, and the Arts*, 12, no. 1.

Kalberg, Stephen. 2012. *Max Weber's Comparative-Historical Sociology Today.* London: Ashgate.

Kirkbright, Suzanne. 2004. *Karl Jaspers: A Biography, Navigations in Truth.* New Haven: Yale University Press.

MacCulloch. 2009. *Christianity; The First Three Thousand Years.* New York: Viking.

Parsons, Talcott. 1937. *The Structure of Social Action.* New York: McGraw-Hill.

———. 1966. *Societies; Evolutionary and Comparative Perspectives.* Englewood Cliffs, NJ: Prentice-Hall.

Schluchter, Wolfgang. 1989. *Rationalism, Religion, and Domination; A Weberian Perspective.* Berkeley: University of California Press.

Stuart-Glennie, John. 1878, 1879, 1880. *The Modern Revolution,* three volumes; *Proemia I: Isis and Osiris; Or the Origin of Christianity as a Verification of an Ultimate Law of History* (reprinted London: Forgotten Books, 2015); *Proemia II: Historical Inductions; Travel and Discussion in Egypt, Sinai, Palestine, and Syria with the Late Thomas Buckle* (reprinted London: Historical Collection from the British Library, no date); *Proemia III: Europe and Asia; Discussion of the Eastern Question in Travels through Independent, Turkish, and Austrian Illyria* (reprinted London: Forgotten Books, 2017).

Weber, Max. 1930. *The Protestant Ethic and the Spirit of Capitalism.* New York: Scribner's.

———. 1946. "Religious Rejections of the World and their Directrions." In *From Max Weber; Essays in Sociology,* edited by Hans Gerth and C. Wright Mills. New York: Oxford University Press.

———. 1951. *The Religion of China.* New York: The Free Press.

———. 1952. *Ancient Judaism.* New York: The Free Press.

———. 1958. *The Religion of India.* New York: The Free Press.

———. 1968. *Economy and Society,* 3 volumes. New York: Bedminster Press.

———. 1988 [1920]. *Gesammelte Aufsaetze zur Religionssoziologie,* 2 volumes. Tübingen: J. C. B. Mohr (Paul Siebeck).

Zimmer, Heinrich. 1956. *The Philosophies of India.* Cleveland: Meridian Books.

4

Shadows of Forgotten Ancestors

Some Forerunners and Followers of Max Weber's Protestant Ethic Thesis in France and Brazil

Roberto Motta

Preliminary Remarks

The "Protestant Ethic" thesis had, as is well known, existed before Max Weber's essays bearing on it.[1] Charles de Villers (1765–1815), Napoléon Roussel (1805–1878), and Émile de Laveleye 1822–1892), among others, dealt with it in the French-writing Europe of the nineteenth century. Weber does not refer to either Villers or Roussel, but he mentions Laveleye in his essay on the *Protestant Ethic and the Spirit of Capitalism.*[2] During the same century, or by the beginning of the following one, Brazilian writers Aureliano Tavares Bastos (1839–1875) and Eduardo Carlos Pereira (1855–1923), among others, in addition to a certain number of missionaries of English and North American origin, also dealt, in Brazil, with the issue of Protestantism and Progress. It is very unlikely that Weber was ever acquainted with Brazilian authors and English-speaking missionaries in South America. In any event, Weber does not refer to all his predecessors, including Tocqueville. He does mention Hegel elsewhere in his oeuvre, but not so in his essays on the *PESC.*[3] Yet, they did share some important points of view concerning the issues dealt with by Weber in the *Protestant Ethic and the Spirit of Capitalism* or in the "Prefatory Remarks."[4]

Most of these forerunners did not reach Weber's level of theoretical sophistication. Hegel and Tocqueville, who will be quoted and briefly commented upon later in this paper, certainly did. The author of the present paper takes it for granted that there is indeed an association between Progress and Protestantism.[5] This simply means that, as a general rule, there seems to be a correlation between a sizable Protestant population in a given country or region, and the economic and other development that takes place in the same country or region. But a distinction should be drawn between, on one hand, the general thesis of the association of some form of the Protestant ethic and some form of economic and cultural progress, and, on the other hand, Weber's specific version of the same thesis. Weber formulates the thesis with a high degree of historical erudition and conceptual sophistication. This includes the emphasis he attributes to predestination, with the anxiety it arouses in believers. This anxiety, as he claims, would be relieved through inner-wordly asceticism.

Predominantly Protestant countries of Europe and of the Americas have exhibited, for the last two hundred years or so, a supremacy over predominantly Catholic countries of the same continents. This supremacy transpires in economic and scientific development, level and quality of education,[6] military might, and so on and so forth.

Concerning the Americas, Protestant uniqueness was recognized by many observers and commentators, including the Protestant Hegel and the ostentatiously Catholic Tocqueville, since the first decades of the nineteenth century. For Europe, one would say that while Napoleonic France was the dominant power (until the battle of Waterloo, in 1815), the idea of Protestant superiority would not meet with unrestricted acceptance. However, such superiority became increasingly evident during the remainder of the century. The defeat in wars with Protestant Prussia of two major Catholic powers, Austria (1866) and France (1871), plus the victory of the United States over Spain in the so-called Spanish American war (1888), probably contributed to a generalized awareness of Protestant supremacy.

The Other Napoléon

The research[7] on which this paper is based has not been exhaustive. Even if the author had wished it to be so, he could hardly have been successful in identifying, in countless libraries, big or small, every publication about the Protestant Ethic thesis, in France and Brazil, let alone in Germany, if he had ventured so far. Let us begin with Napoléon Roussel's (1854, 1855) outstanding book, titled *Catholic Nations and Protestant Nations: Compared in Their Threefold Relations to Wealth, Knowledge, and Morality.*[8] It is a huge treatise in two volumes. Nonetheless, its outline is simple. It is summed up in the following passage on page 2:

> If one happened to find, dispersed in all points of the globe, some peoples whose members are honest, behave righteously, are enlightened and prosperous, would not one exclaim here truth rules? If, at the same time, one finds other peoples who are comparatively miserable, ignorant, immoral, might not one say: here error rules? If this double experience is renewed in several points of the globe, will not those possibilities [concerning the rule of truth or error] turn into certainties? (Roussel 1854, 2)

Roussel moves on to a sample of countries or regions, comparing them according to a certain number of variables, such as the level of literacy and education, industriousness, crime rates, propensity to save, and so on. Among others, he contrasts North and South America, Scotland and Ireland, Protestant Switzerland and Catholic Switzerland, Prussia and Austria, Holland and Belgium, England and Spain. In all of these areas, according to him, Protestants clearly enjoy a greater, often much greater rate of progress, than Catholics.

Roussel takes care to discredit explanations based on climate and race. As he puts it: "I do not know whether I am intelligent because my skin is white. But . . . if you take away my faith from me, the whiteness of my skin will not prevent my giving up myself to injustice and egoism" (Roussel 1854, 436–37). Among students of the Protestant Ethic, Roussel has not been the only author who refused to admit the importance of a "racial" factor. Other commentators, not only in France or Brazil, have done the same, probably due less to a belief that all men are created equal, than to a wish to emphasize the religious, ethical factor.[9]

Roussel seems to be only rarely, if at all, mentioned by later authors.[10] His name is absent from Émile de Laveleye's better known essays, *De l'Avenir des Peuples Catholiques*[11] (1875a) and, translated into English and published with a preface by Gladstone, *Protestantism and Catholicism in Their Bearing upon the Liberty and Property of Nations* (1875b). Nevertheless, it is obvious that Laveleye follows Roussel in his comparisons, involving France, Spain, Italy, England, Scotland, and Ireland, emphasized by him in the two first pages of his booklet (1875a). Roussel and/or Laveleye are also imitated, along the same comparative vein, by Brazilian writer E. Carlos Pereira (1920), who, besides having been a distinguished "homme de lettres," was a Presbyterian minister.

This paper is not meant to meddle in the history of "Outre-Rhin"[12] sociotheological developments. It would seem that in Germany there were more complex motivations. Paul Münch remarks that "Protestantism conveyed to a country a higher culture, greater vitality and dynamic progress. This was missing in the Catholic states. In general, Roman Catholicism appeared as the *religion of the stationary, relatively non-advanced races and nations*. . . . Non-religious causes like nature, climate, or race *could never sufficiently explain the inner, characteristic certainty of a development. At its most basic* it was a matter *of the life, of the spirit . . . living in that confession*. Ten years after these statements were made, Max Weber published his study on the relation between Protestantism and the spirit of capitalism" (Münch 1987, 70).[13]

Münch, transcribing Hummel (1895), adopts a more refined terminology than either the somewhat rustic Roussel's or the more journalistic Laveleye's had done. But substantively he says the same thing as both of them.

Roussel was one of the favorites of American Baptist missionary Zachary C. Taylor (1851–1919), who worked in Northeastern Brazil near the end of the nineteenth century. Taylor, who knew French (or his wife did), translated and published some "polemic tracts" (as he calls them) by Roussel. Yet, in Taylor's precious autobiography, no mention is found to Roussel's main book. Laveleye is the author who is quoted by Taylor when he mentions that he bought in São Paulo the rights to the booklet *The Future of the Catholic Peoples,* with its many comparisons between the progress of Protestant countries and regions and the stagnation of the Catholic ones.[14]

Taylor, in a long and picturesque passage, dwells on this theme, which was seen as a central tenet of Protestant apologetics:

> "Are You a Protestant?" This tract I made from the suggestion of a Southern writer thirty years ago, who mentioned all the principal articles of machinery, cloths, etc., made by Northern for Southern people. "Are you a Protestant?" is the question by the Catholic. "Yes," is the reply of the Protestant, who then

> tells the civilization, progress and advancement of Protestant nations—England, Germany, Switzerland, Holland, Norway, Sweden, Denmark, France, in part, and the United States. Whereas Italy, Spain, Portugal, Mexico, Central and South America, all dominated by priests, or rather by the pope, are rated as third class nations. I showed that quite all the machinery, hardware, cloth, medicine, etc., are made in Protestant countries. The priests ride on Protestant railroads, steam boats, send telegrams over Protestant wires, read their papers through Protestant spectacles, and when they walk in Protestant shoes to see the nuns, they find them sewing on Protestant machines. (Taylor 1900, second notebook, 102–103)

Taylor's passage would seem to echo the phrase of a Protestant theologian quoted in Nipperdey (1987,78): "The machine has something Protestant about it." And the theologian would seem to echo the reverend Taylor. Very likely, such a phrase, or equivalent ones, were uttered by many people, in many countries, in the nineteenth century and later.

Apparently only a handful of scholars and/or theologians, in South America and Northern Europe, still knows something about Roussel and his book. He was superseded by Laveleye, who seems to have benefited from his predecessor's writings without worrying about quotation marks and references. Yet Laveleye's whole work, which exerted for some time a strong influence in cognizant circles, has also been all but forgotten. It is highly doubtful that mainline Weber researchers would care for either of these two French-writing authors.[15]

Roussel will again be mentioned just to note that he was himself very prone to quote—and abundantly so—from authors who could reinforce his opinions. To name only some of these authors—who often deserve attention in their own right—he quotes from Alexis de Tocqueville (1805–1859), Michel Chevalier (1806–1879), Alcide d'Orbigny 1802–1857), Edgar Quinet (1803–1875), Charles de Villers (1765–1815), François Guizot (1787–1874), and others.

Roussel describes concrete situations and seems to be only too often right when stressing the affinities between Protestantism and industriousness. But, excepting the requirement of literacy in order to read the Bible, honesty, righteousness, and other such qualities, he does not delve deeper into the theological characteristics of Protestantism that might ultimately explain such affinities or correlations.

Charles de Villers

Roussel makes a long quotation from Villers[16] all the more important because some of the latter's s ideas are still current in philosophical and sociological circles. Villers emphasizes the discovery of subjectivity, the clear and rational possession of the subject by himself.[17] It is possible that Villers, who was conversant with Kant's philosophy, exerted some influence on Hegel. There are certainly affinities between them. The latter remarks that

> the Spirit comes to its subjective knowledge, its subjective identity. In association with this phenomenon the difference between the Romanic and Germanic peoples comes again to the fore. . . . Spain's chivalrousness has gone to New World, to America, without having first come to itself in its deepest intimacy. So no industry came to exist in the country, as the Inquisition did not allow the rise of Self. (Hegel 1996, 503–504)

Protestant or Philoprotestant authors gloried in the advent of Self, credited to the Lutheran Reformation. Catholic or Philocatholic commentators and, at that, some highly conservative ones, such as Frenchman Charles Maurras (1878–1953) and disciples, also acknowledged Luther's discovery. But they viewed it as a plague, the main one at the root of many others, of modern times. Let us quote from Jacques Maritain (1882–1973),[18] who wrote an essay on *Luther or the Advent of the Self* (Maritain 1970 or 1925):

> It would be astonishing if the extraordinary loss of balance induced by Lutheranism had not had repercussions in all spheres. . . . Man will just have to throw off as an empty theological accessory the cloak of meaningless grace and turn his faith-trust on to himself, and he will become that pleasantly liberated being whose continual and infallible progress delights the universe today. And thus, in the person of Luther and in his doctrine, we are present at the Advent of the Self. (Maritain 1970, 4, 18)[19]

Alexis de Tocqueville

Alexis de Tocqueville shared with Max Weber the view of New England as being a promised land, a good and spacious land, a land flowing with milk and honey. For Weber, New England flowed with the milk of inner-wordly asceticism and the honey of industriousness (the latter resulting from the former). For Tocqueville, who published his *De la Démocratie en Amérique* sixty-nine years before the first edition of Weber's *The Protestant Ethic and the Spirit of Capitalism*, New England flowed with Democracy and, likewise, industriousness. For Tocqueville, a given, precise religion, say, a Congregational or Presbyterian church infused with Calvinist theology, carries no special importance. He views religion, including, indeed stressing, Roman Catholicism,[20] above all from a civic point of view.[21]

In spite of his professions of Machiavellianism, Tocqueville[22] was favorably looked upon by Roussel because, without attributing it explicitly to religious and/or racial factors, he supported the thesis of the slow progress (if any at all) of Catholic areas of the Americas, in contrast to mainly Protestant New England.[23]

One may remark a family air common to Hegel and Tocqueville in their evaluations of South America. Neither had ever visited that part of the world. Hegel died in 1831, before the publication of Tocqueville's *Democracy in America*. It is unlikely that Tocqueville, judging by this book, was acquainted with Hegel's teaching on the philosophy of history. However, the backwardness of South America was a commonplace among voyagers and commentators.[24]

Brazilian Views

Since the first half of the nineteenth century, leading Brazilians authors became aware of the development gap between the United States and Brazil.[25] Indeed, well into the twenty-first century, this gap continues to be a major theme of social science and social thought in Brazil. Why are we not the United States? This is the question. What has always been at stake, the problem Brazilian social thinkers have wished to solve, was that of Brazil's specificity, or, to put it crudely, its backwardness.[26] Why had not Brazil evolved along lines similar to those followed by Northern Europe, and, mainly, North America? Which cause, or causes, could explain this persistent gap?

Racial factors were alleged. The United States had progressed, and Brazil had failed to do so, due to the fact that Europeans did not mix, in the former country, with the African slaves and their descendants. In Brazil, on the other hand, the Portuguese conquerors showed little or no racial exclusiveness[27] and mixed extensively, not only with Amerindians, but also with Africans. The Portuguese themselves were blamed for their backwardness. Brazilians should have chosen better ancestors for the European side of their families.[28] Yet, racial explanations were superseded by cultural explanations. Rather soon in Brazilian intellectual history, the religious factor tended to be viewed as the decisive one. Protestantism was seen by many of its supporters, and also by many who held no religious allegiance to it, as the foundational religion of the United States and as the source of its progress. Although a people cannot change their "race," cultural and religious changes are known to have happened. Brazilians should have converted to Protestantism or, failing this, at least adopted the Protestant ethic. This would have been followed by cultural, social, and economic progress.

Aureliano Tavares Bastos, the so-called Apostle of Progress, is probably the earliest representative of an outwardly nonreligious expression of Philoprotestantism in Brazil.[29] He also expressed the deep feeling of economic, political, and intellectual inferiority of Brazilian vis-à-vis North Americans. He wanted Brazil to gain "a new soul." In order to do so, the country would have to learn from others the recipe for progress.[30]

Readers of Max Weber's *The Protestant Ethic and the Spirit of Capitalism* will notice the affinity between the quotation drawn from Bastos and the treatment Weber gives Protestant sectarianism. Certainly Max Weber had not read Bastos. Hegel's *Lectures on the Philosophy of History* and Tocqueville's book on democracy in America might have been common, though unstated sources.[31]

Bastos may have been influenced by Hegel, known to him, if at all, through French commentators. He might also have read Tocqueville concerning New England. Yet the brunt of his Philoprotestantism may have been derived from his contacts with Presbyterian missionary James Cooley Fletcher, whom he met in Brazil around the middle of the nineteenth century. Fletcher, enlarging considerably on an older book by Daniel Parish Kidder, published a well-known *Brazil and the Brazilians* (1857; Portuguese translation 1941).[32] A kind of holy alliance was formed between the Protestant missions and churches and, on the other hand, the representatives of a conception of historical development, associated, at its highest, with Hegel and Weber. Thanks to the efforts above all of North American missionaries, Protestant churches began to take shape in Brazil by 1850. The message of those churches was, at the same time, both theological and sociological.

This was clearly stated by Brazilian author E. Carlos Pereira, whose book, with the wide encompassing title *The Religious Problem of Latin Amer-*

ica (Pereira 1920), was a best-seller on Protestant apologetics in Brazil.[33] A large part of the book is devoted to Dogmàtics. But he does not forget historical comparisons, largely based on Émile de Laveleye.[34]

Interpreters of Brazil

There is in Brazil a discipline called Brazilian Social Thought. This field is actually the study of about ten eminent authors, acknowledged as the Interpreters of Brazil.[35] They were social thinkers at large, rather than sociologists, anthropologists, or historians in the strict, professional meaning of these terms. They provided the *grands récits*[36] that have been applied to the interpretation of Brazilian society, culture, and history. Max Weber's essays furnished a strong nondenominational, scholarly legitimation to the Protestantism and Progress thesis, many of whose elements were incorporated into some of these meganarratives. This Philoprotestant bias has strongly marked Brazilian social science, down to the present day.

Sérgio Buarque de Holanda stands out among the "*ensaístas*."[37] According to him, there would be, "among people of Hispanic[38] extraction, an invincible repulsion toward every kind of morality based on the value of work" (Holanda 1956, 27).[39] Among the causes he attributes to this state of things were the lackluster, if not outright faulty, translations of the Bible into Portuguese. Thus, according to the Brazilian writer, the words in the Bible that refer to professional activity "lack the distinctive religious ring they have in the Germanic tongues. The Portuguese translations of the Bible have the ethically colorless 'obra,' whereas the Protestant versions use *calling* or *Beruf*."[40]

A similar outlook characterizes another major leading "interpreter," Vianna Moog. In his *Bandeirantes and Pioneers* (1964; original Brazilian version 1956) he opposes the Brazilian ethos of adventure, represented by the *Bandeirantes* (more or less equivalent, but with less panache, to the *Conquistadores* of Spanish-speaking America), who would embody the attitudes Max Weber considers typical of a premodern capitalism associated with "the adventure capitalist [which] has existed throughout the world" (Weber 2002a,155).

Holanda's Weberianism was adopted and exacerbated by Moog, who says that "in the case of the achievements of the United States compared to those of Brazil, it is impossible not to emphasize the differences that distinguish the two cultures on the religious and moral level. These differences would have ultimately led to the progress of civilization in geometric ratio in the United States and in arithmetic rate in Brazil" (Moog 1964, 88).

A Farewell to France

If there had been a quota of French authors to be mentioned in this paper, it would certainly have been met. It is true, however, that the history of Weber's reception in France during the last forty years or so, comprising the translations of his oeuvre and the interpretations or reinterpretations of his ideas, presents a great interest, not only sociological but also ethnographical. It would make highly exciting reading. The French story is not wholly unlike its Brazilian counterpart. In both countries the main "use value" attributed to Weberianism is not quite that of sociological, historical, indeed theological exactitude. This value lies, rather, in the project, attributed to Weber, concerning modernity and development.

Alain Peyrefitte's (1925–1999) two books (1976, 1995) on the subject of Weberianism, the Protestant Ethic, economic development, etc., deserve more attention than they have generally received. Peyrefitte, who was several times a state minister of the French Republic, also prided himself as a scholar. He was for a while a visiting professor at the prestigious Collège de France, a member of several academies, and claimed, among other things, to be an anthropologist. He writes in the style of a Protestant or Philo-protestant reformer, warning the French that, if they do not adopt the Protestant Ethic, France will, in many respects, remain an underdeveloped country (he does not mince words), unable to match Germany or Britain.[41] He adopts with zest Roussel's methodology of comparisons between countries.[42] Thus, at the time of his writing, the twelve economically most advanced Protestant countries enjoyed a mean annual per capita income of US$ 3,500, while the twelve most advanced Catholic countries (among them France, Belgium, and Austria) did not surpass a mean of US$ 2,000 (Peyrefitte 1976, 142–43).[43]

Peyrefitte claims, loudly and clearly, what other French students of Weber state, or would like to state, perhaps in more subtle ways. He is certainly not the only functional equivalent of a Protestant reformer[44] among the recent, or relatively recent, supporters of the *Protestant Ethic* thesis in France.[45] But it is impossible to be acquainted with every new intellectual development, or with every new book or article published in France, on

Weber and other subjects. There are more things along the banks of the Seine than are dreamt of in one's speculations.

Final Remarks

How will this chapter be viewed by its eventual readers? It certainly comprises more than merely a collection of antiqua, curiosa, and exotica. It represents an attempt, in connection with the thesis of the association between Protestantism and Progress, to stress, indeed at times to unearth, the importance of authors from far away and long ago. Among them there are philosophers, historians, political scientists, missionaries and others, such as Hegel, Tocqueville, Roussel, Villers, Fletcher, Laveleye, Taylor, etc., plus some eminent Brazilian authors, like Bastos, Holanda, and Moog.

An idea subjacent to this paper will not necessarily be shared by many readers. It may be hyperbolically expressed by the dictum "from Napoléon to Napoléon nobody like Napoléon." In spite of his pedestrian style and unavoidable exaggerations, Napoléon Roussel worked on the rock of hard fact. In Western or Western-colonized countries of Europe and the Americas, there has been an undeniable correlation between Protestantism and Progress.

Roussel's book, like the ones by Laveleye on the same subject, exerted, in several countries, an undeniable impact upon Protestant apologetics. But they are not quite essays bearing directly on the theological or philosophical roots of the Protestant ethic and their impact on the spirit of capitalism or the spirit of progress. They remain, so to say, on the statistical level. They concern, rather, some practical consequences of that ethic. Other authors, such as Villers and Hegel, dealt right with the ethical spirit[46] of Protestantism and its consequences concerning the wealth of nations, but none, to the present writer's knowledge, did it as exhaustively and as brilliantly as Max Weber. As Kalberg puts it:

> Max Weber . . . created an empirically-based, comparative, and historical sociology of universal breadth. Since his death in 1920, Weber's reputation as the seminal sociologist of our time has continued to grow. In recent years, a wide world renascence of interest in his writings has called forth a veritable flood of literature on all aspects of his sociology. (Kalberg 1994, 1)

What Kalberg says agrees with Karl Jaspers's eulogy of Max Weber, in which Jaspers says that Weber "is the philosopher who presents to history the mirror in which it recognizes itself. He personified his time, its tendencies and its problems" (Jaspers 1988, 36). Weber seized the essential: the rationalization process that permeates every aspect of the society, the culture, and the economy of the leading countries of the West, which have led, influenced, changed, or challenged the rest of the world.

This process is the central subject of Abramowski (1966), who is an enthusiastic Weberian. Yet, he warns the reader that "Weber should be evaluated not by his exactness in details, but rather by the fruitfulness of the questions he raises and of his interpretations" (Abramowski 1966, 12).

The flood of literature on Max Weber's interpretation of history and society keeps increasing. This applies, in a peculiar way, to countries such as France and Brazil, where, as we have seen when dealing with Sérgio Buarque de Holanda and Alain Peyrefitte, intellectuals often express a wish to atone for the Catholicism and the traditionalism of their native societies. In spite of his explicit professions of historical and sociological empiricism, Weber, for certain purposes and from a certain standpoint, is treated less as a sociologist than as the prophet of a new kind of society, in which reason will, once and for all, replace tradition. In a way, this corresponds to a secularized culmination of the Lutheran and Calvinist Reformation.

Notes

1. These essays, first and foremost, are those collected in Weber 2002b, including the "Prefatory Remarks" (Weber 2000a) to these essays and to other essays on the sociology of religion written by Weber (1920).

2. Cf. footnote number 29 at Weber 2002a, 169. "[T]he assertion that such a connection [between Calvinism and the capitalist spirit] exists is not 'new.' E. de Laveleye (1875) and Matthew Arnold [1822–1888] (1906, among others), have addressed this connection. On the contrary, 'new' is only its questioning, which is entirely unfounded. The task here is to explain this connection."

3. The acronym *PESC* will henceforth be used in this paper to designate *The Protestant Ethic and the Spirit of Capitalism.*

4. According to Jean Hyppolite (1983, 25, 26, 27) Hegel's Philosophy of History actually consists in the interpretation of the "spirit" or the "genius" of peoples, a task full of Weberian, sociological, and anthropological implications.

5. Any considerations of Asian countries such as Japan, China, Korea, India, and others, are excluded from this paper.

6. A comparison of scientific development, level and quality of education, and related topics, among Protestants and Catholics, mainly in Germany and France, is very much the subject of Aubert 1963, a book considered by many as a classic on its subject.

7. As different from the effort.

8. Roussel 1854 refers to the French original version of the author's magnum opus. Roussel 1855 is the English translation of the same book. It has not been easy to find the English translation either in France or in Brazil. The copy listed in the catalogue of *Bibliothèque de France* was illegible. Pages had adhered to one another in an irreversible way, due to sheer lack of readers for the last fifty years or so. The French original was in a far better state but, at any rate, was very, very far from qualifying as one of the most often consulted items of that grandiose library. My query caused some embarrassment among the librarians, all very polite and gentle. Thus, in this paper, quotations from a French original were translated into English at the author's own risk. He dealt in the same way with the other French- and Portuguese-writing authors quoted in this paper. Some of them had already been translated into English, but multilingual libraries are not available everywhere. Incurring even greater risks, he also dared to translate into English short passages from Hegel's, Jaspers's, and Abramowski's German.

9. An outstanding example of this tendency is Weber himself, with his disclaimer of racial explanations at the very end of his prefatory remarks to his *Collected Essays in the Sociology of Religion* (Weber 2002a).

10. Although Roussel is rarely mentioned today, references to his main book are occasionally to be found on the internet, in association with what appear to be conservative or fundamentalist Protestant sites. It was through this channel that he was first heard about by the author of this paper, who is an associate foreign member of *équipe de recherches Groupe Sociétés, Religions, Laïcités (GRSL)*, connected to *Centre National de la Recherche Scientifique* and to *École Pratique des Hautes Études*. To his knowledge, no present-day French sociologist of religion, of whatever confessional or ideological persuasion (if any), has ever mentioned Roussel or even heard about him. This is said with the fear of being wrong, the *formido errandi,* strongly recommended by ancient logicians. Nevertheless, the English version of his book was recently reissued in Sweden or Finland, according to information available on the Web (Rousssel 2015).

11. This means "on the future of the Catholic peoples," about which Laveleye, a French-speaking and -writing Belgian with a strong anticlerical tendency, was very pessimistic.

12. That is, "beyond the Rhine," as the French, somewhat improperly, are fond of designating the German lands.

13. In this paragraph, passages in italics are quotations made by Münch of Hummel 1895.

14. Cf. Taylor 1900, 2nd notebook, 101.

15. The full French text of Laveleye's *De l'Avenir des Peuples Catholiques* is available on the internet by courtesy of Harvard University.

16. However, Villers is quoted here according to his own book, which is available on site http://gallica.bnf.fr/ark:/12148/bpt6k5401889s.

17. In his own words, "Protestantism is the force of repulsion, inherent to reason, to drive away from itself all that which wants to take its place. . . . The man who is free in the innermost sanctuary of his soul looks around himself with daring and entrepreneurship. . . . He who is a slave in the core of his being, is also so, without realizing it, in the whole of his behavior, degraded as he is by the stupidity and the apathy that seize his faculties" (Villers 1804, 243–44).

18. Concerning Charles Maurras, see Maurras 1972, E. Weber 1962. Jacques Maritain started his career as a Maurrassian, that is, a strict conservative. In the late 1930s he turned into an international leader of "catholiques de gauche" (liberal Catholics), although in the 1960s he recoiled from many consequences of "aggiornamento" in the Catholic Church.

19. Nipperdey remarks that "the philosophers of the Counterrevolution had singled out Protestantism as the real origin and seedbed of revolution against tradition and authority. The liberals turned the argument around: Protestantism is indeed connected with progress and modernity, but Protestantism is not revolution; it is constant reform. The Catholic countries are the ones with this kind of revolutions, provoked by despotism, corruption and laziness. This kind of argument colored all historical-political reasoning in the first two-thirds of the nineteenth century" (Nipperdey 1987, 77).

20. He thinks of Catholicism, at least as practiced and organized in New England and neighboring areas, as a particularly "democratic" (his own term) form of religion.

21. "Religion sees in civic freedom a noble exercise of man's faculties. . . . Religion knows that its empire is all the better established when it wishes to rule with the exclusive use of its own forces. . . . Freedom sees in religion the companion of its struggles and victories, the cradle of its infancy, the divine fountain of its rights. It looks at religion as the safeguard of morals, and morals as the guarantee of laws and the assurance of its own duration" (Tocqueville 1986, vol. 1, 91). Some pages later, he adds that "[a]lthough it matters to a given individual that he follows what he considers as the only true religion . . . society has nothing to fear or to hope for in another life. What matters to it is not that individuals follow the only true religion, but that they follow a religion at all. Moreover, all sects in the United States merge in the great Christian unity and the morals are the same everywhere in the country. . . . It may be added that many Americans, in the cult they render to the Deity, follow rather their habits than their beliefs" (Tocqueville 1986, vol. 1, 431).

22. Even if one imagined that, in his heart of hearts, Tocqueville was a Philoprotestant, he had to mind his promising career in the post-Napoleonic, conservative France of the monarchical and Catholic "Restoration."

23. "In which part of the world will one find more fertile empty lands, bigger rivers, more richesses of all kinds, still intact and virtually inexhaustible, than in South America? . . . Yet, there are on Earth no nations more miserable than those of South America. . . . I found in New England men ready to leave a country in which they could live comfortably, in order to seek fortune in empty lands. Not too far from them I saw the French population of Canada confining themselves in a space too narrow for them, while the same empty lands were also located situated quite within their reach. While the emigrant from the Unites States acquires, with but a few days of work, a large property, the Canadian pays for his land at the same high price he would pay if he were still living in France" (Tocqueville 1986, vol. 1, 452–53). A number of historians would disagree on this point, among them C. B. A. Behrens, who stresses that "[t]he British colonists prospered and multiplied, while Canada increasingly became an economic liability to the French government. For all this, however, it was the French, not the British, who had the great exploits of daring to their credit. Inspired principally by a love of risk and danger, and by romantic visions of a great empire to lay at the feet of the King of France, it was they who discovered the Great Lakes and the Rockies, found the source of the Mississippi and went down to the Gulf of Mexico" (Behrens 1967, 80.) So much for "confinement in a space too narrow for them."

24. Edgar Quinet summarizes this in the following way: "What can be the reason of this miracle of sterility in a new world, other than Catholicism, essentially conservative for the last 300 years, has outspent its force and creative impulse?" (Quinet 1844, 293).

25. Let us be careful not to overestimate either the economic or the intellectual advance of Brazil in the nineteenth century. There were there a few fine poets and novelists. Yet, by the middle of that century there were in the country only two law schools, two medical schools, and one engineering or "polytechnic" school. (Brazil had, in 1850, about eight million inhabitants.) These schools, geared to the young of the country's elite (but not really immune to infiltration by "parvenus"), seem to have been centers of excellence in their fields and allied ones. Many people in Brazil, considered today as pioneer sociologists, anthropologists, or social thinkers hailed from such schools and were acquainted with the most recent intellectual and political trends fashionable in Europe. Universities, in the Euro-American sense of the term, started being funded in the 1920s. For the last forty years or so, the number of universities in Brazil, public and private, lay and confessional, with undergraduate and graduate courses, has been growing at an exponential rate. Sociologists and anthropologists, at times highly publicized, are today a common feature all over the country.

26. A distinguished American author, Francis Fukuyama, edited a book titled *Falling Behind: Explaining the Development Gap between Latin America and the United States* (Fukuyama 2008). The first chapter of this book deals directly with "Two Centuries of South American Reflections on the Development Gap between

the United States and Latin America" (Donghi 2008). This chapter, like the whole book, downplays the role of religion and other cultural factors in the explanation of the "development gap."

27. This was remarked by keenly perceptive Hegel. Although he did not refer specifically to racial mixture, he wrote that the "Portuguese were more humane than the Dutch, the Spanish and the English. Thus there came to exist along the coast of Brazil [where almost all important cities were located] a greater facility for the Black slaves to become free, giving rise to large concentration of free Africans" (Hegel 1920, 193).

28. The Dutch, who occupied a part of Brazil (the main sugarcane growing area) during nearly twenty-five years in the seventeenth century, are, to this day, often portrayed as those ideal ancestors.

29. Bastos has been partly edited and commented upon by Moraes Filho (2001) and Vieira (1980). The latter emphasizes Bastos's Protestant proclivity.

30. He could recognize this recipe in the "liberal spirit of the Reformation, which had led a small colony, New England, to give rise to the mighty, rich, large, enlightened, free, intelligent, generous, bold republic of the United States of America . . . [which] had not suffered from the stupid fanaticism of the 16th century priests, having instead been settled by Quakers and members of other independent sects. Thanks to the Reformation, the U.S. had been impregnated with the moral consciousness, industriousness, intelligence, perseverance, awareness of human dignity and the sense of personal freedom, which are the message of the Gospel and stand out as the basic features of the races of the North of the Globe" (Bastos 1938, 391).

31. Bastos, trained as a lawyer, was also a keen advocate for American economic interests in Brazil.

32. A recent Brazilian commentator of Kidder's and Fletcher's, Carlos A. Valentim, comments on the thesis, according to which, at least in Brazil, the message of evangelization is the message of civilization. "According to the Presbyterian minister [Fletcher] the progress of civilization was pulled ahead by two main powers: high quality education, on one hand, and, on the other, a religion capable to uplift the morality of the people. His basic idea was to convert Brazil to Protestantism and Progress at the same time. . . . His model of civilization was the United States. To him Protestantism entailed scientific, economic and technological development" (Valentim 2010, 101–102).

33. About Protestant missionary activity in Brazil, see Mendonça 2008.

34. His book ends with the following words: "The political and social inferiority of our race, the moral and religious state of the Ibero-American societies are there to claim against Rome's pernicious influence. . . . Protestantism was born from the freedom of the individual consciousness. . . . Protestantism is everywhere associated with the exuberance of luxuriant and vigorous individual prosperity, like plant life in the Tropics" (Pereira 1920, 426–27).

35. They are also called the "essayists" (*ensaístas*).

36. The expression *grands récits* is used here with the meaning it has in Lyotard 1979.

37. Holanda, to this day, is widely held as one of the intellectual heroes of Brazil. Let us remark that he was, or intended to be, a strict Weberian.

38. Holanda uses the adjective *Hispanic* to designate people with Iberian roots both in Europe and the Americas. The use of this adjective to designate Brazilians (and Portuguese) is, nevertheless, uncommon in either Brazil or Portugal, where *hispânico* applies rather to Spanish-speaking people. The Portuguese might even consider offensive their being dubbed Hispanic.

39. Some of those writers, in Brazil as well as in France, attributing a deterministic value to Protestantism in the advent of economic progress, were far more "Weberian" than Weber himself.

40. Cf. Holanda 1994, 167.

41. Although it is quite improbable that they ever heard of each other, there are striking similarities between Alain Peyrefitte and Sérgio Buarque de Holanda.

42. There are good reasons to suspect that he, or his assistants, had read Napoléon Roussel, although he does not mention his distant predecessor in the bibliography of his 1976 book.

43. Peyrefitte is decidedly unclear concerning the origin of these figures. In a footnote concerning the fifteen wealthiest countries of the world, Peyreffite refers to the 1974 year *Book of the World Bank*. Of the fifteen listed countries, thirteen "belong to the Protestant model," among them, quite unexpectedly, Israel. This may have originated in a tortuous chain of printing mistakes, Israel, which is not a Protestant country, having taken the place of unmentioned, and likewise non-Protestant, Japan. At any rate, this shows a very unWeberian carelessness in Peyrefitte and/or his assistants. Elsewhere in his book he mentions as his sources "1973: Official Statistics of the World Bank; 1975 Early estimates of the World Bank and of the O.E.C.D." (Peyrefitte 1976, 510). But even if Peyrefitte's figures should be wrong lock, stock, and barrel, he would still be representative of a widely diffused frame of mind in France and elsewhere.

44. It is well known that French intellectuals are often informally organized in "coteries," whose members are not always on mentioning, let alone quoting, or even greeting, terms with members of other "coteries." It is quite possible that Peyrefitte's books were successful as best-sellers. This certainly applies to his *Le Mal Français* (1976). It was, after all, a book written by a prominent politician, with a title containing the word *mal,* which, according to subtleties in the way it is spelled and pronounced, may have several meanings in French. The book may even have been mistaken for a kind of Gallic Kinsey report. On top of this, he was a cousin, namesake, and contemporary of sensationalist author Roger Peyrefitte, who wrote several novels whose dominant subject was the private lives of French upper-class ladies and gentlemen. As previously remarked concerning Roussel, references to Peyrefitte by members of the mainline Weberian establishment (or establishments)

in France are difficult to find. Be that as it may, the author of this paper was more than once questioned by French colleagues in the following terms: "What, are you joking? Do you mean that Peyrefitte wrote two books about the issue of the Protestant Ethic and the Spirit of Capitalism? Oh, I see, you mean the Peyrefitte who was a minister of De Gaulle's."

45. The early reception of Weber in France is the subject of at least two publications: Pollak 1986 and Hirschhorn 1988.

46. "Spirit" is a basic category in Hegel's philosophy. But this does not imply that Hegel (as different from Max Weber) gave a full monographic treatment to the issue of the Protestant ethic and the spirit of economic progress.

References

Abramowski, Günter. 1966. *Das Geschichtsbild Max Webers: Universalgeschichte am Leitfaden des okzidentalen Rationalisierungsprozesses.* Stuttgart: Ernst Klett Verlag.

Arnold, Matthew. 1906. *St. Paul and the Protestant Prosperity of Nations.* London: Smith Elder.

Aubert, R. 1963. *Le Pontificat de Pie IX (1846–1878).* Paris: Bloud et Gay.

Bastos, Aureliano Cândido Tavares. 1938. *Cartas do Solitário.* São Paulo: Companhia Editora Nacional.

Behrens, C. B. A. 1967. *The Ancien Régime.* New York: Harcourt Brace Jovanovich.

Donghi, Tulio Halperin. 2008. "Two Centuries of South American Reflections on the Development Gap between the United States and Latin America." In *Falling Behind: Explaining the Development Gap between Latin America and the United States,* edited by Francis Fukuyama, 11–47. Oxford: Oxford University Press.

Fukuyama, Francis, ed. 2008. *Falling Behind: Explaining the Development Gap between Latin America and the United States.* Oxford: Oxford University Press.

Hegel, G. W. F. 1920. *Die Vernunft in der Geschichte: Einleitung in der Philosophie der Weltgeschichte.* Herausg. von Georg Lasson. Leipzig: Verlag von Felix Meiner.

———. 1996. *Vorlesungen über die Philosophie der Weltgeschichte (Berlin 1822/1823).* Herausg. von Karl Heinz Ilting, Karl Brener, u. Hoo Nam Seelmann. Hamburg: Felix Meiner Verlag.

Hirschhorn, Monique. 1988. *Max Weber et la Sociologie Française.* Paris: L'Harmattan.

Holanda, Sérgio Buarque de. 1936. *Raízes do Brasil.* Rio de Janeiro: José Olympio.

Hummel, Friedrich. 1895. "Was gibt der evangelische Protestantismus den ihm zugehöringen Völkern bis heute vor den römisch-katholischen Völkern voraus? Vortrag, gehalten bei der VII. General-Versammlung des Evangelischen Bundes zur Wahrung der deutsch-protestantischen Interessen in Bochum. 9. August 1894." Quoted in Paul Münch, "The Thesis before Weber: An Archaeology." In *Weber's Protestant Ethic: Origins, Evidence, Contexts,* edited by Hartmut Lehman and Guenther Roth, 5–71. Cambridge: Cambridge University Press.

Hyppolite, Jean. 1983. *Introduction à la Philosophie de l'Histoire de Hegel.* Paris: Seuil.

Jaspers, Karl. 1988 [920]. "Max Weber. Eine Gedenkrede." In *Gesammelte Schriften.* München: Pieper.

Kalberg, Stephen. 1994. *Max Weber's Comparative-Historical Sociology*. Chicago: The University of Chicago Press.

Kidder, Daniel Parish, and James Cooley Fletcher. 1857. *Brazil and the Brazilians, Portrayed in Historical and Descriptive Sketches*. Philadelphia: Childs and Peterson.

Laveleye, Émile de. 1875a. *L'Avenir des Peuples Catholiques: Étude d'Économie Sociale.* Paris: Fischbacher.

———. 1875b. *Protestantism and Catholicism in Their Bearing upon the Liberty and Prosperity of Nations.* London: John Murray.

Lehmann, Hartmut, and Guenther Roth, eds. 1987. *Weber's Protestant Ethic: Origins, Evidence, Contexts.* Cambridge: Cambridge University Press.

Lyotard, Jean-François. 1979. *La Condition Postmoderne.* Paris: Les Éditions de Minuit.

Maritain, Jacques. 1970 [1925]. "Luther or the Advent of the Self." In *Three Reformers: Luther, Descartes, Rousseau*, 3–52. New York: Crowell.

Maurras, Charles. 1972. *De la Politique Naturelle au Nationalisme Intégral.* Textes chosis par F. Natier et C. Rousseau. Paris: Vrin.

Mendonça, Antônio Gouvêa. 2008. *O Celeste Porvir: A Inserção do Protestantismo no Brasil.* São Paulo: Edusp.

Moog, Vianna. 1964 [Brazil 1956]. *Bandeirantes and Pioneers.* New York: George Braziller.

Moraes Filho, Evaristo, ed. 2001. *As Ideias Fundamentais de Tavares Bastos* Rio de Janeiro: Topbooks.

Münch, Paul. 1987. "The Thesis before Weber: An Archaeology." In *Weber's Protestant Ethic: Origins, Evidence, Contexts*, edited by Hartmut Lehmann and Guenther Roth, 5–71. Cambridge: Cambridge University Press.

Nipperdey, Thomas. 1987. "Max Weber, Protestantism, and the Debate around 1900." In *Weber's Protestant Ethic: Origins, Evidence, Contexts*, edited by Hartmut Lehman and Guenther Roth, 73–81. Cambridge: Cambridge University Press.

Pereira, E. Carlos. 1920. *O Problema Religioso da América Latina: Estudo Dogmático-Histórico.* São Paulo: Empresa Editora Brasileira.

Peyrefitte, Alain. 1976. *Le Mal Français.* Paris: Plon.

———. 1995. *La Société de Confiance : Essai sur les Origines et la Nature du Développement.* Paris: Odile Jacob.

Pollak, Michaël. 1986. "Max Weber en France: L'Itinéraire d'une Œuvre." Cahier no. 3 de l'Institut d'Histoire du Temps Présent. Paris: Centre National de la Recherche Scientifique.

Quinet, Edgar. 1844. *L'Ultramontanisme ou l'Église Romaine et la Société Moderne.* Paris: Comptoir des Imprimeurs Unis.

Roussel, Napoléon. 1854. *Les Nations Catholiques et les Nations Protestantes Comparées sous le Triple Rapport du Bien-Être, des Lumières et de la Moralité.* Deux thomes. Paris: chez Meyrueis.

———. 1855. *Catholic Nations and Protestant Nations: Compared in Their Threefold Relations to Wealth, Knowledge, and Morality.* Boston: John P. Jewett.

———. 2015. *Catholic Nations and Protestant Nations: Compared in Their Threefold Relations to Wealth, Knowledge, and Morality.* Forgotten Books. The names of the city and the country (Sweden? Finland?) of the publication do not appear on the internet. Förlag Forgotten Books, judging from lists and catalogues, is by no means limited to reissuing fundamentalist Protestant literature.

Taylor, Zachary C. 1900 (approximately). *The Rise and Progress of Baptist Missions in Brazil: An Autobiography*, typescript in three notebooks kept at the library of the University of California at Los Angeles. Access to the typescript was granted to the author of this paper in the late 1990s. The typescript seems to have been translated into Spanish and published, in book form, by Colombia's Cauchita Baptist University Press, in 1969. Neither the author nor, apparently, the librarians at UCLA were cognizant of this publication during the author's research in California.

Tocqueville, *Alexis de. 1986 [1835, 1840] De la Démocratie en Amérique. Two volumes. Paris: Gallimard.*

Valentim, Carlos A. 2010. "O Brasil e os Brasileiros." *Fides Reformata*, 2: 97–107. Universidade Mackenzie, São Paulo.

Vieira, David Gueiros. *1980. O Protestantismo, a Maçonaria e a Questão Religiosa no Brasil.* Brasília: Editora Universidade de Brasília.

Villers, *Charles de. 1804. Essai sur l'Esprit et l'Influence de la Réformation de Luther. Paris: Henrichs; Metz: Collignon.*

Weber, Eugen. 1962. *Action Française.* Stanford: Stanford University Press.

Weber, Max. 1920. *Gesammelte Aufsätze zur Religionssoziologie* 3 Bände. Herausgegeben von Marianne Weber. Tübingen: J. C. B. Mohr (Paul Siebeck).

———. 2002a. "Prefatory Remarks" to *Collected Essays in the Sociology of Religion*, translated by Stephen Kalberg. In *The Protestant Ethic and the Spirit of Capitalism*, translation and introduction by Stephen Kalberg, 149–64. Los Angeles: Roxbury.

———. 2002b. *The Protestant Ethic and the Spirit of Capitalism.* Translated and introduction by Stephen Kalberg. Los Angeles: Roxbury.

———. 2003. *L'Éthique Protestante et l'Esprit du Capitalisme, suivi d'autres essais.* Édité, traduit et présenté par Jean-Pierre Grossein avec la collaboration de Fernand Cambon. Paris: Gallimard.

5

Images of Natural Order and Rulership by Measure, Number, and Weight in the Hellenistic-Roman Era

A Study of Intercivilizational Encounters

Donald A. Nielsen

Introduction

The following pages present a case study of intercivilizational encounters in the Ancient Mediterranean world between Greece, Ancient Judaism, Rome, and early Christianity. Explorations of such encounters provide a particularly useful entry into the study of civilizational structures, since they highlight differences among civilizations as their representatives experience them, rejecting, accepting, modifying, and otherwise adapting and putting to new uses ideas, symbolic designs, and institutions from other settings. The focus on specific aspects of encounters, rather than on the direct comparison of whole civilizations in all their complexity, also allows us to avoid becoming lost in a welter of "big structures, large processes and huge comparisons."[1]

My focus is on the ways in which images of natural order and rulership by measure, number, and weight were deployed by civilizational elites during the Hellenistic-Roman era. As such, this study is a contribution to the research program initiated by Durkheim, Mauss, and their school into the historical sociology of the categories of the human spirit (see Nielsen 1998). In particular, it deals with aspects of the categories of quantity and number and imagery derived from those categories.[2] At the same time, I hope to contribute to the understanding of the development of what Max Weber called theoretical rationality (see Kalberg 2012, ch.1) by examining how partial rationalization processes in philosophy, religion, and law occurred in the ancient world through the use of a particular set of theoretical rationales.

This analytical focus on central categories of the human spirit and images of order, and their connection to processes of partial theoretical rationalization, belongs to the study of historical structures of consciousness, that is, the making of minds and frameworks of thought, as they are modified through and within intercivilizational encounters. In my view, a research agenda that fails to account for the key emerging categories and intercivilizational rationales or "structures of reasons" (Nelson 1981, 70) that constitute the structures of consciousness of civilizational actors will provide a highly incomplete picture of the conjunctures enhancing our interest in changing human experience and expression (see Nielsen 2004).

The temporal focus on intercivilizational encounters in the Hellenistic-Roman era represents a shift away from the study of what has variously been called "axial age" civilizations (Jaspers 1949) or "seed bed" cultures (Parsons 1966) and toward the period in which later encounters took place, ones involving the precipitates of those earlier civilizational "breakthroughs." I have been calling this later period a "second axial age" because of its importance in the formation of ideas and symbolic systems vital to later European history (see Nielsen 2002). The similarity between the Hellenistic-Roman era and our current globalizing and intercivilizational conjuncture adds greater interest to the study of this historical period.

I will begin by briefly examining the uses of the images of order and rulership by measure, number, and weight in a "pivotal" Hellenistic Jewish text, the *Wisdom of Solomon*. This text establishes my topical focus. In accordance with the metaphor of its "pivotal" character, it also allows us to move in varying historical directions, without claiming that, despite its historical influence, this particular text was necessarily the only one of decisive historical significance. These will include the origins of the image among the ancient Greeks, its further uses in Hellenistic Judaism and early Christianity, and its deployment by Roman jurists. The essay will conclude by looking briefly at this imagery's longevity and the surprising uses to which it has been put in later Western European civilization.

The *Wisdom of Solomon*: A Pivotal Text in the Encounter of Judaism and Hellenism

The encounter between Judaism and Hellenism is clearly illustrated in the text of the *Wisdom of Solomon* (hereafter abbreviated as Wisd). It was written in Greek by a Jewish writer steeped in Greek thought in Alexandria sometime in the first century BCE or the middle of the first century CE (see Winston 1979). It is not the first or only text embodying this encounter. This era saw the translation of the Old Testament into Greek (the Septuagint) and the deep penetration of Hellenic ideas into Jewish life and thought (see, e.g., Hengel 1974). The Alexandrian setting is particularly central. Alexandria was a Greek city with a large Jewish population. It was also a central dissemination point for Plato's ideas. Thrasyllus in the first century CE assembled what is still viewed as the full collection of Plato's texts. Alexandria also saw the syncretistic development of Jewish Hellenistic thought in the writings of Wisd and Philo and was a key site in the emergence of early Christian theology in the work of Clement, Origen, and others. Plotinus studied there with Ammonius Saccus, who was also Origen's teacher and, thus, neo-Platonism saw its proximate origins in Alexandria. The formula developed by Wisd in this context is our particular initial concern.

Wisd has features common to other literature of this period, including an encomium to the personified figure of Wisdom (*sofia*), which places it within the international current of wisdom literature common to ancient Judaism, Greece, Egypt, and Babylonia. The lengthy praise of wisdom is connected with a discussion of the Jewish exodus from Egypt and the punishments meted out by God to the Egyptians. In the process, it reconfigures the idea of creation. Wisd argues that God could have punished the Egyptians by all the power at His disposal, but did not do so, since "thou hast arranged all things by measure and number and weight" (Wisd 11, 20). God's creation is seen as terms of precise quantitative forms and, perhaps more importantly, God is seen as submitting His own powers to reward and punish (though in principle unlimited) to the same limits implied by the measure, number, weight formula. Indeed, submission to the quantitative laws now embedded in the creation is portrayed as the source of divine mercy as He reconfigures the creation itself to create punishments fitted to the Egyptians' precise sins.

This new use of "mirroring punishment," with its emphasis on precise quantitative values, goes beyond the usual concept of *lex talionis* common to this era. The merger in Wisd of the Biblical image of a creator God with the idea of natural order determined by measure, number, and weight, which as we shall see is ultimately a Hellenic Greek complex of ideas, marks the text as one emerging from the encounter of Judaism and Hellenism, and unlikely to emerge under any other combination of circumstances (see Nielsen 1996b; 2002).

The text has a "pivotal" quality in two respects. It became a historically important text. It influenced later Jewish Alexandrian writers such as Philo (or, given chronological uncertainties, operated in parallel to other efforts such as Philo's). It was adopted by early Christian thinkers and was finally given greater authority by Jerome and others through inclusion in the Latin translation of the Bible, the Vulgate, in the fourth century. In turn, it was transmitted to later Western European medieval writers working exclusively in Latin.

Also, the text is "pivotal" in a second sense. It allows us to "pivot" and turn historically in a variety of directions from the Wisd text to not only the aforementioned Jewish and Christian thinkers, but also to the origins of the measure, number, weight formula among fifth and fourth century BCE Greek thinkers. It also allows a turn to earlier biblical images of creation and rulership by precise quantity, and, finally, a turn to the related uses by the Roman jurists, as well as later medieval and early modern European thinkers. This locates Wisd at a central confluence of civilizational traditions and developmental phases. Its key imagery provides a good reference point for our investigation.

Origins of the Image in Greek Thought

The precise trichotomy of measure, number, and weight is undoubtedly of Greek origin. The image appears in a variety of Greek texts of the fifth and fourth centuries BCE and may go back to an earlier period. It emerges in a broader contest of Hellenic civilization, which emphasized the role of polar opposites in experience, along with the further ideas of equality, harmony, balance, measure, limit, and the mean as a way of resolving the contradictions between opposing forces and creating the best forms of life, whether in the polis, the individual soul, or the wider natural order (see Lloyd 1992; Nielsen 1996a). The measure, number, and weight complex needs to be understood as a particular linguistic expression of this wider civilizational matrix.

One usage of our formula is found in Euripides's tragedy the *Phoenician Women*, first presented around 411–09 BCE (see Cornford 1957, 169–70). The main scene for present purposes is the speech of Jocasta to her son Eteocles, where she pleads with him to honor the prior agreement with his brother Polyneices to share rulership of Thebes. Eteocles now wishes instead to retain rule beyond the one year formerly agreed and not share rule with Polyneices. Jocasta warns not to pursue the Goddess of Ambition, who creates strife in families and cities, but instead heed Equality, who has "set up men's weights and measures, given them numbers" (Grene and Lattimore 1959, 479).[3] The use of the image to support the idea of justice in rulership is striking, as are its links to the idea of equality, here personified as a God. Euripides is known for his frequent use of anachronism, placing contemporaneous ideas from his own time in the mouths of the mythical figures portrayed in tragedy. This suggests that our imagery was at least current enough during Euripides's time to be recognized by his audience as a rhetorical form. The play's date (411–09 BCE) also marks the trichotomy's pre-Platonic origins, since Plato was born in 428 BCE and would have been only in his late teens at the time.

Apart from Euripides's usage, Plato's writings became the main source of the imagery which later appears in Wisd and others. The image is used by Plato in several texts for differing purposes, especially in his *Republic* and *Laws.* In Plato's work, as with Greek civilization generally, it is often linked to the aforementioned ideas and ideals as well as to a variety of geometrical and mathematical images. These latter ideas are apparently Pythagorean in origin and reflect the influence, along with Socrates, of Pythagoreanism on Plato's emerging philosophy.

In the *Republic,* emphasis on the role of measure, number, and weight appears as a rationale, that is, a complex of reasons, used to combat error and the illusory and destructive influence of poetry, painting, and other imitative arts and instead lead the soul upward toward the higher levels of consciousness. As such, it occupies a vital place in the education of the citizen, especially in the training of ruling elites (see Sterling and Scott 1985, 293). In the *Laws,* the measure, number, and weight formula is repeated as a method for balancing the competing political virtues of monarchy (actually oligarchy as the translator Pangle notes) and democracy and forming a more perfect polis (see Pangle 1988). Thus, in these two major political works of Plato our formula serves as a rationale for differing purposes, both connected with the creation of more perfect rulership in the polis.

Plato's frequent use of these and other quantitative philosophical images is probably derived from Pythagorean sources and the question arises whether or not Pythagoras or his followers were the ultimate historical source of this trichotomy. In my view, it is indeed likely that Pythagorean ideas formed the implicit matrix of thinking that led to the later, more precise trichotomy. Pythagoras formed a religious community guided by a variety of ritualistic rules, but also believed that reality could be understood as number, an idea developed further by his more mathematically inclined followers (see Burkert 1972; De Vogel 1966). Their philosophy apparently evolved from its pre-Parmenidean forms to later ones current during Plato's lifetime. As a result, they cannot easily be described in terms of a coherent system, nor their precise chronological relationship with Plato's work be determined with any certainty. However, at the heart of their philosophy was the tacit assumption that arithmetic number was to be identified with geometrical points and both in turn with the physical atom (see Kirk and Raven 1971, 247). Cornford has expressed this implicit view by the term *number-atomism* (Cornford 1957, 205). This complex led the Pythagoreans to a view of cosmogony and natural order which could readily have formed the basis of our key imagery. To summarize perhaps a bit too systematically, the Pythagorean number philosophy argued that the One (not itself conceived as a number) served as an originating force for cosmic evolution and was identified with Limit. Confronted by the Unlimited, the One extended itself into Two, which created the line, then Three, which created the plane, and then Four which gave rise to three-dimensional bodies. Thus, the Pythagorean view of creation through the implicit number-point-atom identity yields the combination of the three figures in our key image: number, measure, weight (although the last named term is only implied by the existence of solids, and the quality of weight is not explained). In Cornford's account, this process creates the three dimensions of space (Cornford 1957, 206–207). Although the Pythagoreans did not directly utilize the formula (i.e., measure, number, and weight), like other Greek thinkers they do seem to have created the implicit assumptions and arguments that made such a later formula possible. The early date of this tacit assumption and ensuing philosophy is further supported by the fact that the famous "paradoxes" of Zeno of Elea were a direct critique of this Pythagorean formulation and Zeno's work dates to the mid-fifth century BCE, well before the uses of the trichotomy by Euripides or Plato (see Lee 2014).

In his *Metaphysics*, Aristotle had already critiqued the Pythagoreans by arguing that their number philosophy, with its purely quantitative approach, could not account for the diverse qualities of real objects. Thus, number and measure might still help understand empirical reality (as it had in Plato's extension of Pythagorean ideas in his *Timaeus*), but weight, color, etc., were qualities which could not be explained by a purely geometrical and arithmetical philosophy, even with its atomistic additions (Aristotle 1966, 705–706). However, through its distinction between the two categories of quantity and quality, Aristotle's critique provides indirect support for my suggestion of a congruency between the Pythagorean cosmology and the measure, number, and weight imagery. It is precisely the failure of the Pythagoreans to develop a clear distinction between the categories of quantity and quality which led them to restrict their cosmogony to purely quantitative terms and assume that the three-dimensional world emerging from number's creative powers would also account for the diverse qualities of things.

The development of the various schools of Greek philosophy after Aristotle created a complex philosophical environment during the Hellenistic-Roman era. Thinkers became adherents of one or another of the established schools or combined ideas from differing sources. In the process, they created philosophies amalgamating Platonic, Aristotelian, Stoic, Epicurian, and other motifs. The accent was frequently placed on Platonic ideas, with Pythagorean, Stoic, and others joined to support the dominant images drawn from Plato. The result of this eclectic philosophical complex has been called "middle Platonism" (Dillon 1996). It provided much of the philosophical material utilized by Wisd, Philo, Origen, and other thinkers of this period, especially those emerging, as noted, from Alexandria.

The Encounter of Hellenism with Ancient Judaism and Early Christianity

The image from Wisd forms part of a trajectory of ideas and symbols from the Old Testament and other Judaic writings prior to Wisd through other Hellenistic Jewish writers and to those of early Christians. In these pages I can briefly examine only a selection of these works.[4] I will first compare some uses of related imagery in the Old Testament, the Apocrypha and the Pseudepigrapha with the Wisd formula and then look at selected figures in the Hellenistic-Jewish world (especially Philo of Alexandria) and early Christianity.

Biblical texts contain a variety of images congruent with Wisd. However, the precise Greek trichotomy does not appear. Many of the Biblical texts deploy images of God's creation and judgment through measurement and balances. Such rationales are common in the Prophets and various wisdom texts. They utilize metaphors drawn from commercial and architectural practices to capture God's workings. Here are some examples. In Job we read that during the creation, "[H]e [God] gave to the wind its weight and meted out the waters by measure" (Job 28:25). Proverbs tell us that when God judges the soul, "the lord weighs the spirit" with "a just balance and scale" (Prov. 16:2). Elsewhere, Proverbs writes that "every way of man is right in his own eyes," but that God "weights the heart" (Prov. 21:2).[5] In a particularly evocative combination of images, Isaiah writes that God has "measured the waters" and "marked off the heavens with a span, enclosed the dust of earth in a measure and weighed the mountains in scales and the hills in a balance" (Isa. 40:12). In the Book of Enoch we read that the "actions of men are weighed in the balance," a trope found elsewhere in Enoch (see Charles 1913, 212–13). Related usages are found in IV Ezra (or 2 Esdras), where the fulfillment of apocalyptic prophecy involves the precondition of the creation of a particular number of righteous persons and involves God's weighing of the age in a balance and measuring the times (Charles 1913, 567). These quotes represent only a few of the many usages of such images in the Bible, Apocrypha, and Pseudepigrapha as rationales to describe especially the processes of divine creation and judgment. What is equally remarkable is the absence of the precise formula found among many earlier Greek writers, especially Plato. The difference between these texts and the Wisd usage is clear. Only with the fuller interpenetration of Judaism and Hellenism, especially in a setting of intercivilizational encounter such as Alexandria, do we see the full rationalization of the inherited Biblical ideas through the use of the Greek measure, number, and weight formula. In a related vein, Koester (1968) has shown that this setting also saw the fullest development of the idea of "laws of nature."

The self-imposed limitation of God's fuller powers should especially be noted. The awesomely powerful and often capricious God of the Old Testament now limits himself to rewards and punishments in accordance with the quantitative laws now embedded in his own creation. While the emphasis remains on the—in principle—unlimited divine rulership, this rule is now tempered and God works His will through the laws embedded in His creation. To adapt Max Weber's terminology, used by him in a different context, the "substantively irrational" God of the Old Testament is replaced by a more "substantively rational" and self-constraining creator and judge who even shows mercy to sinners precisely through the means of quantitative measure, number, and weight (see, e.g., Weber 1968: 85–86, 655–57).

Philo of Alexandria represents another central figure in our story. His work was contemporaneous with Wisd, emerged from the same Jewish-Hellenistic Alexandrian milieu of intercivilizational encounter, and utilizes the same measure, number, and weight imagery along with a variety of other numerological symbolisms. These are mostly connected with Philo's discussions of Divine creation, but also involve ways of expressing his ideas about punishment, retribution, and natural order. For example, Philo directly employs our trichotomy when he writes that "Moses held that God, and not the human mind, is the measure and weighing scale and numbering of all things" (see the citation in Nielsen 2002, 272). This remarkable passage directly parallels Wisd and is only one of the most striking ones in which such similar quantitative images appear. Philo does several things here. First, he attributes the Platonic idea that God is the measure of all things to Moses who, in his view, had influenced Plato. Second, in good Platonic fashion, he opposes Protagoras's idea that "man is the measure of all things" (see Pangle 1988, 103; Cornford 1934, 31). Philo's debt to Plato and middle Platonism is well known, but his use of the Platonic rationale to legitimate the Mosaic text's theological priority is striking. He remains committed to his Jewish religious traditions, while employing Greek philosophical ideas to more fully rationalize and defend them. Moreover, Philo's work is filled with other arithmetic and numerological images, most often in the context of his treatment of divine creation. These are used to support his key image of creation and rulership by measure, number, and weight (for a fuller discussion see Nielsen 1996b; 2002).

The early Christian theologian Origen also gestures to the Wisd formula (which he views as canonical), but with modifications. In his work *On First Principles*, he writes that God "made all things by number and measure" and adds that "when the scripture says that God created all things 'by number and measure' we shall be right in applying the term 'number' to rational creatures or minds . . . whereas 'measure' will correspondingly apply to bodily matter," which God used in the appropriate quantity for ordering the world (see the citation in Nielsen 2002, 280). He draws on Wisd's Hellenistic-Jewish imagery, yet modifies it significantly in light of his new, developing Christian consciousness, which emphasizes Divine creation of the physical world by measure and the creation of mankind in a precise number of rational creatures. Man is a unique type of creation endowed with the light of reason, a Platonic image now attached to the Jewish and emerging Christian God. Measure and number continue to place a central role, but weight has dropped out of the picture. Its absence seems to imply a relative devaluation of the physical world in the emerging Christian worldview.

Among early Christian thinkers of a somewhat later period, Augustine employs the Wisd image of creation by measure, number, and weight perhaps most extensively. With its translation in the Vulgate, it has now achieved full legitimacy and authority. He uses it to construct his image of creation, but also deploys it in his aesthetics and his analysis of the Trinity (see Dunham 2008; Harrison 1988; Roche 1941). In his *Confessions* he quotes the Wisd passage and uses the trichotomy to attack astrology and Manichaeism (Augustine 1961, 95). Like Origen, he sometimes omits reference to the third idea of weight (and sometimes even to measure) and emphasizes only number (see, e.g., Augustine 1950, 375, 401). Indeed, Augustine, like Philo, employs a complex Christian numerology in his work.

Although it is not directly related to our theme, there were parallel, yet strikingly different developments outside the orbit of Jewish and early Christian writers. Plotinus's philosophy emerged directly from Plato and other Greek sources that were central to the neo-Platonic philosophy. Plotinus's treatise on numbers in the *Enneads* constructs a three-tiered hierarchy of quantitative images of ultimate reality: the One (not a number, but a force identified with the Good from which all things emanate); mathematics as the forms of numbers used in creation or emanation; numbers as measures of the object world (see Nielsen 2002, 282–83).[6] Although Plotinus was, with Origen, a student of Ammonius Saccus at Alexandria, he does not quote the Wisd text or use its precise image. He constructs an alternative, purely Greek philosophical system free of the commitments that led Hellenistic Jewish and early Christian writers to merge some variant of the Greek idea of order by measure, number, and weight with the inherited Biblical texts and their general religious commitments.

The Image and Its Uses in Roman Jurisprudence

The intercivilizational encounters of the Hellenistic-Roman world include reference to Rome, which in its imperial expansion brought together a variety of intellectual influences from Greek, Jewish, early Christian, and Near Eastern civilizations. In these pages, I can examine only those outcomes of intercivilizational encounters related to Roman law and, in particular, those which involve the uses of the rationale of measure, number, and weight.

The influence of Greek ideas is once again decisive in this regard. With the expansion of the Roman Republic into Greece, in a Mediterranean cultural climate already heavily Hellenized by the prior efforts of Alexander the Great, Greek philosophical approaches were adopted by Roman jurists and Greek rhetorical styles were increasingly used in defense of clients by courtroom advocates. At Rome, the court advocates were separate from the jurists, who did not represent clients. As a result, the uses of a rhetorical art imitating Greek models were confined to the courtroom and had no influence on the developing Roman legal science, which was in the hands of the jurists. This was in keeping with the general tendency of the Hellenistic world toward professional specialization of the arts and sciences.

Actual Greek substantive law had only a selective impact on Roman law. Roman jurists recognized particular Greek laws and those of other peoples as part of the *ius gentium,* which the jurists in turn increasingly saw as a manifestation of the *ius naturale.* It was among the jurists that Greek ideas had their greatest impact. Greek philosophy (e.g., Plato, Aristotle, and the later Greek schools) were known to the jurists. They borrowed methods of "collection and division" from texts such as Plato's *Sophist*, the idea of *diaeresis* (differentiation) from Aristotle, and dialectic from Greek thinkers more generally to create a systematic classification of cases and laws into genera and species. This led to an increasing level of abstraction in juridical reasoning and aided the Roman jurists, who usually worked casuistically with concrete cases, to assemble a more rational and systematic organization of cases and laws into general categories (Schulz 1936, esp. ch. 4; 1953, 62ff.; Jolowicz 1967, 425–28).

The results of this work can be seen in the *Institutes* of Gaius, a work of the second half of the second century CE, around the time of Marcus Aurelius's reign (i.e., 160 CE). It is the only surviving Roman juridical text of the Principate (about 80 percent has survived) providing an organization of legal science for purposes of teaching and instruction. His work starts with a general introduction to legal ideas, including the relationships among the civil law, *ius gentium,* and *ius naturale,* one that is later reproduced with modifications in the *Institutes* of Justinian (circa 532 CE). It classifies laws into those of persons, property, and actions, although the substantive legal materials worked into this classification are often arranged confusingly.

The use of the particular rationale of measure, number, and weight appears in Gaius in the context of the law of contracts. I would immediately add that the imagery appears as what Genzmer (1952) has called a "formula" regularly used in precisely the same way in Roman law. It was undoubtedly taken by Gaius and the Roman jurists directly from Greek philosophical sources, probably Plato, although the precise lines of transmission remain obscure. It could not have been adopted from Wisd at a time when Jewish and Christian texts carried no authority among Romans. Moreover, among the Roman jurists, the formula always appears in the order "weight, number, and measure" (a reversal of Wisd's and other Hellenistic Jewish writers' usage of measure, number, and weight). This further confirms the fact that the jurists took the term independently from Greek philosophy, where the order is not as uniformly or consistently stated.

The Roman law broadly divided contracts into informal and formal ones and had historically recognized four types of contracts: formal, literal, real, and consensual. The real contracts were, in turn, divided into four other types: *mutuum*, *commodatum*, pledge, *fedeicommisa*. It is *mutuum* that concerns us here (see Jolowicz 1967, 292–301). The contract of *mutuum* was an informal, real contract of some antiquity, which only became legally actionable sometime during the late Republic. It was a contract of loan for consumption. Money or goods (e.g., wine, corn, grains, etc.) were transferred from the lender to the recipient. Real contracts involved the direct conveyance of the thing (*res*) from one party to the other. The recipient necessarily gained title of ownership to the goods loaned, unlike the other three related real contracts, where only possession was conveyed. The goods were to be used or consumed and, upon the due date, if one was specified, were to be returned to the lender in the form of goods of a similar quality and of an equal weight, number, and measure (Buckland 1966, 462–65).[7]

This formula reappears in the *Digest* of Justinian (532 CE). It is represented there by Ulpian and other third-century CE jurists in connection not only with *mutuum,* but also various legal forms such as legacy and *fideicommissa* (gifts upon death of the testator to individuals separate from those things bequeathed to the heir and promises by the testator of legacies to third parties, which are binding on the heir as promises made in "good faith").

It is of added interest that the contract of *mutuum* did not involve any interest (*fenus*), but only the return of the same quantity of the loan. The Roman *mutuum* later became a reference point for medieval European debates over usury and was cited as a rationale by traditionalist defenders of the Deuteronomic prohibition against usury (see Nelson 1969, 84–85, 149). In sum, the weight, number, measure formula served the evolving needs of Roman jurists who used a more theoretically rationalized and standardized form of Greek thought for the adaptation of an inherited Roman legal practice to changing circumstances.

Episodes in the Later History of the Measure, Number, Weight Image

The complex of ideas and images discussed above had a future. It was repeatedly reborn and put to varied uses by theologians, philosophers, and pioneers of the new science and mathematics. In conclusion, we will mention only a few noteworthy instances in a history that would require a much fuller treatment.

The translation into Latin of the biblical texts in the Vulgate included the *Wisdom of Solomon*, and our key images were passed on to Medieval Europe. With the revival of learning in the twelfth and thirteenth centuries, there was an increased interest in quantitative thinking in several quarters, practical and theoretical. The older religious dichotomy of Heaven and Hell was modified with the invention of Purgatory, whose punishments were now seen as temporary and measured in accordance with the severity of the sinner's offenses (see LeGoff 1984). With the growth of cities and the revival of commerce, interest in mathematics and more precise systems of numbers and accounting increased the relevance of inherited religious texts, which had been collected by such figures as Isidore of Seville and had already been devoted to an image of God as the great mathematician (Crosby 1997; Chenu 1968, 106). Biblical wisdom literature, including the text of Wisd, also saw a revival and the image of a world arranged by measure, number, and weight began a new life. Solomon (as Wisd was called in the Vulgate) was subject to commentaries and quotations from the text multiplied (see Smalley 1952, 324–25). With the coming of the Renaissance, classical texts from Plato other than the *Timaeus*, which had previously been central to Platonic commentaries, were now rediscovered. Along with ideas and images drawn from Pythagorean sources, they added new dimensions and authority to those images already inherited from Wisd. Figures such as Marcello Ficino drew on Wisd to envision the world as a hieroglyphic where measure, number, and weight ruled (Allen 1994, esp. Appendix 3).

The pioneers of the early modern revolution in philosophy and science drew on a variety of images in their efforts to understand nature. The precise formula from Wisd was never entirely lost despite its partial displacement by Cartesian and Galilean geometry and the idea of a book of nature written in mathematical script. Leibniz's hope of creating a universal characteristic in which all of reality could be expressed in numbers drew explicitly on Wisd for inspiration (Leibniz 1989, 5). The world of political and social organization was also drawn into this movement of thought. The attempt to create a "social physics" was already in progress in the seventeenth century long before Auguste Comte proclaimed his invention of this new science (see Sorokin 1928, ch. 1). Richard Petty's project for a new political arithmetic referred directly to the Wisd formula, a fact that did not escape the notice of Karl Marx, who as late as 1859 called attention to Petty's use of the Wisd formula to legitimate his new political arithmetic (see Finkelstein 2000: Marx 1970, 52–53). Between Petty and Marx lay Jeremy Bentham, whose felicitous calculus of pleasure and pain attempted the reduction of all moral and political questions to quantitative terms and laid the foundation for current cost-benefit analysis.

The continued existence and uses of the Wisd formula is perhaps not surprising. Ideas die hard, but this complex of ideas actually grew stronger rather than weaker as it became firmly embedded in Western European structures of consciousness and, thus, took possession of the early modern European mind. The uses of the Wisd formula served the purpose especially of cloaking new, often revolutionary ideas in a traditional, religious form. It legitimated intellectual innovations in culture, politics, and society through a now traditional and respected rationale. It communicated the idea that innovators were merely discovering what God had already deposited in His creation. In the words of Henry Sumner Maine, the formula served as a "fiction" in the service of "progressive" changes (Maine 1970, 25).

Concluding Remarks on the History and Theory of Intercivilizational Encounters

The foregoing discussion has traced aspects of the history of a complex of ideas born especially in Greece, adapted to related images in ancient Judaism, and further developed for their own purposes by early Christian thinkers. It has also shown some of the uses to which the classical Roman jurists put this image, adopting it directly from Greek sources through a separate intercivilizational encounter, without reference to Jewish and Christian thinkers. Finally, it has gestured more briefly to the rich and varied subsequent uses of this image in Western European intracivilizational history. In all these cases, variations on the category of quantity or number were put to use in the creation of images used as rationales for differing philosophical, political, theological, and juridical purposes. At the same time, the adoption of images derived from the category of quantity or number advanced the fuller theoretical rationalization of these same cultural spheres.

In particular, we have argued that the central image of a world created, judged, and ruled by measure, number, and weight and the ways it was employed by intellectual elites—philosophers, theologians, jurists—in differing contexts, emerged from a series of intercivilizational encounters. It was unlikely to have developed independently in any other way or merely within the context of any one cultural setting. While our key image owes a special debt to ancient Greek thinkers, as we have seen, it is not exclusively from the "spirit" of any single civilization that new intellectual innovations associated with it were born, but rather from the confluences of ideas flowing from varying sources across national boundaries into a wider stream in which civilizational actors were immersed. Actors caught up in the maelstrom of such encounters forge new ideas and images, often in defense of their own cultural traditions, often to elaborate new structures of consciousness from their own basic stock of ideas, and sometimes merely to add important formulae to better capture existing ways of thinking.

In all these cases, there is the transfer of the sort of spiritual values that Marcel Mauss (2000) discovered at the heart of gift exchange. By contrast, civilizations that harden their inherited traditions against such "alien" ideas in the name of retaining the "purity" of their civilization are likely to miss opportunities for further transformation in the long term of historical development. These civilizations will find themselves isolated from other civilizations, which repeatedly borrow and adapt—and, in this way, change and grow. Our case study leads to this conclusion.

Notes

1. The phrase is adapted from Charles Tilly's book by that title.

2. This essay does not examine the history of mathematics, only ideas and images derived from the category of number. For the role of our central image in the history of mathematics see Hoyrup (1994).

3. Euripides's text contains fourth-century interpolations, none of which touch on our key passage (see Grene and Lattimore 1959). Craik (1988) and Mastronarde (1994) note this passage and both emphasize the notion of equality, but neither cites the trichotomy or its later significance.

4. This section draws selectively on my previous research (see Nielsen 1990, 1996b, 2002).

5. Proverbs' image of God weighing the heart clearly derives from earlier Egyptian sources, in particular, the ancient Egyptian judgment of the soul by weighing the heart found in the Papyrus of Ani (circa 1200 BCE). I cannot now pursue this further indication of an intercivilizational encounter between ancient Egypt and emerging Jewish civilization. However, Egyptian myths of creation and rulership do not appear to have employed any of the quantitative imagery present in the Bible (see Morenz 2013, 160–63; see also the pictures of measuring devices contemporaneous with Ani in Robinson 2007, 48 and opposite title page).

6. Barker notes the prevalence of arguments from triads in neo-Platonic thought without exploring its implications or comparisons with Jewish and Christian thinkers (Barker 1966, 365). The entire subject requires further investigation.

7. Goudy (1910) argues that this formula is an aspect of the more general practice of conceptualization by trichotomy in Roman law. Schulz (1953) opposes this idea as too broad. Schulz's view seems more historically correct, although Goudy's view raises important and interesting problems.

8. Hopper cites Wisd and its popularity in Medieval Europe, but, ambiguously, either misquotes the text by writing, "God has arranged all things by number and measure" (Hopper 1938, 75), or perhaps implies, without explanation, that medieval thinkers, following Origen and Augustine, had dropped the reference to weight.

References

Allen, Michael. 1994. *Nuptial Arithmetic: Marsilio Ficino's Commentary on The Fatal Number in Book VIII of Plato's* Republic. Berkeley: University of California Press.

Aristotle. 1966. *The Basic Works of Aristotle.* Edited with an Introduction by R. McKeon. New York: Random House.

Augustine. 1961. *Confessions.* Translated with an Introduction by R. S. Pine-Coffin. London: Penguin.

———. 1950. *The City of God.* Translated by Marcus Dods. New York: Modern Library.

Barker, Ernest, ed. and trans. 1966. *From Alexander to Constantine.* Oxford: Clarendon Press.

Buckland, W. W. 1966. *A Textbook of Roman Law: From Augustus to Justinian.* Cambridge: Cambridge University Press.

Burkert, Walter. 1972. *Lore and Science in Ancient Pythagoreanism.* Cambridge: Harvard University Press.

Charles, R. H., trans. *Apocrapha and Pseudepigrapha of the Old Testament in English,* Vol. 2: *Pseudepigrapha.* Oxford: Clarendon Press.

Chenu, M. D. 1968. *Nature, Man and Society in the Twelfth Century*. Translated by J. Taylor and L. Little. Chicago: University of Chicago Press.

Cornford, Francis M., ed. and trans. 1934. *Plato's Theory of Knowledge (The Theaetetus and the Sophist of Plato)*. New York: Humanities Press.

———, ed. and trans. 1937. *Plato's Cosmology: The Timaeus of Plato*. New York: Harcourt, Brace.

———, ed. and trans. 1939. *Parmenides and Plato*. New York: Humanities Press

———. 1957 [1912]. *From Religion to Philosophy*. New York: Harper Torchbooks.

Craik, Elizabeth. 1988. *Euripides: Phoenician Women*. Edited with a translation and commentary. Warminster: Aris and Phillips.

Crosby, Alfred W. 1997. *The Measure of Reality: Quantification and Western Society, 1250–1600*. New York: Cambridge University Press.

De Vogel, C. J. 1966. *Pythagoras and Early Pythagoreanism*. Assen: Vsan Gorecum.

Dillon, John. 1996. *The Middle Platonists: 80 B.C. to A.D. 220*. Ithaca: Cornell University Press.

Dunham, Scott A. 2009. *The Trinity and Creation in Augustine: An Ecological Analysis*. Albany: State University of New York Press.

Finkelstein, Andrea Lynn. 2000. *Harmony and Balance: An Intellectual History of Seventeenth Century English Economic Thought*. Ann Arbor: University of Michigan Press.

Gaius. 1946. *The Institutes of Gaius*. Text with Critical Notes and Translation by Francis de Zulueta. 2 vols. Oxford: Clarendon Press.

Genzmer, Erich. 1952. "Pondere, Numero, Mensura." Archives d'Histoire du Droit Orientale. *Revue Internationale du droits de l'Antiquite* 1: 469–94.

Goudy, Henry. 1910. *Trichotomy in Roman Law*. Oxford: Clarendon Press.

Grene, David, and Richard Lattimore, eds. 1959. *The Complete Greek Tragedies, Vol. IV: Euripides*. Chicago: University of Chicago Press.

Harrison, C. 1988. "Measure, Number, and Weight in St. Augustine's Aesthetics." *Augustianum* 28, no. 3: 591–602.

Hengel, M. 1974. *Judaism and Hellenism*. 2 Vols. Philadelphia: Fortress Press.

Hopper, Vincent F. 1938. *Medieval Number Symbolism*. New York: Columbia University Press.

Hoyrup, Jens. 1994. *In Measure, Number, and Weight: Studies in Mathematics and Culture*. Albany: State University of New York Press.

Jaspers, Karl. 2016 [1949]. *The Origin and Goal of History*. Boston: Routledge.

Jolowicz, H. F. 1967. *Historical Introduction to the Study of Roman Law*. 2nd Ed. Cambridge: Cambridge University Press.

Joost-Gangier, Christine. 2007. *Measuring Heaven: Pythagoras and His Influence on Thought and Art in Antiquity and the Middle Ages*. Ithaca: Cornell University Press.

Kalberg, Stephen. 2012. *Max Weber's Comparative Historical Sociology Today*. Boston: Routledge.

Kirk, G. S., and J. E.Raven, ed. and trans. 1971. *The Presocratic Philosophers.* Cambridge: University Press.

Koester, H. 1968. "Nomos Physios: The Concept of Natural law in Greek Thought." In *Religion in Antiquity,* edited by J. Neusner, 521–41. Leiden: Reidel.

Lee, H. D. P. 2014 [1936]. *Zeno of Elea.* Translated with an introduction and notes. Cambridge: Cambridge University Press.

LeGoff, Jacques. 1984. *The Birth of Purgatory.* Translated by Arthur Goldhammer. Chicago: University of Chicago Press.

Lloyd, G. E. R. 1992. *Polarity and Analogy.* Indianapolis: Hackett.

Maine, Henry Sumner 1970 [1861]. *Ancient Law.* Introduction and notes by F. Pollock. Boston: Peter Smith.

Marx, Karl. 1970 [1859]. *A Contribution to the Critique of Political Economy.* New York: International Publishers.

Mastronarde, Donald J. 1994. *Euripides: Phoenician Women.* Edited with an introduction and commentary. Cambridge: Cambridge University Press.

Mauss, Marcel. 2000. *The Gift.* New York: W. W. Norton.

Morenz, Sigfried. 2013. *Egyptian Religion.* Hoboken: Taylor and Francis.

Nelson, Benjamin N. 1969 [1949].*The Idea of Usury.* 2nd Rev. Ed. Chicago: University of Chicago Press.

———. 1981. *On the Roads to Modernity.* Edited by Toby Huff. Totowa, NJ: Rowman and Littlefield.

Nielsen, Donald A. 1990. "Max Weber and the Sociology of Early Christianity." In *Time, Place, and Circumstances: Neo-Weberian Studies in Comparative Religious History,* edited by William H. Swatos, 87–102. Westport, CT: Greenwood.

———. 1991. "Natural Law and Civilizations: Intracivilizational Polarities and the Emergence of Heterodox Ideals." *Sociological Analysis* 2, no. 1 (Spring): 55–76.

———. 1996a. "Pericles and the Plague: Civil Religion, Anomie and Injustice in Thucydides." *Sociology of Religion* 57, no. 4 (Winter): 397–407.

———. 1996b. "La Misura Divina: creazione e retribuzione nel libro della Sapienza e in Filone." *Religioni e Societa* 24, Anno XI: 9–21.

———. 1998. *Three Faces of God: Society, Religion, and the Categories of Totality in the Philosophy of Emile Durkheim.* Albany: State University of New York Press.

———. 2002. "Civilizational Encounters in the Development of Early Christianity." In *Handbook of Early Christianity: Social Science Approaches,* edited by Anthony Blasi, Paul-Andre Turcotte, and Jean Duhaime, 267–90. Twin Oaks, CA: Altamira Press.

———. 2004. "Rationalization, Transformations of Consciousness, and Intercivilizational Encounters." In *Rethinking Civilizational Analysis,* edited by Said Arjomand and Edward A. Tiryakian, 119–31. Thousand Oaks, CA: SAGE.

Pangle, Thomas L., trans. 1988. *The Laws of Plato.* Chicago: University of Chicago Press.

Parsons, Talcott. 1966. *Societies: Evolutionary and Comparative Perspectives.* Englewood Cliffs, NJ: Prentice-Hall.

Robinson, Andrew. 2007. *The Story of Measurement.* London: Thames and Hudson.

Roche, W. J. 1941. "Measure, Number, and Weight in Augustine." *The New Scholasticism* 15 (October): 350–76.

Schulz, Fritz. 1936. *Principles of Roman Law.* Oxford: Clarendon Press.

———. 1953. *History of Roman Legal Science.* Oxford: Clarendon Press.

Smalley, Beryl. 1952. *The Study of the Bible in the Middle Ages.* New York: Philosophical Library.

Sorokin, P. A. 1928. *Contemporary Sociological Theories.* New York: Harper and Row.

Sterling, Richard, and Phillip Scott, trans. 1985. *Plato: The Republic.* New York: W. W. Norton.

Watson, Alan, trans. and ed. 1998. *The Digest of Justinian.* 2 vols. Philadelphia: University of Pennsylvania Press.

Weber, Max. 1968. *Economy and Society.* 3 Vols. Totowa, NJ: Bedminster Press.

Winston, David, ed. 1979. *The Wisdom of Solomon* (Anchor Bible Vol. 43). New York: Doubleday.

6

The Pioneers of Islamicate Civilizational Analysis

Saïd Amir Arjomand

In the classical period of sociology in France and Germany, which I have identified with the first generation of comparative sociologists (Arjomand 2010), the critical importance of the sociology of religion is generally acknowledged. In Germany, Max Weber strongly linked the spread of the world religions with the development of the major civilizations of the world. Germany had already witnessed, in the closing decades of the nineteenth century, the emergence of a sociological analysis of Islam in the work of a leading proponent of the so-called Higher Criticism of the Bible, Julius Wellhausen, whose influence was combined with that of Max Weber in the work of one of the latter's students, C. H. Becker.

The second generation of comparative sociologists in the third quarter of the twentieth century saw major developments alongside the Weberian paradigm on the development of civilizational patterns out of the world religions of salvation by Karl Jaspers, who formulated the idea of the Axial Age and included Mohammad among the paradigmatic individuals who had changed human history.[1] Influenced by Weber and Jaspers, Marshall Hodgson worked specifically on the civilizational analysis of Islam, focusing on the religious input into the development of what he called the Islamicate civilization. Meanwhile, a Durkheimian sociology of Islam emerged in France with the work of Joseph Chelhod, while Benjamin Nelson in the United States offered a model for the analysis of intercivilizational encounters.[2]

In the third generation of comparative sociologists from the last quarter of the twentieth century to the present, S. N. Eisenstadt reinforced the civilizational consequences of the world religions in Weber while developing Jaspers's idea of the Axial Age into axial civilizations, including Islam and its civilizational pattern. Bryan S. Turner and Saïd Amir Arjomand have written on Islam extensively, developing their implicitly comparative analysis alongside the tracks laid down by the pioneers of the sociology of Islam in the first two generations. This chapter charts the manner in which all three generations, albeit in distinct ways, saw a close interweaving of the great religions and the axial civilizations.

European Pioneers in the First Generation

Émile Durkheim, as we all know, sought the sociological essence of religion in its origins and turned to the most primitive society in the world to draw empirical evidence for it. Durkheimian sociology had a considerable impact in Egypt in the interwar period, and in Egypt and Iran in the 1950s and 1960s, producing ideologically interesting sociologies of Islam in Arabic and Persian which were, however, pronouncedly normative and, as such, beyond the scope of this chapter (Arjomand 2013). In the Francophone world, however, Joseph Chelhod, a Lebanese sociologist writing and teaching in France, embarked on a sociological study of Islam that remained strictly faithful to Durkheim's positivism, and applied Durkheim's theory of religion to the rise of Islam in pagan Arabia fairly exhaustively. His *Introduction to the Sociology of Islam* (1958) was, significantly, titled, "From animism to universalism." In The *Elementary Forms of Religious Life* (1912), Durkheim was greatly influenced by W. Robertson Smith's *The Religion of the Semites*, published in 1889, and the latter was in turn deeply influenced by the great German scholar of the so-called Higher Criticism of the Old Testament, Julius Wellhausen (d. 1918). Robertson Smith had translated Wellhausen's *Prolegomena to the History of Ancient Israel* (1878) into English. Chelhod's sociology of Islam was thus indirectly influenced by Robertson Smith and Wellhausen, and probably also directly by Robertson Smith's *Kinship and Marriage in Early Arabia* (1886).

According to the older sociological interpretation, the gods of the Arabian Peninsula had their sanctuaries in the territory of a tribe, and they were usually shared by allied tribes or those in the vicinity able to visit them. Such sharing of the divinities, and participation in common fairs and festivals around their sanctuaries, made for religio-cultural unity (Chelhod

1955, 123–25). The sacred enclave was called *hijr*, where common rituals of initiation, pilgrimage to and circumambulation of the sanctuary shrine (*hajj*) with shaven heads were performed. The most important divinities were Manāt, the goddess of the tribes of Aws, Khazraj, and Ghassān, the Lāt, goddess of the Thaqif, and the ʿUzzā, goddess of Mohammad's tribe, the Quraysh, as well as the Kināna, the Khuzāʿa, and of the Mudar tribal confederacy in general. Chelhod takes Q.53.19–20 to mean that the three goddesses were considered the daughters of the paramount god, Allah. Rival religious and tribal cleavages could overlap, producing intermittent conflict, as they did between Mecca and Tā'if (Chelhod 1958, 97, 113). This was inevitable as long as the religio-culturally unified and economically integrated tribal society of Western Arabia remained segmented and without any central or otherwise unified political authority structure. In the early 1960s, Chelhod extended the same theoretical framework to the study of Arab mythology under the influence of the fellow-Durkheimian Claude Lévi-Strauss (Chelhod 1962), and directed research on a project on the history and civilization of the Yemen (Chelhod 1985). The Durkheimian theory, amplified by Lévi-Strauss's idea of bricolage as the guiding principle of the *pensée sauvage,* found an impressive historicized application in Jacqueline Chabbi's reconstruction of Mohammad's presentation of his new religion to his kinsmen and others in the tribal society of Mecca before migrating to Medina, where elements in Islam that were "foreign" to the Arab tribal society came to predominate (Chabbi 1997). With this, the Durkheimian purchase on Islam reaches its limit, leaving the subsequent development of Islam as a world religion to alternative theoretical approaches.

The limitations of sociology of ancient Arabia in Chelhod and Chabbi were precisely those of Durkheim's sociology of religion: translocal or those transcending one society were excluded. Thus, for instance, from subsequent archaeological research we know the three so-called daughters of Allāh to be attested as minor but translocal goddesses in ancient southern Arabia (Robin 2000), where the paramount god, Il, happened to have three (different) daughters. In Mohammad's Hijāz by the seventh century, they were evidently considered the daughters of the paramount god, Allāh. In the Aramaeco-Greek ecumene of the first half-millennium after the Common Era, Allāt, ʿUzza, and to a lesser extent Manāt, who had scattered local betyls and shrines, were identified with major ecumenical goddesses, notably Aphrodite and Ishtar, though name changes and transfer of epithets were not infrequent and polynymy common (Al-Azmeh 2014, 173–82). Nevertheless, the same limitations imposed by Chelhod's Durkheimian model marks Aziz Al-Azmeh's neo-Durkheimian *Emergence of Islam in Late Antiquity* (2014).

Al-Azmeh's analytical framework for the period of the emergence of Islam under Mohammad, suggestively labeled Paleo-Islam, can be considered neo-Durkheimian not so much because of its dependence on Durkheim but on Wellhausen whose influence through Robertson Smith had helped shape the Durkheimian theory of religion. Wellhausen (1883, 1887) had turned from the religion of ancient Israel, with which he had begun his career, to the far better documented study of early Islam. As the ultimate common source to both Durkheim and Al-Azmeh, Wellhausen's influence gives the latter's reading of Arabian religion a distinctly neo-Durkheimian flavour. Thus, following Wellhausen's insistence on the primacy of cult and ritual in Semitic religion, Al-Azmeh (2014; 2018b, 30) plays down the significance of beliefs and highlights the function of the cultic associations around sacred enclaves of betyls and their shrines in the Arabian peninsula. Religion, he maintains, was primarily conceived in terms of the rituals, especially sacrifice (Al-Azmeh 2018b, 29).

In continuing his attempt to understand the *Urgestalt* of the religion of Israel, Wellhausen (1887) had traced the emergence of Allah as a trans-tribal, higher god, tending to universality, and a god without a cult in pagan Arabia. Al-Azmeh renews Wellhausen's search while maintaining the latter's insistence on the primacy of ritual and of the cultic sodalities organized around the sacred enclaves (singular, *haram*) centered on the shrines of deities in late antique Arabia. Al-Azmeh emphatically excluded any overarching theological template that might derive from Judaism or Christianity, and meticulously traces the evolution of Mohammad's conception of God from the Lord (*rabb*) of the sacred Meccan enclave along the path of monolatry and henotheism through what he later called "Mohammad's henotheistic diplomacy of the divine" (Al-Azmeh 2018a, 358) to the pure monotheism as the worship of Allah as the One and only God, whose description he leaves to others. Although Mohammad's revolutionary break with Arabian cultic practice by ending the intercalation in Arabian ritual calendars is well noted by him (Al-Azmeh 2014; 2018a,360), he has little, if anything, to say about the reconstructive rationalization of beliefs that preceded and went along with the ending of intercalation. As this example shows, what Al-Azmeh's impressive analysis leaves out entirely is Mohammad's new revolution in the Abrahamic religious tradition that used Arabian pagan religion as a springboard.

To Max Weber we owe the seminal idea of the world religions of salvation as the kernel around which distinct civilizations, or, to use Weber's own words, *Kulturkreise* (cultural worlds) grow.[3] Weber did have a colleague who applied some of his idea to Islam: Carl Heinrich Becker (d. 1933), who founded a major journal in Islamic studies, *Der Islam*, in 1910. Becker had studied with Max Weber at Heidelberg before the latter began to consider himself a sociologist and participate in the foundation of the German Sociological Association in 1910, and still considered Weber a cultural historian when acknowledging his indebtedness to him for understanding "comparisons of varied working out of ideas" (Becker 1967, 1, 33) This is significant because Becker was influenced by Weber's early idea of causal adequacy on the basis of counterfactuals, which Weber himself did not put to too much use, and he applied the idea to his analysis of civilizational encounters in antiquity. The result was epitomized in his famous counterfactual, "Ohne Alexander den Grossen keine islamische Zivilisaation!" (Becker 1967, 1, 16) In "Der Islam in Rahmen einer allgemeinen Kulturgeschichte" (1921), Becker applauded Ernst Troeltsch's application of Weber's idea that each cultural world has its own pattern of development, but refuses to follow the latter in considering these as self-contained, and proceeds to compare the divergent paths of development of the Hellenistic heritage in the Christian/Western and Islamic/Near Eastern civilizations (Becker 1967, 1, 24–39). Becker had identified the role of religion in the distinctive "developmental path (*Entwicklungsprozess*)" of the civilization of Islam in an earlier essay (Becker 1967, 1, 5) He nevertheless succumbed to the then-typical classicist prejudice of seeing Islam as an offshoot of Hellenism, as reflected in the above-mentioned counterfactual statement that the Islamic civilization was only made possible by Alexander as the propagator of Hellenism. The same prejudice surfaces in Al-Azmeh's (2014, 28) claim that the rise of Islam was "the ultimate consequence of Hellenistic fermentation." In the final part of the *Emergence of Islam*, he presents the transition from the "Paleo-Islam" of Mohammad to the Islam of the Umayyad empire as the "theological sublimation" aimed at bringing the Arabian religion into line with the Hellenistic rationalism of late antiquity (and the Caliphate into the political theology of the late Roman empire) under the unspecified but allegedly imperative requirements of empire[4] (Al-Azmeh 2014, 99, 518).

Weber himself uses the term *Entwicklungsform,* which I have translated as "developmental path" (Arjomand 2016b) and have applied to the distinct pattern of sectarian development and differentiation of the religious and political domains during the formation of Islam as a world religion (Arjomand 2014). In contrast to Becker's and Al-Azmeh's reading of the rise of Islam as the extension of the Hellenism of Late Antiquity, I see the developmental path of the Islamicate civilization as a distinctive one set by Mohammad's religious revolution as an architectonic rationalization of the Abrahamic tradition in which Greek philosophical rationalism at best played a secondary part.

Becker also drew on the exemplary work of Weber's above-mentioned older contemporary Julius Wellhausen, who considered the rise of Islam as a religious revolution that found expression in a social polity and thereby underwent change "from being an individual to being a political religion" (Wellhausen 1883, 553). Becker took over this emphasis on the political dimension of Islam. In his study of the institutionalization of the Friday congregational prayer (Becker 1967, 1, 472–500), for instance, he emphasized that it was a platform for the governors to expound the ruling ideology during the first century of Islam from the "political mosque" at the capital cities (*amsār*) (Wellhausen had called the pristine mosque the "drilling ground"). Wellhausen's Protestant theological convictions, however, focused his interest on the origins of Islam as a world religion and its sectarian offshoots, and he found the long-term developmental process of institutionalization boring. Becker, in contrast, was most interested in the development of the Islamic(ate) civilization out of Islamic religion (van Ess 1980, 43–44).

Becker was nevertheless somewhat ambivalent toward Max Weber and had a tendency to prioritize other nonreligious factors in that process of development. In any event, he turned to politics at the age of forty in 1916 to become Prussia's minister of cultural affairs after World War I. Weber himself was actively engaged in and writing on politics at that time, and formally returned to academic life only in the last year of his life. He did not have time either to pursue his project of a sociology of Islam or to create a Weberian school of comparative sociology. The one area in which Weber's last project went beyond incidental remarks and amounted to a significant contribution was in the section of the chapter on the sociology of law in the *Economy and Society* on religious laws (Weber 1954). In an impressive paper published in *Der Islam* (1935), Joseph Schacht (d. 1969) developed Weber's treatment in that chapter of Islamic law as a religious "jurists' law." This was a significant step in the sociology of Islamic law, but it had little immediate impact. In short, Weber's influence was not transmitted beyond Germany until the subsequent generations of comparative sociologists in the United States. Meanwhile, Schacht left Nazi Germany for Egypt in 1934 and migrated to Britain and then the United States, producing his pioneering *Origins of the Muhammadan Jurisprudence* in 1950 and his classic study, *An Introduction to Islamic Law*, in 1964.

The Second Generation: Marshall Hodgson

I have identified the second generation of comparative sociologists with the Comparative Social Anthropology of Civilizations Project at the University of Chicago in the late 1940s and 1950s, which was directed by Robert Redfield (d. 1958), who elaborated its analytical framework in terms of the "societal" and the cultural structures of a civilization and linked the two via its "historical structure" consisting of relations of temporal hierarchy between a Great Tradition and its Little Traditions. The project's most immediate impact was felt on the study of Indian civilization through Milton Singer, who took over after Redfield's retirement, but it also recruited prominent orientalists working on China and Islam (Arjomand 2010). The major contribution to the project on Islam was by a member of the University of Chicago Committee on Social Thought, Marshall Hodgson.

Marshall G. S. Hodgson (d. 1968) received his PhD from the same Committee on Social Thought (founded by Redfield) in 1951, and after a postdoctoral year in India, began his academic career at the University of Chicago. He was much more suited for relating Islam as a world religion to the civilization that grew around it than his mentor, who had joined the Redfield Project before him. Hodgson believed that his mentor G. von Grunebaum was too dependent on Arabic sources, and mostly neglected the Persian ones. He therefore followed Arnold Toynbee rather than his mentor, drawing on the latter's distinction between an Iranic and an Arabic Islamic civilization in *A Study of History* (Hodgson 1993, 189). Hodgson called the cultural traditions that grew on the basis of the Persian language "Persianate." He further contrasted the continued vitality of the "Persianate zone" with the early flourishing of the "Arabic zone" of the Islamicate civilization, going so far as to divide the latter historically "into an earlier 'caliphal' and a later 'Persianate' phase" (Hodgson, 1974, 2, 293–94).

Hodgson subscribed to Redfield's theoretical framework for the comparison of civilizations, and accordingly developed an approach to world history that was in sharp contrast to that of his colleague, William McNeill, in *The Rise of the West* (1963), which he considered Eurocentric and therefore parochial. Hodgson was, furthermore, influenced by John U. Nef in his approach to modernity. Nef (1960) argued that the so-called breakthrough to modernity in the West resulted from a happy confluence of a whole number of contingent circumstances all at the same critical time. Hodgson explored the possibility of a similar confluence of sociopolitical developments that might have opened an alternative Islamicate path to modernity, and highlighted as one such possibility the failed but remarkable attempt by the late 'Abbasid Caliph al-Nāsir li-Din Allāh (r. 1190–1225) to integrate Sufi orders and *fotovvat* associations of the young men and artisans of the city-quarters under the caliphate, with the advice of his Persian counselor and spiritual master, Shaykh Abu Hafs ʿOmar Sohravardi (d. 1234) (Hodgson 1974, 2, 386–436).

At the time of his death, Hodgson was working simultaneously on a book on the unity of world history and on his magnum opus, *The Venture of Islam*, as he strongly believed the first was necessary for the proper understanding of the second.[5] His unfinished work on Islamic civilization and culture was posthumously edited by Reuben W. Smith and published in three volumes under the title of *The Venture of Islam. Conscience and History in a World Civilization* (1974). His manuscript on "The Unity of World History" remains unpublished, though his earlier published essays on world history were later collected and edited by Edmund Burke III in *Rethinking World History* (1993).[6] Hodgson's early interest in the history of Shiʿism (Hodgson 1955a; 1955b; 1962) enabled him, in *The Venture of Islam*, to give the period of Islamic history, beginning with the Buyid conquest of Baghdad, followed by the Fatimid conquest of Egypt and Syria, and ending with the Saljuq overthrow of the last Buyid sultan of Iraq, as "the Shiʿite century" (945/334–1055/447) (Arjomand 2015).

Hodgson's main contribution to the sociology of Islam, however, was a novel Weberian approach to Islam as an Abrahamic world religion, which he considered the culmination of the "kerygmatic movement" in world history. Hodgson's elaboration and consequent conceptual innovations became widely known only after the posthumous publication of *The Venture of Islam.* To distinguish Islam as a world religion from the civilization that grew around it in the "agrarianate-citied" region from the Nile to the Oxus (conceived as a major part of what McNeill called the Afro-Eurasian *ecumene* [Oikoumene]), Hodgson reserved "Islam" for the religion but coined the term *Islamicate* to describe the culture and civilization that developed around it and expanded throughout the *ecumene.* This made his approach more world-historical than Weber's. For him, the transformation of the Western world in modern times was "unthinkable" without the institutional innovations in the Afro-Eurasian *oikoumene* (Hodgson 1993, Pt. I) This world-historical perspective saw the modern transformation as the aggregate result of varied responses through institutional innovation to common challenges and changing conditions faced by different regions of the *oikoumene.* Different regions shaped and contributed to the core content of this process of modern transformation. The "unity of history" consists in the continuous interaction of specific historical trajectories across regions, and thus speaks to the general issue of locating human or societal agency in time and space (Islamoğlu 2012, 458).

Three influential concepts formulated by Hodgson to describe the five phases or stages of the development of the Islamicate civilization amount to a typology of Islamicate political regimes. The caliphal phase, covered in the first volume of *The Venture of Islam*, culminated in the early ʿAbbasid age of "caliphal absolutism," which already bore the imprint of the pre-Islamic Persian tradition of autocracy. In the second volume, Hodgson rejected the ideal types applied to the Islamic world by Max Weber—namely, "patrimonialism" and, with better reasons, sultanism—and instead offered two ideal types of his own in their place: "the *aʿyān-amir* system" in the Seljuq period, and "the military-patronage state" of the post-Mongol era. The former describes the regime that emerged with the development of the *iqṭāʿ* system of land tenure, in which large land grants were made to the military elite. In this system, social power of the notables (*aʿyān*) in cities was subordinated to the domination of the military elite (*amir*s), commanding the garrisons and using enormous landholdings for the maintenance of their tribal contingents. With the weakening of bureaucracy and decentralization of land assignments that resulted from the increase in the size of the *iqṭāʿ*, on the one hand, and the amalgamation of fiscal revenue collection and prebendal grants for military and administrative service, on the other, the system ineluctably developed in a military direction. Furthermore, the power of women in Turkic royal families, in interaction with the absence of primogeniture and indivisibility in nomadic kingdoms, laid the foundation for a novel political regime. The appanage of a young Seljuq prince was de facto governed by his tutor (*atabeg*), whom his widowed mother tended to marry. The *aʿyān-amīr* system thus changed into an extremely decentralized system in the latter part of the twelfth and early-thirteenth centuries.

Hodgson at one point considered the Sufi orders "the pivotal late medieval institution" and discussed it in conjunction with the emergence of the Persianate world (Hodgson 1993, 184–90). Nevertheless, he ignored the phenomenal growth of popular Sufism after the thirteenth century (Burke 1993, 326), and did not put Sufi-informed Persianate Islam as an organizing principle of society in the middle period on par with the "*Sharʿi*-minded piety."

Hodgson's third ideal type for the post-Mongol period is "the military-patronage state," which is modeled quite closely on the Mamluk sultanate in Egypt and Syria. The slave generals, Mamluk *amīrs,* elected the ruler (*sultān*) from their own ranks, and the Mamluk kingdom was thus taken over as a whole by him and never divided among the princes of the royal house as appanages. Egypt's Mamluk regime was similar to the Delhi Sultanate as an Islamicate polity under a complex system of collective rule by military slave generals. Given their relatively small number among the population, the Mamluk Sultans of Egypt and Syria and their families developed an extensive network of patronage, through endowments (*awqāf*), over civic, educational, and charitable foundations run by the civilian elite.

Last but not least, in the third volume of *The Venture of Islam* Hodgson adopted the idea of "gunpowder empires" for the early modern Muslim empires, namely the Ottoman, the Safavid, and the Mughal. He did so in part to draw attention to the fact that military technology in the sixteenth century made them the center of gravity in the Eurasian landmass outside China. It should be pointed out, however, that his emphasis on this later impact of military technology on social organization does not remedy Hodgson's blind spot on the fundamental significance of nomadic pastoralism in the Nile-to-Oxus region, which he primarily conceived as an agrarianate-citied civilization.

The Second Generation: Ernest Gellner

If nomadic pastoralism and Sufism were not integrated into Hodgson's theoretical framework, they were the focal points of treatment of Islam by Ernest Gellner (d. 1995). ʿAbd al-Rahmān Ibn Khaldun (d. 1406) who considered himself the founder of the rational science of history and is widely considered by Gellner and others as a sociologist *avant la lettre,* offered an ingenious model of the dynamics of the power/culture nexus in the Islamicate civilization. There were two basic and radically different forms of organization of human life, the nomadic life of the desert, and the settled life of the cities. The former developed in the desert periphery of the Islamicate civilization, the latter in its urban centers. Ibn Khaldun placed the production of group solidarity (*ʿasabiyya*) as the source of power in the desert while equating civilization (*ʿumrān*) as the source of culture in its urban centers.[7] Military power generated in the tribal periphery, when aided by religious reformers trained in the *madrasa*s of the urban centers, enables the leader of a tribal coalition to conquer the cities and form a dynasty. Law-abidingness, education, and the luxuries of city life are militarily and politically debilitating, however, and make the city-dwelling dynasty of nomadic origins prey to a newly formed tribal confederation from the desert periphery, and the pendulum swings back to the formation of a new dynasty (Gellner 1981, 25–27). At this point, Gellner extends the causal role Ibn Khaldun attributed to religious reformers in unifying tribes to the consequences of the dynastic cycles they triggered. The doctors of scriptural Islam of the cities displace and weaken the tribal maraboutic saints with each turn of the cycle, thus deepening the penetration of scriptural Islam of the imperial centers into the tribal periphery (Hall 2010, 279–80). Here, Gellner's reading of Ibn Khaldun is completely forced, with the hindsight of his hypothesis on Islamic reform as modernization to be discussed presently. What he reads into Ibn Khaldun is David Hume's idea on the oscillation between enthusiasm and superstition in religion,[8] equated respectively with maraboutic anthropolatry and scripturalist deism in Islam (Anderson 1984, 114–16). The Humean oscillation in religion is superimposed on the Khaldunian purely political swing that describes the cycle of rise and fall of dynastic states.

This aspect of Gellner's theory was developed somewhat further by S. N. Eisenstadt (d. 2010). Drawing on Gellner's depiction of Ibn Khaldun's model of the cycle of the rise and fall of puritanical Muslim dynasties as the Khaldunian pendulum's swing, and perhaps also on Hodgson's idea of uninstitutionalized social activism, Eisenstadt (2002) offers a relatively simple model of constant tension between an Islamic primordial utopia—the ideal of the Golden Age of pristine Islam—and the historical reality of patrimonial Sultanism, coexisting with an autonomous public sphere protected by Islamic law and dominated by the religious elite, the *ulema*.

Moving beyond North Africa, the empirical locus of Ibn Khaldun's and his own theory, Gellner (1981, 73–77) offers a structural model of the unhinging of Ibn Khaldun's pendulum through what he calls the Mamluk Option in order to accommodate the Terrible Turk. "Mamluk" means "the owned," or "slave," and the Mamluks were the slave soldiers employed by Muslim rulers whose recruitment the Ottomans regularized and perfected as the Janissaries, who were made a pillar of their long-lasting empire. The nomadic conqueror cannot rely on his tribesmen for long, Gellner argued, and he has to turn to mercenaries or slave soldiers. The reason is that "the lack of separation between their civil and military roles made them excessively responsive to pressures other than the long-term plans of the supreme command. Notoriously, they went home when it suited them, oblivious to strategic considerations" (Gellner 1990, 113). If the use of *civil* for tribesmen is jarringly Gellneresque, so is his assimilation of the Mamluks as the ruling stratum to Plato's guardians: "The fact that these elites were to be called slaves was relatively unimportant. The state owned them, but they owned the state" (Gellner 1990, 114).

This brings us to Gellner's noted theory of nationality as the generic form of identity required by modern states. Unlike particularistic tribal and ethnic identities, the passive democratization of the *Rechtsstaat* offered a universalistic identity for the "modular" individuals functioning in modern industrial societies. The generic identity of the individuals in what other observers called mass society is the structural element from which modern nationalism springs (Gellner 1984). Once more in a typically Gellneresque surprise, he assimilated the modern mobile bourgeois to the socially unattached eunuch, Mamluk, and celibate cleric of old: we are all clerks! "It is only in our modern world that everyone becomes employable on bureaucratic terms, that the Mamluk condition becomes universalized" (Gellner 1981, 77).

Gellner was quick to see, however, that his theory of nationalism did not fit the Muslim world he knew, and whose exceptionalism he accounted for as follows: As the lower urban strata continue to be impotent after postcolonial independence, they "can only console or express themselves in terms of their Islamic purity: for a nationalist expression of the *ressentiment* is not open to them" (Gellner 1981, 66). Now in French Algeria, the Islamic puritanism of the reformist doctors (*ulema*) who led the opposition to colonial rule and were progenitors of nationalism, equipped the Mamluks of the postindependence state and industrial society with a puritanical ethic suited for modernity. Gellner thus turns to Max Weber to explain what appeared as Islamic exceptionalism in terms of his theory of nationalism but is now seen to fit the logic of Weber's comparative sociology of world religions: Islam is the only world religion that is "secularization-resistant," because it is already this-worldly and can readily generate its own puritanical ethic adaptable to modernization (Hall 2010, 286; Turner 2013, 15–17). Just as he had imposed a religious oscillation on Ibn Khaldun's political one, here too, Gellner offers a cultural supplement to his structural model of pendulum unhinging in the contemporary world by the positing the spread of puritanical, scripturalist Islam in lieu of his generic nationalism. He grafts a Weberian analysis of Islamic puritanism onto his model of the historical dynamics of North African dynastic cycles derived from Ibn Khaldun. Gellner assumed the Berber religious reformers of the medieval Berber empires, the Almoravids and the Almohads, were in a similar, inherently ambiguous position to the marabout holy lineages of High Atlas he studied. "They must serve tribal, non-urban ends, but they must also link the tribes with a wider and urban-oriented ideal of Islam." They thus "keep the door open for the propagation of 'purer' Islam by endorsing it in the course of the very practices in which they deviate from it" (Gellner 1981, 130). This statement threw considerable light on the so-called neo-Sufi fundamentalism, notably that of the Naqshbandi Order, found elsewhere in the Muslim world since the eighteenth century.

In the twentieth century, however, he detects a very different fundamentalist and puritanical urban trend, for whose explanation Weber alone provides the guideline. For Weber, the this-worldly asceticism of the Puritans would, under favorable circumstances, be secularized into the spirit of capitalism. Talcott Parsons (1963) generalized this idea into secularization as the privatization of religion as the final stage in the evolution of Christianity. Peter Berger (1967) generalized it further into the Judaeo-Christian cultural foundation of secularism, while Oestreich (1969) and later Gorsky (1995; 2003) extended the Weberian Protestant Ethic thesis more narrowly to explain the ethos of state-building in early modern Europe. In a similar vein, Gellner saw Protestantism as the harbinger of nationalism. "Equal access to a scripturalist God paved the way to equal access to high culture" (Gellner 1984, 142). Protestantism thereby transforms Western societies in the direction of "a generic Protestantism, equalitarianism, democracy and nationalism," and thus into "a more homogeneous humanity" (Gellner 1988, 262–63).

But Gellner also found a Muslim replica of ascetic Protestantism, in the interwar Islamic reform movement (*islāh*), known as the Salafiyya, in Middle East and North Africa (Merad 1967). Basing his argument on the double-edged struggle of this movement for orthodox reform against maraboutism and Westernism in French Algeria and for the recovery of the pure Islam of the pious ancestors (*al-salaf al-sālih*), Gellner (1981, 171) concluded that Islam's "this-worldliness, conjoined to a puritanical stress on Koranic rule-observance, would seem a Weberian ethic indeed." It should be noted that James Peacock (1983) provided solid empirical support for the strength of this Weberian ethic among the fundamentalist as compared to the nominal Muslims in Indonesia. The post–World War II and postindependence period is marked by the sharp decline of popular Sufism and a corresponding rise of puritanical, fundamentalist, or scripturalist Islam (Geertz 1968). Hence, the Gellner thesis on Islam as the sole "secularization-resistant" world religion.

Truth to tell, however, contemporary Islam is not alone among the world religions in its resisting secularism by its vigorous assertion in modern politics. D. E. Smith (1970) detected the politicization of religion as a global tendency long before it reached its culmination at the end of the twentieth century. Before the onset of modernization, religion is a mass phenomenon, politics is not. As modern societies become political societies that incorporate masses in some form or other, religion becomes politicized to varying degrees as an instrument of political mobilization.

The Third Generation: S. N. Eisenstadt

In the third generation of comparative sociologists, S. N. Eisenstadt did not write much on Islam explicitly, but his influence is evident in many of that generation who did. Eisenstadt's seminal concepts of axial age and multiple modernities are integrally connected and have their common roots in his dissatisfaction with the modernization theory he had helped develop in the 1960s. Modernization theory ignored the major issue of the "continuity and reconstruction of tradition," and Eisenstadt began with coining the term *post-traditional societies* (1972) and finally settled for "multiple modernities"[9] (Eisenstadt 2000). Tradition and modernity were combined in "new foci of collective national identity" (Eisenstadt 1972, 7).

In Max Weber's comparative sociology, the impact of the world religions was transmitted through the social strata or classes that constituted their respective social bearers or carriers (*Träger*). The notion of rationalization as a developmental pattern links the institution building of the formative periods to the religious solutions to the problem of the meaning of human life. These define the ideal interests of the bearers of the world religions that must be brought into some meaningfully consistent reconciliation with material conditions and historical contingencies. Part III of my *Sociology of Shiʿite Islam* is devoted to a systematic analysis of the emergence of the cultural bearers of Shiʿism after the cessation of the historical Imamate in the ninth century, and their gradual transformation in Iran into a hierocracy in the sixteenth, and eventually a theocracy in the last quarter of the twentieth century (Arjomand 2016b). As the leading figure in the third generation of comparative sociologists, S. N. Eisenstadt presented a sketch of the inner dynamics of Islamic civilization, which he was to elaborate further (Eisenstadt, Hoexter, and Levtzion 2002). The main feature of this model was the oscillation between military regimes with limited pluralism and intolerant, "proto-fundamentalist" and "Jacobin fundamentalist" ones. This model is appealing for its simplicity and for discarding the Eurocentric view of social evolution and dynamics. It leaves out, however, the heterodoxy whose importance Eisenstadt highlights in his general civilizational analysis—namely, the radical Shiʿite apocalyptic utopia of the millenarian revolutions from the Ismāʿili Fatimids in the tenth to the Bābis in the nineteenth century. In adopting the pendulum swing model into a Khaludnian ideal type of revolution, for which I claim applicability beyond the Muslim world, I shifted the focus to the generation of revolutionary movements on the periphery as opposed to the center, and to the effect of religion and ideology on group solidarity (*ʿasabiyya*), Ibn Khaldun's key sociological concept (Arjomand 2009, 10–112, 214).

Eisenstadt's comparison of the articulation of culture and power in the Islamic and Indian civilizations can also be mentioned as an illustration of his comparative civilizational analysis. It was focused on the constitution and development of political arenas, and highlights the varying salience of the public sphere. The two civilizations vary in terms of the relevance of the political order to salvation and therefore the relative strength of its religious regulation. In Muslim societies, Eisenstadt (2006, 7) found that a "very vibrant and autonomous public sphere" was decoupled from "access to the political arena," which remained restricted. The religious motive to uphold the moral order was clearly strong in Islam, and the frustrated urge to restructure the mundane world often found expression in movements of protesters who sought to restore pristine Islam as a primitive utopia. Meanwhile, the rulers were expected to maintain public order and defend the community while the clerical estate, the *ulema*, acted as the guardians and regulators of its basic norms and thus the "bearers" of Islam and its transcendental vision. In the Indian civilization, by contrast, we have relatively wide access to the political arena combined with "rather minimal tendencies to the reconstitution of the political order" (Eisenstadt 2006, 9). The latter feature is explained by the religio-cultural centrality of the caste system. The caste system organized the social order in terms of duties rather than rights "in highly hierarchical relations and in collective ways" (Eisenstadt 2006, 10), and, as a system of social power, thus circumscribed the scope of political authority. Within the circumscribed political sphere, the ruler regulated the relations among collective actors who had relatively easy access to him.

Armando Salvatore (2007) traces the impact of Aristotelian public reasoning on Latin Christianity and Islam, resulting in the shaping of their respective public spheres within the framework of S. N. Eisenstadt's paradigm of axial civilizations. The comparison centers on the idea of the *res publica christiana,* with special reference to the thought of Thomas Aquinas

(d. 1274), and *maslaha ʿāmma* (public good/interest), notably in the work of the Muslim jurist Abu Ishaq al-Shatibi (d. 1388). The most questionable premise of this comparison is that the concept of *maslaha* occupies a central position in the Islamic tradition comparable to that of *respublica christiana* in the Christian tradition, whereas in fact it is a somewhat marginal notion in Islamic jurisprudence. Furthermore, al-Shatibi's treatment of it has had nothing like the tremendous impact of Aquinas's philosophy of law in the West. Despite many erudite details on the Christian-Muslim intercivilizational dialogue, Salvatore's ambitious attempt at civilizational analysis is therefore inconclusive.

Returning to Eisenstadt's comparison of Hinduism and Islam, a more systematic comparison of the bearers of Islam and Hinduism is certainly called for. The Brahmins were the guardians and regulators of the basic values and norms of the Hindu civilization, as the *ulema* were of the Muslim one, and in both cases independently of the rulers and the state. This similar function was however performed very differently, in an ethical and juristic style by the *ulema,* and in a ritual style by the Brahmins. The civilizational consequences of this difference in the orientation of the bearers of the two religions could then be systematically explored. There is, furthermore, a corresponding similarly in the function of rulership and its religious autonomy in the two cases, which I highlighted in my contribution to the Eisenstadt *Festschrift* (Arjomand 2005). In neither civilization were the rulers the guardians of religion and articulators of its transcendental vision. Eisenstadt's treatment of the two cases is not symmetrically consistent, however. He underlines the autonomy of kingship in India and notes the revisionist argument in Indian historiography for its legitimacy as "semi-sacral" power and yet not derived from the authority of the Brahmins. The autonomous legitimacy of kingship is thus considered an important feature of the Indian normative order. What I consider very similar normative autonomy of kingship in the Islamic civilization after the separation of the Caliph and the Sultan is, by contrast, presented by Eisenstadt as merely de facto. The ancient symbolism of power in the form of universal monarchy survived Islam, as sacral kingship survived Buddhism and Brahminism. Surely this much is even implied by Eisenstadt's latest idea of 'multiple axiality' as the result of the interaction between axial and pre-axial civilizations (Eisenstadt 2005, 531).

Eisenstadt also emphasized the degree of autonomy of the elites representing orthodoxy in relation to the ruler and political power as a determinant of the strength of their civilizational impact. I have similarly treated the degree of the autonomy of the Shiʿite hierocracy from the patrimonial state in different periods as a key determinant of their cultural impact on Iran (Arjomand 1984). According to Eisenstadt (1993), whether Islam remains confined to the religious sphere or might have a broader impact in a civilization largely depends on their autonomy from the rulers. This explains the different civilizational impact of Islam in sub-Saharan Africa and Southeast Asia, where we do not find the *ulema* as a strong independent sodality (*Rechtsgenossenschaft*), as compared to the Middle East and North Africa, where we do.

For Eisenstadt, the dynamics of axial civilizations continues unimpaired into the global age. Multiple modernities that result from the interaction between Western-inspired modernization and the continued social dynamics of axial civilizations in the global era give rise to a distinct "civilization of modernity" (Eisenstadt 2003, 2, 493–571). As in the original Western modernity, the civilization of modernity includes the Jacobin variety, which comprises contemporary fundamentalist movements, including Islamic fundamentalism. What Eisenstadt calls the Jacobin version of modernity in fact combines the political radicalism of the eponymous French revolutionaries with the reactive impulse of contemporary fundamentalists to preserve axial traditions. This combination needs unpacking. In *Rethinking Civilizational Analysis* (2004),[10] Edward Tiryakian and I replaced Norbert Elias's Eurocentric notion of *the* civilizing process by two sets of processes. Intracivilizational processes, to borrow Redfield's key terms, are developmental patterns that rest on the continuous approximation of local Little Traditions to the central Great Tradition of the respective civilization. Intercivilizational processes represent encounters or dialogue between different world civilizations. The two types of civilizational process can, and usually do, occur simultaneously and intersect. This is a matter of considerable importance in the global context, where intracivilizational processes intermingle with intercivilizational ones as well as with the development of what Eisenstadt in the same volume calls a distinct, albeit composite "civilization of modernity." The intracivilizational processes of Sanskritization and Islamicization is another. Each of these intracivilizational processes intersects with Westernization (modernization after the creation of the United Nations), and lately with globalization as an intercivilizational process. This intermingling inevitably produces tension, tension that can be resolved by compromise and assimilation, or can result in violent clashes. The inter- and intracivilizational processes constitute the appropriate context for considering the clash of civilizational elements within each and every world civilization, and within the composite civilization of modernity (Arjomand and Tiryakian 2004).

The Third Generation: Bryan S. Turner and Saïd Amir Arjomand

In the third generation of comparative sociologists should be included Bryan S. Turner's *Weber and Islam* (1974) and my *Shadow of God and the Hidden Imam* (1984). We both attempted to see what Max Weber's projected sociology of Islam might have looked like, and how it could be developed. In the following decades, Turner developed his own Weber-inspired approach in a number of studies, now collected under the title of *Sociology of Islam* (2013), and I continued to use and develop a Weberian theoretical framework for studying Shi`ite Islam as a world religion in a number of essays that are published as *Sociology of Shi`ite Islam* (2016).

As a contributor to Eisenstadt's axial civilizations and multiple modernities, furthermore, I also drew on the civilizational analysis of Islam of Benjamin Nelson (1980) who placed the (divergent) inception of modernity in the West around the thirteenth century. In this period, Thomas Aquinas commissioned the translation of Aristotle's *Politics*, the one major work of his that was not translated into Arabic (Arjomand 2001). In a later article, I revisited the Islamic city and its pattern of politics on two opposite eastern and western regions of the Islamicate world (Arjomand 2004). For the western lands, I drew on the urban politics of the Maghreb, as described by Ibn Khaldun in his history of the Berbers in detail and independently of his general model of dynastic cycles, and compared it with those of Andalusia conquered by Spain. The logic of this comparison rested on the revealing encounter between the politico-legal traditions of the two civilizations that took place with the reconquests by James I of Aragon (1213–1276), which brought *mudéjar* (Spanish Muslim communities) communities into a relationship of vassalage with him. James, who commissioned Thomas Aquinas's *Summa Contra Gentiles* for the education of the Dominicans and Franciscans to preach among his Muslim subjects, granted the *mudéjars* municipal self-government on the basis of *fueros* similar to charters of the other cities of his realm. For eastern Islamic lands, I put Hodgson's hypothesis, or more precisely, the urban and constitutional reforms, through which Caliph al-Nāsir sought to enhance urban solidarity as a new basis for the reassertion of the enfeebled Caliphal power against the Sultans, in the context of pre- and post-Mongol urban politics. My conclusion was that

> Caliph al-Nāsir's civic reforms did have a lasting effect in the eastern Islamic lands, and that the growth of Akhi/Futuwwa confraternities made for a conspicuous presence of plebeian urban groups not known in the Maghreb as surveyed by Ibn Khaldun. Nevertheless, this development did not constitute an irreversible stride on the path to modernity. Self-government remained a matter of default and soon gave way to autocracy and/or the establishment of a new dynasty. In none of the three cases analyzed . . . do we find a development of a new theory of government or any normative justification of self-rule and consolidation of the practice of municipal self-government. (Arjomand 2004, 244)

Municipal self-government is a striking feature of the medieval West not found in the Islamicate civilization, while the unavailability of the *Politics* in the Muslim world was a further obstacle to the development of a new theory of government.[11] This conclusion was in line with the negative conclusion of the 1999 study that the absence of the concept of corporation in Islamic law hampered the autonomy of the *madrasas* in comparison to the rise of the universities in the West on the basis of the idea of corporation in Roman law.

Eisenstadt's pioneering comparisons in civilizational analysis are of great heuristic value, but they share the limitation of global civilizational ideal types and must be historicized. I have accordingly treated the relative strength vis-à-vis the patrimonial states of civil society and civic institutions as variables. The charitable and educational institutions that dominate the public sphere of Muslim societies were shown to undergo a few major historical and geographical variations. Likewise, I critically assessed Hodgson's ideal-type of "military-patronage state" in view of its underestimation of the significance of nomadic polities in the east, and proposed a further division of his military-patronage type between the Turko-Mongolian empires in Iran and Central Asia. In the Turko-Mongolian empires, the Turkish ruling estate was overwhelmingly dominant over and segregated from the civilian subject estate without needing to make any great concessions to the Persian civilian elite. In the Mamluk regimes in the Delhi Sultanate and Egypt and Syria, by contrast, a numerically much smaller Turkish military elite without any roots in local society needed the support of the Arab civilian elites much more critically, and the latter were consequently greater beneficiaries of its patronage system (Arjomand 1999).

It goes without saying that the above analysis draws heavily and directly on Max Weber. It is likewise with my contribution to the study of multiple modernities. Modern politics profoundly affects the authority of the guardians of tradition, especially that of the bearers of the world religions. Max Weber (1978, 2, 1195) noted this effect of modern mass politics in general terms: "Hierocracy has no choice but to establish a party organization and to use demagogic means, just like all other parties." Nowhere was this done as radically and as effectively as by the Shi`ite hierocracy in Iran in the 1970s under Khomeini's revolutionary leadership. I find it difficult to escape the conclusion that under Khomeini's charismatic leadership, the Islamic Revolution in Iran resulted in "both the traditionalization of a modernizing nation-state and the modernization of the Shiʿite tradition, a tradition endowed with the usual transformative potential of the world religions of salvation" (Arjomand 1989, 117).

The dialectic of tradition and modernity in fact became the dominant theme in the public sphere in postrevolution Iran in the 1990s after the revolutionary Islamic ideology had subsided. Although its political impact during the presidency of Mohammad Khatami (1997–2005) was minimal and the return of the reformists to power was prevented by flagrant electoral fraud in June 2009, the long-term significance of the movement should not be minimized. The so-called religious intellectuals in the 1990s elaborated a critical theoretical framework for understanding the dialectic of tradition and modernity. The focus of this critical perspective was not on the transition from tradition to modernity but on the continuous tension between modernity and religion (Arjomand 2009, ch. 5). The search for an alternative modernity in postrevolutionary Iran through the dialectic of tradition and modernity has had a considerable impact in many parts of the Muslim world, Even though Islamic terrorism and global jihad may be more spectacular than reformism, it is equally a manifestation of multiple modernities, albeit of the Jacobin variety.

Many aspects of Bryan Turner's sociology of Islam, too, can be related to the insights of Gellner and Eisenstadt. Eisenstadt did not carry his analysis of the bearers of different forms of Islam to the present. Gellner, however, presented the doctor/jurists (*ulema*) and the Sufi saints (*marabouts*) as rival carriers of different forms of Islam, noting the decline of the authority of the latter who had enjoyed the backing of the French colonial rulers. He highlighted the challenge to the authority of the *ulema* by a new socially mobile and educated urban middle class with Western degrees who espouse the ethic of the Islamic reform of pre-independence doctors (Turner 2013, 284). History does not stand still, however, and we can now see the severe challenge to Gellner's middle-class Muslim Puritans by the largely unemployed lumpen-intelligentsia of Muslim countries, and especially those hailing from the underclass of the Muslim diaspora in Western Europe, as the bearers of radical political Islam and global Jihad. It should be noted that the bearers of these new tendencies are not self-sufficient but rely on those of a particular Islamic tradition for which they have the closest elective affinity. The Salafi scripturalism was adopted the Hanbalite theology (Merad 1978, 141–54), and when the global Jihadists established their Islamic State of the Caliphate in occupied Iraq and Syria, they imported twelve Wahhabi judges who follow the Hanbalite rite from Saudi Arabia (*The Economist*, 9/20/2014, 43).

Concluding Remarks

Of pioneers in the civilizational analysis of Islam, Hodgson is clearly the most systematic and historical, and thus comes closest to Max Weber's project for the sociology of Islam as a world religion. Nevertheless, his work on *The Venture of Islam* was unfinished at the time of his death, and his companion world history never completed or published. Although Bryan Turner (2013, 77–78) takes him to task for his immunization of faith from contamination by sociological factors, what could be posthumously put together on the rise of Islam in fact does not get beyond economic and sociological factors and by omission gives a highly reductionist account that misses the transformative effect of Islam as a new faith altogether. Furthermore, with the world history manuscript remaining unpublished, what he offers explicitly by way of comparison with Christianity is meager, and I do not find it convincing.

Gellner and Eisenstadt rightly celebrate Ibn Khaldun as a great sociologist and offer us specific insights into certain aspects of contemporary processes in the Islamicate civilization without, however, claiming to be comprehensive. The Weberian project of grounding the Islamicate civilization in Islam as a world religion is yet to be completed, and scholars such as Bryan Turner and myself are engaged in completing it.

Notes

1. See chapter 4, by Victor Lidz.

2. See chapter 5, by Donald Nielsen.

3. See the Introduction.

4. This alleged functional/teleological requirement of empire acts as a *deus ex machina* in Al-Azmeh's explanatory framework, and it contradicts his methodological claim (2014, xii) that "nowhere will the end product be used to color the interpretation" of the emergence of Islam. In my view, by contrast, empire is a possible consequence of the centralization of power characteristic of one ideal type (the Tocquevillean) of revolution. In this view, the Umayyad empire was a long-term consequence of what I call Mohammad's constitutive revolution in Arabia (Arjomand 2019, ch.8).

5. Private communication with Professor Reuben Smith.

6. Burke's subsequent *Islam and World History: The Ventures of Marshall Hodgson* (The University of Chicago Press, 2018) was not available to me at the time of this writing.

7. This reading is possible, given Ibn Khaldun's ambiguity and inconsistency in using the term. Strictly speaking, however, Ibn Khaldun's fundamental distinction is between *'umrān hadari* and *'umrān Badawi,* where the two terms, according to his explicit definition, should be translated as urban and nomadic societies/social organizations and not civilizations (Dale 2015, 27–28).

8. Hume's idea was drawn upon already in the eighteenth century by Gibbon in his explanation of the rise of Christianity in the Roman Empire.

9. Neither "post-traditional,' nor "multiple modernities" were terms in common use.

10. The book was based on a special issue of *International Sociology* published in September 2001.

11. It meant continued unawareness of many key Aristotelian political concepts that became available to Aquinas and others in the thirteenth century and shaped Western political thought, such as the commonwealth (*res publica*) and the rule of law (government by laws and not men), with the citizen being the ruler and the ruled at the same time (Aquinas, 138–39).

References

Al-Azmeh, A. 2014. *The Emergence of Islam in Late Antiquity. Allah and His People.* Cambridge: Cambridge University Press.

———. 2018a. "Paleo-Islam: Transfigurations of Late Antique Religion." In *A Companion to Religion in Late Antiquity*, edited by J. Lőssl and N. J. Baker-Brian, 345–68. Oxford: Wiley Blackwell.

———. 2018b. "Implausibility and Probability in Studies of Paleo-Qur'anic Genesis." In *Islam in der Moderne, Moderne in Islam*, edited by F. Zemmin, J. Stephan, and M. Corrado, 15–40. Leiden: Brill.

Anderson, J. W. 1984. "Conjuring with Ibn Khaldun: From an Anthropological Point of View." In *Ibn Khaldun and Islamic Ideology*, edited by B. B. Lawrence, 111–21. Leiden: Brill.

Aquinas, T. 1965. *Aquinas Selected Political Writings*. Edited by A. P. D'Entreves, translated by J. G. Dawson. Oxford: Basil Blackwell.

Arjomand, S. A. 1989. "History, Structure and Revolution in Shi`ite Tradition in Contemporary Iran." *International Political Science Review* 10, no. 2: 109–17.

———. 1999. "The Law, Agency, and Policy in Medieval Islamic Society: Development of the Institutions of Learning from the Tenth to the Fifteenth Century." *Comparative Studies in Society and History* 41, no. 2: 263–93.

———. 2001. "Perso-Indian Statecraft, Greek Political Science, and the Muslim Idea of Government." *International Sociology* 16, no. 3: 455–73.

———. 2004. "Transformation of the Islamicate Civilization: A Turning Point in the Thirteenth Century?" In *Eurasian Transformations, 10th to 13th Centuries: Crystallizations, Divergences, Renaissances*, edited by J. Arnason and B. Wittrock, 213–45. Leiden: Brill.

———. 2005. "Political Culture in the Islamicate Civilization." In *Comparing Modernity, Pluralism, and Hegemony*, edited by E. Ben-Rafael and Y. Sternberg, 309–26. Leiden: Brill.

———. 2009. *After Khomeini: Iran under his Successors*. Oxford: Oxford University Press.

———. 2010 "Three Generations of Comparative Sociologies." *Archives européennes de sociologie/European Journal of Sociology* 51, no. 3: 363–99.

———. 2011. "Axial Civilizations, Multiple Modernities, and Islam." *Journal of Classical Sociology* 11, no. 3: 327–35.

———. 2013. "Multiple Modernities and the Promise of Comparative Sociology." In *Worlds of Difference*, edited by S. A. Arjomand and E. Reis, 15–39. London: Sage.

———. 2014. "Crystallization of Islam and Developmental Patterns in the Islamicate Civilization." In *Social Theory and Area Studies in the Global Age*, edited by S. A. Arjomand, 203–20. Albany: State University of New York Press.

———. 2016a. *Sociology of Shi`ite Islam. Collected Essays*. Leiden: Brill.

———. 2016b "Developmental Path (*Entwicklungsform*): A Neglected Weberian Concept and Its Usefulness in Civilizational Analysis of Islam." In *The Art and Science of Sociology: Essays in Honour of Edward Tiryakian*, edited by R. Robertson, J. Simpson, and D. Buhari-Gulmez. New York: Anthem Press.

Arjomand, S. A., and E. A. Tiryakian. 2004. "Introduction." In *Rethinking Civilizational Analysis*, 1–13. London: Sage.

Becker, C. H. 1967[1932]. *Islamstudien*. 2 vols. Hildesheim: Georg Olms.

Burke, E. 1993. "Conclusion: Islamic History as World History: Marshall G. S. Hodgson and *The Venture of Islam*." In *Rethinking World History: Essays on Europe, Islam, and World History*, 301–27. Cambridge: Cambridge University Press.

Chabbi, J. 1997. *Le Seigneur des tribus. Islam et Mahomet.* Paris: CNRS Éditions.

Dale, S. F. 2015. *The Orange Trees of Marrakesh. Ibn Khaldun and the Science of Man.* Cambridge: Harvard University Press.

Eisenstadt, S. N., ed. 1972. *Post-Traditional Societies.* New York: W. W. Norton.

———. 1993. "Religion and the Civilizational Dimensions of Politics." In *The Political Dimensions of Religion*, edited by S. A. Arjomand, 13–41. Albany: State University of New York Press.

———. 1999. "Weber's Analysis of Islam and the Specific Pattern of Islamic Civilization." In *Max Weber and Islam*, edited by T. E. Huff and W. Schluchter, 281–94. New Brunswick, NJ: Transaction.

———. 2000. *Fundamentalism, Sectarianism, and Revolution.* Cambridge: Cambridge University Press.

———. 2003. *Comparative Civilizations and Multiple Modernities.* 2 vols. Leiden: Brill.

———. 2005. "Axial Civilizations and the Axial Age Reconsidered." In *Axial Civilizations and World History*, edited by Johann P. Arnason, S. N. Eisenstadt, and Bjőrn Wittrock, 531–64. Leiden: Brill.

———. 2006. "Revolution in Early Islam: The Rise of Islam as a Constitutive Revolution." *Yearbook of the Sociology of Islam* 7: 125–57.

———, M. Hoexter, and N. Levtzion, eds. 2002. *The Public Sphere in Muslim Societies.* Albany: State University of New York Press.

Geertz, C. 1968. *Islam Observed.* Chicago: The University of Chicago Press.

Gellner, E. 1981. *Muslim Society.* Cambridge: Cambridge University Press.

———. 1984. *Nations and Nationalism.* Oxford: Blackwell.

———. 1988. *Plough, Sword, and Book.* London: Collins Harvill.

———. 1990. "Tribalism and the State." In *Tribes and State Formation in the Middle East*, edited by P. S. Khoury and L. Kostiner, 109–26. Berkeley: University of California Press.

Gorski, P. S. 1995. "Protestant Ethic and the Spirit of Bureaucracy." *American Sociological Review* 60, no. 5.

———. 2003 *The Disciplinary Revolution. Calvinism and the Rise of the State in Early Modern Europe.* Chicago: The University of Chicago Press.

Hall, J. A. 2010. *Ernest Gellner: An Intellectual Biography.* London: Verso.

Hodgson, M. G. S. 1955a. "How Did the Early Shiʿa Become Sectarian?" *JOAS* 75, no. 1: 1–13.

———. 1955b. *The Order of Assassins; The Struggle of the Early Nizârî Ismâʿîlîs against the Islamic world.* The Hague: Mouton.

———. 1962. "Al-Darazî and Hamza in the Origin of the Druze Religion." *JOAS* 82, no. 1: 5–20.

———. 1974. *The Venture of Islam. Conscience and History in a World Civilization.* Chicago: The University of Chicago Press.

———. 1993. *Rethinking World History: Essays on Europe, Islam, and World History.* Edited by Edmund Burke III. Cambridge: Cambridge University Press.

Islamoğlu, H. 2012. "Islamic World Histories?" In *A Companion to World History*, edited by D. Northpot, 447–63. Oxford: Blackwell.

Merad, A. 1967. *Le Réformisme musulman en Algérie de 1925 à 1940.* Paris:

———. 1978. "ISLĀH. (i) The Arab World." *Encyclopedia of Islam.* 2nd ed. Vol. 4. Leiden: Brill.

Nef, J. U. 1960. *Cultural Foundations of the Industrial Civilization.* New York: Harper and Row.

Nelson, B. 1980. *On the Roads to Modernity: Conscience, Science, and Civilizations. Selected Writings.* Totowa, NJ: Rowman and Littlefield.

Oestreich, G. 1969. *Geist und Gestalt des frühmodernen Staates.* Berlin: Duncker und Humbolt.

Parsons, T. 1963. "Christianity and Modern Industrial Society." In *Sociological Theory, Values, and Sociocultural Change*, edited by E. A. Tiryakian, 33–70. New York: Harper Torchbooks.

Robertson Smith, W. 1972 [1889]. *The Religion of the Semites. The Fundamental Institutions.* New York: Schocken Books.

Robin, Ch. 2000. "Les 'filles de Dieu' de Saba á la Mecque: Reflexions sur l'agencement des patheons dans l'Arabie ancienne." *Semitica* 50: 113–92.

Salvatore, A. 2007. *The Public Sphere: Liberal Modernity, Catholicism, Islam.* London: Palgrave Macmillan.

Schacht. J. 1935. "Zur soziologischen Betrachtung der Islamischen Rechts." *Der Islam* 22.

Smith, D. U. 1970. *Religion and Political Development.* Boston: Little, Brown.

Turner, B. S. 1974. *Weber and Islam: A Critical Study.* London: Routledge and Kegan Paul.

———. 2013. *The Sociology of Islam. Collected Essays of Bryan S. Turner.* Edited by B. S Turner and K. M. Nasir. Farnham: Ashgate.

van Ess, J. 1980. "From Wellhausen to Becker: The Emergence of *Kulturgeschichte* in Islamic Studies." In *Islamic Studies: a Tradition and its Problems*, edited by Malcolm Kerr, 29–51. Malibu: Undena Publications.

Weber, M. 1954. *Max Weber on Law in Economy and Society.* Edited with introduction and annotations by Max Rheinstein. Translation from Max Weber, *Wirtschaft und Gesellschaft*, 2d ed. (1925), by Edward Shils and Max Rheinstein. Cambridge: Harvard University Press.

Wellhausen, J. 1883. "Mohammendanism." *Encyclopedia Britannica.* 10th ed., vol. 26. http://firstsearch.oclc.org.proxy.library.stonybrook.edu/WebZ/FSQUERY?-format=BI:next=html/records.html:bad=html/records.html:numrecs=10:session-id=fsapp7-52030-ij33lfwg-iu5q8d:entitypagenum=3:0:searchtype=advanced.

———. 1957[1878]. *Prolegomena to the History of Ancient Israel.* New York: Meridian Books.

———. 1927 [1887]. *Reste arabischen Heidentums.* Berlin and Leipzig: Walter deGruyther.

7

More (or Less) than a Civilizational "Formation"?

Islam as the "Black Hole" of Comparative Civilizational Analysis

Armando Salvatore

Introduction: Formation or Consummation?

Within the civilizationally oriented comparative historical sociology spearheaded by Shmuel Eisenstadt and developed in a variety of (more or less compatible) directions by Said A. Arjomand, Johann P. Arnason, Bjorn Wittrock, and other scholars especially since the 1980s, Islam has been conceptualized as a civilizational formation in its own right. Within the framework of comparative civilizational analysis, Islam has not surprisingly gained (on the surface at least) a legitimate space and growing importance. However, its membership in the civilizational club has been also subjected to new and more thorough scrutiny. Islam sometimes still appears as an odd and potentially embarrassing late-night invitee, rather than a full member of the club. This chapter operates an inversion maneuver by revising the idea of civilizational formation from the angle of Islam's transcivilizational, more than merely civilizational, dynamics. To this purpose, it redevelops some key ideas of Marshall Hodgson, while reframing them in the context of debates unfolding both within comparative civilizational analysis and within historically and sociologically oriented Islamic Studies (see Arnason 2010, 11; Salvatore 2010; Salvatore 2016).

Karl Jaspers's equalization of a variety of world civilizations via his framework of the "Axial Age" (Jaspers 1953 [1949]) entailed a move to overcome the Euro-Christocentric approach inherited from the nineteenth century's comparative study of "world religions." The move was facilitated by the catastrophe of two world wars and occurred in coincidence with the beginning of decolonization, which unsettled Europe's enduring hegemony on a global scale, not just politically but also culturally and, as it were, civilizationally. While the myth of Europe's civilizing mission had by that time already been discredited as the fig leaf of its imperial will to power, Jaspers's move went deeper than that. It rolled back the Hegelian idea that Europe and the Enlightenment had completed a spiritual advancement prefigured by the Christ. For Jaspers, the real breakthrough reached back to a period, which he termed the "Axial Age," preceding the advent of the Christ by several centuries (approximately 800 to 200 BCE) and embracing a variety of civilizations of the West and East of the Afro-Eurasian landmass, variably—yet profoundly—influenced by a spiritual revolution. In this new framework Christianity and its civilization, namely Christendom (in due time hegemonized by its Western, Latin variant) still played a crucial role in human history, but, as more recently conceptualized by Shmuel Eisenstadt, rather as the manifestation of a "secondary breakthrough" of the axial spirit.

Likewise, the beginning of the consideration of Islam as joining the same axial civilizational family via a "tertiary breakthrough" occurring in late antiquity, may have been helped by Islam's erupting onto global headlines since the late 1970s, and even more after 9/11 and the well-known, latently or patently Islamophobic trivializations of the civilizational idea infamously tied to the name of Samuel Huntington. Additionally, it should not be underestimated that the main proponent of Islam's inclusion in the axial club, Shmuel N. Eisenstadt, was a leading Israeli sociologist. Israel's controversial political position at the core of the Middle East and the ongoing vicissitudes of the Arab-Israeli conflict may have facilitated a fair, contrastive scholarly appreciation of Islam's relation to Judaism as a replacement for the Western canonical juxtaposition (or, inversely, "twinning") of Judaism and Christianity. As formulated by Eisenstadt (2002, 148–49),

> The emphasis on the construction of a political-religious collectivity was connected in Islam with the development of a principled ideological negation of any primordial element or component

> within this sacred political-religious identity. Indeed, of all the Axial Age civilizations in general, and the monotheistic ones in particular, Islam was, on the ideological level, the most extreme in its denial of the legitimacy of such primordial dimensions in the structure of the Islamic community . . . .In this it stood in opposition to Judaism, with which it shared such characteristics as an emphasis on the direct, unmediated access of all members of the community to the sacred.

To sum up, Islam's cooptation into the family of Axial Age civilizations was facilitated by developing the idea of Islam as the outcome of a "tertiary" breakthrough (Cook 1986, 478), or in any case as the "latest" (Eisenstadt 1992, 153) such civilization—coming after the original, primary ones of the first millennium BCE and the "secondary" formations such as Christianity; or, less schematically, as a late eruption or manifestation of the axial formational and transformational impetus (Arnason, Salvatore, and Stauth 2006, 10–11). Islam would, on this account, qualify as an axial civilization, since the label *axial* emancipated itself, mainly thanks to Eisenstadt's intervention, from a strict dependence on a chronologically circumscribed Axial "age." By time, this axial tag became a noun, namely "axiality," probably in analogy with "modernity," of which it was considered as a precursor (Arnason, Eisenstadt, and Wittrock 2005, 4), and, as modernity, not entirely confinable to an era and area.

This cooptation of Islam into the gravitational field of axiality has made more complex the theoretical debate on what is a civilization and how civilizations should be compared. Eisenstadt's just-quoted certification of Islam as not just a legitimate member of the axial civilizational club but as the most radical among them in rejecting the archaic or "primordial" substratum of pre-axial religions adds to this complexity. Yet several implications of such an inclusion of Islam have remained understated and underexplored.[1]

A detailed scholarly exploration of such implications would be probably necessary but cannot be conducted within the framework of this chapter. I will limit myself here to raise the question, as provocatively as possible, whether Islam fits the notion itself of "civilization," which comparative civilizational analysis as a branch of historical sociology has inherited from those disciplines within the humanities at large dealing, separately or conjointly, with religions, languages, and cultures. Generally speaking, and cutting a long story short, we should admit that this concept of civilization has proved to be suitable if applied to Western Europe (or to the "West" in general, as the result of Western Europe's dramatic expansion through the settler colonies of the Americas and Australia), China, or India. On a further step, comparative civilizational analysis has refined the notion and coined the somewhat sharper idea of a civilizational "formation," which corroborates the concept of civilization in sociological terms, both in analogy and in contrast to the sociologically fundamental notion of "society," also by invoking classic authors such as Durkheim and Mauss (Arnason 2003, 126).

Without indulging in an overly theoretical consideration of the concept, suffice here to observe that, paradoxically (and even anachronistically), the emergence of Western Europe, China, or India as well-delimited civilizational units and the possibility itself of their becoming the object, from Weber onward, of a civilizational comparison, was to some variable extent (strongest in the case of India, moderate in the Chinese case) influenced by their confrontation with (or at least exposure to) the more fluid, yet, from their viewpoint, threatening transcivilizational spillover of Islam (see Arnason 2006 and 2010; Salvatore 2010).

In order to proceed, we would need to revise the sociological critique of essentialism in the analysis of Islam. To be suspected of an essentialist reductionism in this case is less the analysis of Islam as a cohesive discursive tradition than as a civilizational unit that neatly corresponds to other presumably comparable units: most notably, Western Christendom (decisively shaped by the Axial Hellenic and Hebrew civilizations), later to become Western Europe, India (for whose civilizational formatting at a late, yet crucial, stage Islam's presence in the subcontinent has been, positively and negatively, seminal), or, even more today, China. While China's largely self-centered civilizational formatting was based on a selective absorption of non-Chinese civilizational influences (the most spectacular of which concerned Mahayana Buddhism), the extent to which its relations to the Islamic ecumene played a significant role should not be underestimated, even if falling short of the more intensive relationship with Islam involving Western Christendom and India. China's imperial centers interacted with an expansive Islam ever since the latter's emergence across the vital lines of long distance trade and military attritions and confrontations engaging China with its mobile western frontier, where Islam replaced Buddhism as a major commercial, military, and cultural force earlier than the second millennium. The role played by Turkic and Mongol nomadic confederations and dynasties in state-formation processes within both the Islamic ecumene and China contributed to fuel the interaction, particularly after the majority of those formations were Islamized on China's Western frontier. One could also argue that China's selective integration of cultural and civilizational influences along the Silk Road shows a wide disparity in its dealing with Buddhism and Islam. This occurred in spite of the fact that religious offers coming from the West were hardly ever classified in terms of an allegedly less congenial Abrahamic or monotheistic versus a more congenial non-Abrahamic or nontheistic nature. This was shown by how Nestorian Christians and Manicheans were often perceived in China's centers as Buddhist sects among others (Foltz 2010 [1999]; Elverskog 2010). One might also argue that the way Islam's transcivilizational ecumene impacted Chinese civilizational formatting often took the more indirect form of establishing a Chinese Han centrality against what Andre Gunder Frank (1992) defined as "the centrality of Central Asia." That China today through its transition to a superpower status has been intensifying the policing of its internal and external borders with Muslim populations shows, however, that even the geopolitical game is recurrently nourished by the fear (or pretext thereof) of Islam's and Muslims' amorphous civilizational identity and potentially anarchic disturbance of China's new hegemonic status.

Thus, one should probably invert the terms of the discussion and raise the question of whether Islam, by having provided the whirling hub to a hemisphere-wide proto-globalization from the middle of the Afro-Eurasian landmass (Salvatore, Arnason, Rahimi, and Tottoli 2018, 18–22), and taking a definite shape during the intermediate period between the axial and the modern breakthroughs (stretching from "late antiquity" to the "ecumenical renaissance": see Fowden 1993 and Wittrock 2001), could provide the necessary (both "formational" and "transformational") benchmark for the comparison among the members of the civilizational club—rather than being ever and again subjected to a (mildly successful) inclusion test in the club. This recalibration of what determines a civilizational benchmark can occur to the extent that an "Islamic perspective" is adopted as a key to formulate the following counterquestion: How can the other, geographically and historically less central Afro-Eurasian civilizational formations pass the test of being acknowledged as becoming, quite literally, singular civilizational formations (Western Europe, India, China)? In other words, acquiring the character of a civilizational "formation," rather than simply providing a pole to a hemisphere-wide civilizing process, may have depended on a trajectory of disengaging from the Islamic centrality (and, to some substantial extent, hegemony) in the said proto-globalization. Becoming a civilizational formation in the premodern, prenational era would go along with developing into a relatively autonomous regional hub (the "West," the "Indosphere," the "Sinosphere": for the latter two terms, see Duara 2015) and, more recently, with becoming a competitor for hegemony in the modern and contemporary globalizing processes.

In other words, the hypothesis I am formulating here is that, far from being from their axial beginnings neatly autonomous civilizational "formations," the West, India, and China emerged as idiosyncratic, half-insulated singularities only as byproducts of a wider, long-term Afro-Eurasian transcivilizational dynamics wherein Islam occupied the center stage both geopolitically and historically well into the beginning of the modern era. It was Michael Cook himself who, after launching the idea of Islam as a "tertiary" axial civilization in the 1980s, certified this "centrality of the Islamic civilization" in a recent study included in *The Cambridge World History* (Cook 2015). "Tertiarity" and centrality combine in creating a benchmark (from an Islamic perspective) for assessing the tradeoff between transcivilizational hegemony and singular formation.

The opening of an Islamic perspective from within the core of comparative civilizational analysis has the potential to critically question the view on civilizational transformations (axial, postaxial, or otherwise) as preparing the singular type of Western, transatlantic modernity that offset the primacy and centrality of Islam within the Eastern hemisphere. The Islamic perspective might complexify this somewhat Weberian view much more than comparative civilizational analysis has done thus far with its half-hearted inclusion of Islam in a scheme biased toward other formations or transformations and their comparisons (most notably, the Weberian comparison between the "West," China, and India). With such a suspicion would come the opportunity not to reject notions such as civilizations, formations, or even modernities, but rather to rewrite them from an Islamic perspective. Far from being peripheral, this perspective should qualify as central, for having emerged at the core of the Afro-Eurasian civilizational realm in the crucial intermediate period between the axial and the modern breakthroughs.

It is precisely Islam's historically eccentric positioning vis-à-vis Western-centered modernity, in the eyes of a wide array of Western orientalist, neo-orientalist and post-orientalist scholars (see Masud and Salvatore 2009), that might contribute to make a corrective maneuver pivoted on such an Islamic perspective not just plausible, but perhaps necessary. Marshall Hodgson started one of his key essays on the subject with the following provocation: "In the sixteenth century of our era, a visitor from Mars might well have supposed that the human world was on the verge of becoming

Muslim" (Hodgson 1993, 97). This provocation synthesizes how investing fully into the Islamic perspective inevitably induces some sort of conceptual estrangement in the reader. The oddity of the issue is therefore not intrinsic to Islam as a "civilizational formation," but depends on the rise of the West and particularly on its transatlantic deployment and colonial expansion. This development put to rest the transcivilizational centrality of Islam in the Eastern hemisphere, where "the greater part of the key historic lands of citied culture . . . from Athens to Benares, were under Muslim rule" (Hodgson 1993, 98): a centrality that would have been so obvious to a visitor from Mars.

In contrast, the Weberian comparative perspective was explicitly rooted in the singular, though hegemonic, views and concerns of "the son of the modern European cultural worlds" (Weber 1920, 1). For it, Islam was largely an internal other within the wider West (Salvatore 1996). In spite of all revisions, this Weberian perspective and the matching, ad hoc semi-orientalization of Islam continue to haunt comparative civilizational analysis. The shift of perspectives that I propose could dislodge the son of the modern West from the center of the civilizational universe without trashing social theory and comparative historical analysis, which postcolonial critique tends to see as incorrigibly complicit with Eurocentric social sciences. The shift, however, does not recenter the perspective on a new privileged observer. It would not be a mere concession to poststructuralist fashions (by themselves, no longer *en vogue*) or effect any mere "provincialization" of the West. To explain the move, let me use a cosmological metaphor. Think of a universe where not just formations like stars and constellations like galaxies develop, but also, given certain processes, black holes—whereby "black holes, far from representing just odd discontinuities or cases of perilous decay, are the units that guard the constitutive codes of the multiverse" (Salvatore 2016, 258). The black hole here, originating from a supernova explosion,[2] would be Islam itself, absorbing civilizational "matter" and de-singularizing it to some degree. The work of corroborating this hypothesis should by necessity start again with Hodgson, who was uniquely well positioned to pay adequate tribute to an Islamic perspective. This was not intended as a sheer antiorientalist provocation but as an unexplored resource for comparative civilizational analysis. As maintained by Edmund Burke III, "Marshall Hodgson clearly saw that Islamic history was a strategic point from which to undertake a critique of the discourse on Western civilization" (Burke 1993, xv). I have just proposed that it was even more than that.

The Multiverse Hypothesis

A coordinated investment into an Islamic perspective as first coherently formulated by Hodgson can build on the strengths of Hodgson's work in the light of the forty and more years of scholarship that have lapsed since his premature death, during which the inner diversity of traditions and the significance of cross-civilization encounters have been subjected to ever deeper scrutiny (Arjomand 2016; Salvatore 2016; Salvatore, Rahimi, and Tottoli 2018). Such developments feed into comparative civilizational analysis within sociology but also invest in the importance of a sustained exchange between historical comparative sociologists and professional historians.

Hodgson's approach entailed a theoretically grounded, strong criticism of the provincialism of Western orientalist views on Islam. These views traditionally privileged not only Islam's Mediterranean projection (most notably due to the long drawn-out rivalry of Western Christendom with the Ottoman Empire and the resulting "Turkish Threat," which featured so central to the fears of early modern Europe and its burgeoning public sphere), but even more its Arabian origin. The result was to disregard the key fact, in the construction of a big picture of Islam as a civilization, that from the beginning not just its expansive flourishing but also its intrinsic vitality presupposed cross-cultural exchanges with other civilizational realms (Hodgson 1993, 104).

For now, following this, like other key tracks of Hodgson's work on Islam (see Arnason 2006), one should be provisionally satisfied with a mild (and still blurred) alternative to the idea of civilizational formation as applied to Islam. Hodgson's view of "Islamdom" as a quite transcivilizational type of ecumene and social nexus (Salvatore 2010; Salvatore 2016) appears here as such a promising, yet ambivalent alternative: on the one hand, as previously explained, it might help provide the parameters to the conditions of emergence of Islam as a civilizational formation; on the other, Hodgson's overall approach, if duly renewed, is probably bound to transcend those same parameters. The idea of Islamdom, coined by Hodgson in analogy with Christendom in order to neatly differentiate Islam as a religion from the "Islamicate" civilization, suffered from some of the same pitfalls that it intended to offset. This differentiation between religion and civilization does not neatly apply in the case of Islam: not because Islam conflates various realms, but for the simple fact that religion in this case cannot be reduced to a field such as the one delimited by the Latin *religio* and derivative terms in various Western languages (Turner 1976; Karamustafa 2017). The way the word *religion* is understood in Western social sciences is inevitably the long-term outcome of the emergence of a Westphalian order centred on sovereign states delimiting a religious field, and, with it, of the view of the son of the modern West (Salvatore 2010). If a carefully delimited religious field is not available for historical and political reasons, it becomes difficult to justify a matching civilizational notion.

It is also important to add, following Hodgson, that the implications of how an Islamic/Islamicate civility[3] originally reshaped religious, social, and political institutions and their mutual demarcations became ever more visible after Islam's inception and fully evident in the course of its even more accelerated expansion across the Afro-Eurasian landscape during the post-Caliphal era. Seeing Islam deploying as a transcivilizational ecumene shifts the focus from the idea that Islam was predetermined by its beginnings toward appreciating that a gradual crystallization of its flexible institutional grid only occurred in the epoch that Hodgson dubbed the "Middle Periods," from the tenth to the fifteenth century. Hodgson was particularly eager to emphasize that the bulk of these institutions and norms were decisively shaped through the contribution of the farthest eastern fringes of the "Nile to Oxus" region. This was the wider area that Hodgson identified as an "Irano-Semitic" civilizational realm preexisting the rise of Islam and providing fuel to its development and expansion well beyond its cradle, the Hijaz, in the Western part of the Arabian peninsula. Most notably, he saw this wider region as culturally gravitating around areas such as Khurasan, which is quite central to the Eurasian landscape but rather removed from Mediterranean Syria, seat of the Omayyad caliphs (Salvatore 2016, 262). The importance of Khurasan was not just contingent on the 'Abbasid revolution, though. The main traction to Islam's transcultural expansion beyond the "Nile to Oxus" region came quite consistently from the continuously shifting Eastern frontier regions. As a way of comparison, one should recall that Hodgson tended to consider quite negligible the civilizational contribution to Islamdom of the much celebrated, far-Western region of al-Andalus. The popularity of this region is due to a fully different set of reasons than those we are examining here: namely, for representing the flip side of the modern European states' cultural homogenization and one major symbolic reference for later Muslim anticolonial resentment (cf. Salvatore 2005).

As emphasized by Hodgson, far from entering a process of implosion after the demise of the golden age of the caliphate, "Muslim society flourished grandly in its post-caliphal form. Even where Muslim rule was absent or had been overthrown, Islam often continued to flourish, although thrown on its own" (Hodgson 1974, 271). Hodgson's remark that Islam flourished while "thrown on its own" reveals one interpretative key for evaluating the trajectory that interests us: during the Middle Periods, Islam's structures of governance were quite neatly distinguished from the dynamics of sociocultural connectedness (ranging from long-distance trade to the unfolding of scholarly and Sufi networks), which in turn were ultimately responsible for the spectacular, largely entropic expansion of the Islamic ecumene across the hemisphere during this epoch. Islam's being "thrown on its own" was a badge of social autonomy and of the primacy of connectedness over sovereignty.

More particularly, the geographic centrality of Islamdom within the Afro-Eurasian landmass was matched by a cultural centrality (which Hodgson often liked to see as originating from a kind of "cultural pressure," a force determining a mild level of homogeneity over long distances) depending on a unique combination of a quite apolitical cosmopolitanism and a highly social egalitarianism (Hodgson 1993, 97). This impetus could even extend into a sort of populism *avant la lettre,* offsetting the absence of a permanent legitimization of a fully sovereign, charismatic type of state of the kind that developed in Western Europe as a successor to the fragile medieval paradigm of the *res publica christiana.* These premises, which Hodgson called "populist," might amount to a kind of super-*shari'a,* that is to say, an ideal of Islamic normativity working more broadly as a cultural idiom than as a strictly normative code, and, additionally, as centered on flexible visions of the "common good" (*al-maslaha al-ʿāmma,* a quite central notion of Islamic legal theory: Salvatore 2007, 133–71). The long-term expansive pressure facilitated by these cultural norms may be considered a rather "multiversal" sublimation of the legal/moral code strictly conceived, operating via the cumulative, yet specialized discourse and institutions of *fiqh* (jurisprudence). This sublimation might in turn be understood as the culmination of the ethical prophecy that innervated the Irano-Semitic civilizational realm from earlier epochs (basically from the onset of axial transformations). The "black hole" is still an Irano-Semitic one, but it is able to absorb scattered materials from various Afro-Eurasian provenance, east and west of the "Nile to Oxus."

Particularly the Later Middle Period (ca. 1258–1453, from the Mongol occupation of Baghdad to the Ottoman conquest of Constantinople) represents the climax of a longer epoch of hemispheric integration, of dense transcivilizational dynamics in the Afro-Eurasian landmass (including vast portions of North and East Africa). The simultaneous consolidation and expansive spin of several key norms and institutions (both Islamic and Turko-Mongol, thus, originally non-Islamic) played a central role in the process. Hereby Hodgson's focus, for the subsequent epoch of early modernity, on the three powerful "gunpowder empires," the Ottoman, the Safavid, and the Moghul, might reflect his own underestimation of the complex dynamics of the Later Middle Period, which cannot be reduced to the impact of Mongol rule on the structures of connectedness and government of the three empires. Translocal solidarities were shaped alongside a pattern of significant yet limited stabilization of the legitimacy and corporate identity of religious, social, and political institutions.

What might additionally upset familiar Eurocentric schematizations is that the Islamic expansive trajectory during the "ecumenic renaissance" of the early second millennium CE (Wittrock 2001), roughly matching Hodgson's Earlier Middle Period, displayed some factors of change that could be closely compared to those at work in Western Europe, in particular with regard to the paradigm of distinction and reconciliation between the religious and political spheres. However, such comparable developments concealed an accentuation of divergent rhythms in the cultural reproduction of social power. The main convergence was represented by the rise of mystically oriented movements, whereby "mystical" here means nothing more (or less) than an investment into direct access to the ultimate source of power, with a modicum of specialized cultural mediation represented, in the Islamic case, by Sufi rituals, rules, and sociability. These movements drew on the imagination and needs of the commoners, who were primarily city dwellers, and, increasingly during the Middle Periods, nomadic populations of Turkic origins. These movements were largely integrated into the sociopolitical mainstream and influenced its institutional reconfiguration within both Latin Christendom and Islam, with enduring consequences lasting till our days. They were equally significant, in both civilizational realms, in enhancing the importance of the commoners and promoting their "desire for a renewal of norms of life conduct within wider socio-economic transformations spawned by thriving urban economies and cross-regional trade" (Salvatore 2016, 135; cf. Arjomand 2004 and Rahimi 2006).

Overall, the European orientalists' privileged focus on Islam's origin (neatly mirrored by some brands of twentieth-century and contemporary Islamic fundamentalists/Salafis) looks past—and often conceals from sight—the key issue of entropic unfolding here discussed. The early Islamic integration of the "Nile to Oxus" region could still occur on the basis of patterns of relative continuity with the cultural and religious traditions of the Irano-Semitic civilizational zone. However, the subsequent leaps into the heartland of Sanskritic and Hellenic cultural environments (such that the core of Islamdom now became a much wider "Balkans to Bengal" macroregion) entailed both a more genuine transcivilizational integration and the risk of a new kind of disintegration. It is in this context that the originality and strength of the soft institutional toolkit of legal means, moral codes, and rules of conduct and good life (*adab*) transcending conventional understandings of the *shari'a* came to full fruition, while also showing their limit as a long-term integrative solution that might be good for all epochs (Salvatore 2019).

In this historical, geographic, and civilizational context, the capacity of key Islamic actors to combine such distant repertoires as Roman law, Indic self-cultivation, Central Asian (therefore non-Arab) codes of nomadic rulership and solidarity, and more ancestral, nonaxial rituals based on unstable equilibriums between patriarchal and matriarchal elements[4] reached a historic peak. Yet such developments left behind a potential, or excess, for a further, yet underimplemented integrative impetus: a potential that, first curbed and then seemingly annihilated by the unstoppable European global and imperial expansion, was to be retrieved in the late–twentieth-century, *post*-postcolonial era. Recent, though sharply divergent developments, from the Iranian revolution of 1978–79 through the "Arab Spring" to the rise of ISIS have retrieved a capacity to capitalize on specifically Islamic, and yet ambivalent, features of "transnationalization." These features provide the flip side to the ambivalent reconstruction of Westphalian patterns adopted via European colonialism and embraced, mostly in sharply authoritarian forms, by Muslim-majority postcolonial states. In the most recent processes and transformations, new brands of nationalisms are both integrated and resisted by emergent anti-Westphalian trends (if not yet "formations").

The Dialectics of Power and Knowledge

According to a streamlined rendering of civilizational analysis (which I am synthesizing here for reasons of convenience), all civilizations that claim an axial pedigree, including Islam, and which have developed a notion of accountability of the rulers to some sort of authority transcending the sphere of naked power, are structured via a differentiation between two realms that one can roughly designate as those of "power," on one hand, and "culture" or "knowledge," on the other (whereby for civilizational realms prior to the development of modern capitalism we may have to subsume the pursuit of "wealth" under the dimension of "power"). Such civilizations institute a dynamic relationship between the sphere of knowledge production, centered on transcendent visions, and the power incorporated in institutional arrangements. In this framework, momentous new foundations of religions, such as the rise of Christianity and the emergence of Islam, are considered as new systematizations of older axial repertoires. These legacies have provided patterns for distinguishing, and yet connecting, the realms conventionally designated, in standard Eurocentric parlance, as "religion" and "politics" (or the "state," provided we intend this category as inclusive of premodern power formations).

Shmuel N. Eisenstadt has reaffirmed the high suitability of Weber's malleable (and as such not irremediably Eurocentric) understanding of the relations between culture and power for a comparative approach valuing civilization-specific combinations and trajectories, in contrast to what he considered the much more Eurocentric views of Marx and Foucault (Eisenstadt 2006). In this neo-Weberian approach, religion, however, is not as autonomous a sphere as it may appear, anachronistically, from the viewpoint of Western European, modern, or, better, "Westphalian," state formations. Religion constitutes, rather, a meta-institutional source for channeling human power and a field for its contestation. In this sense, religion is, at least potentially, nothing other than the socially most powerful component of knowledge and culture and the key to their crystallization into institutional formations. Here, a Durkheimian element, prefigured by the eighteenth-century Neapolitan thinker Vico, is retrieved, according to which religion is *the* proto-institution of human society before being or becoming a specific, differentiated one: the former, rather holistic function surviving in a latent form even if the latter takes the upper hand (Salvatore 2007, 194; for a recent analysis, see Arnason 2017).

The problem here is that if seen from a Western, Westphalian viewpoint, the Muslim world has been lacking a viable, centralized, and strongly legitimized state, supported by a clear-cut corporate identity and a corresponding self-limiting religion (or rather a religion effectively contained and redesigned by the state so as to become a "field" providing coherence to individual beliefs). If subjected to such Westphalian yardsticks, the transcivilizational impetus of Islam simply evaporates. Yet by fully investing into the kind of Islamic perspective indicated by Hodgson, what from a Eurocentric viewpoint appear as cultural factors of blockage (boiling down to the reluctance of Islamic cultural carriers to sacralize corporate identities and so to strongly legitimize state formations) are a reflex of a specific civilizational perspective. This in turn derives from a trajectory determined by a cultural construction of power that, at more careful scrutiny, opens ups significant transcivilizational horizons. Reinterpreting Hodgson, this Islamic trajectory appears more "ecumenic" (and therefore transcivilizationally constructive) than the Western building of a singular and hegemonic civilization, the civilization of Western modernity, originally grounded in a plurality of self-entrenched Leviathans ultimately regulating (and at times limiting) competition in a global capitalist arena.

The Western European articulation of the power/knowledge dialectics facilitated by a sort of axial "eccentricity," measured by a sentiment of distance and estrangement from—and new bridging of—the twin axial sources of "Athens and Jerusalem" (an argument famously put forth by Remi Brague 2002 [1992]), ultimately ushered into a modern secular sacralization of political authority, which clearly sublimated the combined axial input (Salvatore 2009). In contrast, in the early development of Islam its political elites were faced in a much more direct way with models of sacral rulership that had hitherto dominated the Irano-Semitic civilizational region. During the Middle Periods, also through the interventions of religio-cultural elites of various provenance and not restricted to orthodox Sunni *'ulama,'* political authority was increasingly decoupled from ideas and practices of the caliphate and imamate as religiously inspired rule and community leadership. Transversal coalitions of political and cultural elites promoted the idea of a divine delegation of power to the "commoners" mediated by egalitarian patterns, a process that was also favored by an extreme, symbolically grounded downgrading of several key attributes of terrestrial power (Salvatore 2007, 99–241; but see also van Ess 2006). This theme had provided a major arrow to the teaching of intellectual and spiritual leaders from the Axial Age, East and West. Robert Bellah was particularly keen to emphasize Islam's capacity to promote what could be seen as a proto-secular core of the sociopolitical bond, leading to a quite thorough divestment of the sacral attributes of human power (Bellah 1970, 146–70). Later developments would allow for a re-sacralization of political rulership only via appropriation of the Islamic notion of saintliness (*walaya*). This, however, could never be claimed as an exclusive kingly prerogative, unlike the peculiar forms of re-sacralization that took form in the early modern European Westphalian framework, in the shadow of Leviathan (Salvatore 2018).[5]

The fact itself that the Islamic perspective on the primacy of social connectedness and the consequent de-sacralization of terrestrial power does not lay a premium on the same type of separation between the realm of the state and the domain of religion as inner belief should prompt us to shed off the residual conceptual misunderstanding lurking behind Hodgson's compact idea of "Islamdom," understood as the social nexus and civilizational matrix transcending the alleged kernel of Islam as religion or "piety." The fact that Islamdom could never institutionally match a civilizational formation such as Western Christendom feeds into the idea of a transcivilizational ecumene. The yet unfulfilled scholarly goal is to explain Islam's rise and formation as a continual expansion and an almost entropic spin over vast distances, rather than as a self-feeding, and territorially delimited, institutional crystallization into religious versus political forms of authority. To this end, one might profitably invest in one of the fundamental formulas of civilizational analysis—namely, to follow the ways knowledge (or culture at large) legitimizes power and power promotes or limits knowledge (Arnason 2003).

Against this background, we can see that the knowledge/power equation that promoted Islam's long-term expansion and transformation did not consecrate a separation of religion from the body politic and what we might call an inversion of the equation into a power/knowledge syndrome of a Foucaultian kind—whereby the state ultimately directs and regulates knowledge production, including specifically religious forms of knowledge. The knowledge/power equation unfolds in the Islamic case through the building of expansive patterns of connectedness, wherein religion is the source of a common, mildly normative idiom, while not being identical to that idiom. We have here a process of differentiation *from* religion of the sociocultural glue represented by what we may call civility (Salvatore 2016). This notion might be preferable to the idea of a civilizational formation. Islamic patterns of civility can develop a quite high self-transcending potential compared with the self-feeding institutional configurations of the previously mentioned three major civilizational "formations" of the Eastern Hemisphere, namely, the Sinitic and Indic civilizations, and Western Latin Christendom, the kernel of what will become later Western Europe or even the "West" or "Occident."

Conclusion: Islam as the Hub of a Hemisphere-wide Transcivilizational Dynamics

To conclude, what through the experience of Western Christendom is called "religion" is in the case of Islam an ensemble of knowledge and practice that is absorbed into highly variable patterns of both local and translocal connectedness. This view is by necessity contrasting with the one long prevalent among European orientalists, namely that the core or essence of Islam is its "religious law," in turn inscribed into its "origin." Against this view, law can only become the source of a strong normative idiom to the extent that it feeds into and adapts to the patterns of connectedness. Islam appears to us as a civilization sui generis, if not as a transcivilizational ecumene—a multiverse more than a universe, originally blending key components of what in the wake of European colonial and global hegemony became distinguished as the "Occident" and the "Orient" (Salvatore 2016).

By proposing the idea of a transcivilizational ecumene and the metaphor of the multiverse I have not only stressed the evanescence of a civilizational core (both in political and cultural terms) in the case of Islam—in spite of converging, relentless efforts by orientalists and fundamentalists/Salafis alike to identify such a center. I have also highlighted the impossibility of a one-to-one relationship between the Muslim allegiance of faith, its traditions and institutions, on the one hand, and the prestige and attractiveness of the wider, mildly normative frameworks accompanying Islam's expansion, on the other: Islamic civilization being erroneously seen, by both orientalists and Salafis, as the rather smooth convergence of both.

The idea of an Islamic transcivilizational ecumene as an inflationary multiverse can replace the stale metaphor of a self-contained civilizational universe or galaxy. The new notion, however, could still be tributary to a revised understanding of Islam's "core," no longer tied to a fixed "origin," but fed by a continual, aggregative whirlpool that works like a supermassive black hole favoring cultural consummation, amalgamation (and sometimes occultation) of surrounding cultural "matter" and its multiple "origins." In this sense, the rise of Islam is really, as evidenced by Hodgson, the "culmination" of an older, axial dynamics originating within the Irano-Semitic civilizational realm. Staying within the astronomical metaphor, the originality of the rise of Islam out of that constellation represents the stage of a supernova explosion of what used to be a more compact star, namely, the Irano-Semitic, urban-based ethical egalitarianism—an explosion sending shock waves through larger regions, recombining ethical egalitarianism with a variety of other axial patterns of accountability and ego-alter connectedness, and prefiguring the recession of the egalitarian star-supernova into a powerful black hole with a high capacity for transcivilizational absorption and processing.

More than a late or tertiary axial breakthrough within the Irano-Semitic realm, the rise of Islam was the consummation of its axial civilizational impetus and egalitarian program. More than a beginning, it was an end, the release of centrifugal forces from an increasingly mobile core. The initially explosive and enduringly entropic process, unfolding over vast distances that sharply transcended the "Nile to Oxus" region, fed into the aspirations to sociocultural autonomy of a transversal stratum of postaxial administrators of the moral code. Composed of Sufi masters and practitioners no less than *'ulama,'* they felt empowered to tame the historic, hemisphere-wide hegemony of aristocratic gentries and armed bands and, when times and circumstances allowed, to create new Islamically inflected cultures and solidarities across class cleavages.

In order to survive and thrive, the egalitarian impetus of the Irano-Semitic realm had to transcend itself into cosmopolitanism. Nonetheless, as we are increasingly aware, a centripetal reconstruction of a supposedly original "essence" of the realm in the guise of a civilizational "universe" of egalitarian cosmopolitanism for all Muslims was, and more than ever still is, an open possibility. Ignited by the European obsession with origins manifested through colonial orientalism, and due to the concomitant release of anticolonial resentment among Muslims worldwide, what is identified as the Islamist option was born around a century ago. It nowadays thrives alongside a powerful and yet unpredictable retrieval of the older, centrifugal dynamics. A new balancing between these two in principle mutually opposing forces is probably in the cards, and maybe tentatively in the making, in more than one locale (Malik 2018).

Notes

1. It is quite revealing that in the first edited collection dedicated to the topic, Eisenstadt (1986) introduced a section on Islam in less than a half-page at the end of a more than five hundred pages–long volume. The section only includes a short essay by the well-known Islamic Studies scholar Michael Cook, featuring the mentioned remark on the "tertiary" axial character of Islam, which Eisenstadt quoted in later talks that I also attended. In the follow-up, three-volume edited collection on the Axial Age (which is only available in German), Islam is featured in the third volume, within a much larger section, and a more substantial introduction by Eisenstadt (1992); the section included a number of essays by other well-known scholars of Islam such as Ira M. Lapidus and Ernest Gellner.

2. I first used the "supernova" metaphor in a paper I prepared for a conference that took place on May 23 and 24, 2011, in Helsinki and featured as speakers, among others, Johann P. Arnason, Sverre Bagge, Garth Fowden, Jaakko Hämeen-Anttila, Jonathan Shepard, and Bo Stråth. I was not able to attend the workshop and my paper was never published. However, Johann P. Arnason, whom I thank here, provided comments to that paper. The present chapter makes use of

some of the materials from that unpublished paper. More recently I saw the use of the supernova metaphor with regard to the rise of Islam used by none less than Peter Brown (2017). He did not develop it into a "black hole," though, which I saw as a predictable follow-up metaphor that I hope will not be misunderstood here. Also within lay perceptions of the physics of black holes it is clear that blackness and hollowness are *not* their main characteristics.

3. We may find a milder and more plastic alternative to civilization in the notion of "civility," which also matches the concept of *adab* (Salvatore 2019).

4. To these we should add, to a quantitatively minor yet significant extent, Sinitic patterns of cosmic and moral order (Murata 2000).

5. The trajectory of the Shiʿa represents both a resistance to such trends and their selective, original absorption into a restatement of the power of charismatic elites (Arjomand 2016).

References

Arjomand, Said A. 2004. "Transformation of the Islamicate Civilization: A Turning Point in the Thirteenth Century?" In *Eurasian Transformations, 10th to 13th Centuries: Crystallizations, Divergences, Renaissances*,edited by Johann P. Arnason and Björn Wittrock, 213–45. Leiden and Boston: Brill.

———. 2016. *The Sociology of Shi'ite Islam: Collected Essays*. Leiden and Boston: Brill.

Arnason, Johann P. 2003. *Civilizations in Dispute: Historical Questions and Theoretical Traditions*. Leiden and Boston: Brill.

———. 2006. "Marshall Hodgson's Civilizational Analysis of Islam: Theoretical and Comparative Perspectives." In *Islam in Process: Historical and Civilizational Perspectives*, vol. 7, *Yearbook of the Sociology of Islam*, edited by Johann P. Arnason, Armando Salvatore, and Georg Stauth, 23–47. Bielefeld: Transcript; New Brunswick, NJ: Transaction.

———. 2010. "Introduction: Domain and Perspectives of Civilizational Analysis." *European Journal of Social Theory* 13, no. 1: 5–13.

———. 2017. "Theorizing the History of Religions: The Weberian Agenda and Its Unresolved Issues." *Social Imaginaries* 3, no. 2: 109–43.

Arnason, Johann P., Shmuel N. Eisenstadt, and Björn Wittrock. 2005. "General Introduction." In *Axial Civilizations and World History*, edited by Johann P. Arnason, Shmuel N. Eisenstadt, and Björn Wittrock, 3–18. Leiden: Brill.

Arnason, Johann P., Armando Salvatore, and Georg Stauth. 2006. "Introduction." In *Islam in Process: Historical and Civilizational Perspectives*, edited by Johann P. Arnason, Armando Salvatore, and Georg Stauth, 8–19. vol. 7, *Yearbook of the Sociology of Islam*. Bielefeld: Transcript; New Brunswick, NJ: Transaction.

Bellah, Robert N. 1970. *Beyond Belief: Essays on Religion in a Post-Traditional World*. New York: Harper and Row.

Brague, Rémi. 2002 [1992]. *Eccentric Culture: A Theory of Western Civilization*. South Bend: Saint Augustine's Press.

Brown, Peter. 2017. "At the Center of a Roiling World." *The New York Review of Books*, May 11.

Burke III, Edmund. 1993. "Introduction: Marshall G. S. Hodgson and World History." In Marshall G. S. Hodgson, *Rethinking World History: Essays on Europe, Islam, and World History*. Cambridge: Cambridge University Press.

Cook, Michael. 1986. "The Emergence of Islamic Civilization." In *The Origins and the Diversity of Axial Age Civilizations*, edited by Shmuel N. Eisenstadt, 476–83. Albany: State University of New York Press.

———. 2015. "The Centrality of Islamic Civilization." In *The Cambridge World History*, Vol. 5: *Expanding Webs of Exchange and Conflict, 500ce–1500ce*, edited by Benjamin Z. Kedar and Merry E. Wiesner-Hanks, 385–413. Cambridge: Cambridge University Press.

Duara, Prasenjit. 2015. *The Crisis of Global Modernity. Asian Traditions and a Sustainable Future*. Cambridge: Cambridge University Press.

Eisenstadt, Shmuel N. 1986. "Introduction: The Axial Age Breakthroughs: Their Characteristics and Origins." In *The Origins and the Diversity of Axial Age Civilizations*, 1–25. Albany: State University of New York Press.

———. 1992. "Die Geschichtserfahrung des Islam." In *Kulturen der Achsenzeit II. Ihre institutionelle und kulturelle Dynamik*, Vol. 3: *Buddhismus, Islam, Altägypten, westliche Kultur*. Frankfurt: Suhrkamp.

———. 2002. "Concluding Remarks: Public Sphere, Civil Society, and Political Dynamics in Islamic Societies." In *The Public Sphere in Muslim Societies*, edited by Miriam Hoexter, Shmuel N. Eisenstadt, and Nehemia Levtzion, 139–61. Albany: State University of New York Press.

———. 2006. "Culture and Power: A Comparative Civilizational Analysis." *Erwägen Wissen Ethik/Deliberation Knowledge Ethics* 17, no. 1: 3–16.

Elverskog, Joann. 2010. *Buddhism and Islam on the Silk Road*. Philadelphia: University of Pennsylvania Press.

Foltz, Richard. 2010 [1999]. *Religions of the Silk Road: Premodern Patterns of Globalization*. New York: Palgrave Macmillan.

Fowden, Garth. 1993. *Empire to Commonwealth: Consequences of Monotheism in Late Antiquity*. Princeton: Princeton University Press.

Gunder Frank, Andre. 1992. *The Centrality of Central Asia*. Amsterdam: VU University Press.

Hodgson, Marshall G. S. 1974. *The Venture of Islam: Conscience and History in a World Civilization*, vol. 2, *The Expansion of Islam in the Middle Periods*. Chicago: University of Chicago Press.

———. 1993. *Rethinking World History: Essays on Europe, Islam, and World History*, Cambridge: Cambridge University Press.

Jaspers, Karl. 1953 [1949]. *The Origin and Goal of History*. New Haven and London: Yale University Press.

Karamustafa, Ahmet. 2017. "Islamic Dīn as an Alternative to Western Models of 'Religion.'" In *Religion, Theory, Critique: Classical and Contemporary Approaches and Methodologies*, edited by Richard King, 163–71. New York: Columbia University Press.

Malik, Jamal. 2018. "The Sociopolitical Entanglements of Sufism." In *The Wiley-Blackwell History of Islam and Islamic Civilization*, edited by Armando Salvatore, Roberto Tottoli, and Babak Rahimi, 585–606. Oxford: Wiley-Blackwell.

Masud, Muhammad Khalid, and Armando Salvatore. 2009. "Western Scholars of Islam on the Issue of Modernity." In *Islam and Modernity: Key Issues and Debates*, edited by Muhammad Khalid Masud, Armando Salvatore, and Martin van Bruinessen, 36–53. Edinburgh: Edinburgh University Press.

Murata, Sachiko. 2000. *Chinese Gleams of Sufi Light*. Albany: State University of New York Press.

Rahimi, Babak. 2006. "The Middle Period: Islamic Axiality in the Age of Afro-Eurasian Transcultural Hybridity." In *Islam in Process: Historical and Civilizational Perspectives*, vol. 7, *Yearbook of the Sociology of Islam*, edited by Johann P. Arnason, Armando Salvatore, and Georg Stauth, 48–67. Bielefeld: Transcript; New Brunswick, NJ: Transaction.

Salvatore, Armando. 1996. "Beyond Orientalism? Max Weber and the Displacements of 'Essentialism' in the Study of Islam." *Arabica. Revue d'Études Arabes/Journal of Arab Studies* 43, no. 3: 412–33.

———. 2005. "The Euro-Islamic Roots of Secularity: A Difficult Equation." *Asian Journal of Social Science* 33, no. 3: 412–37.

———. 2007. *The Public Sphere: Liberal Modernity, Catholicism, Islam*. New York: Palgrave Macmillan.

———. 2009. "From Tension to Dialogue? The Mediterranean between European Civilization and the Muslim World." In *Civilizational Dialogue and World Order. The Other Politics of Cultures, Religions, and Civilizations in International Relations*, edited by Michális S. Michael and Fabio Petito, 217–37. New York: Palgrave Macmillan.

———. 2010. "Repositioning 'Islamdom': The Culture-Power Syndrome within a Trans-Civilizational Ecumene." *European Journal of Social Theory* 13, no. 1: 99–115.

———. 2011. "Eccentric Modernity? An Islamic Perspective on the Civilizing Process and the Public Sphere." *European Journal of Social Theory* 14, no. 1: 55–69.

———. 2016. *The Sociology of Islam: Knowledge, Power, and Civility*. Oxford: Wiley-Blackwell.

———. 2018. "Sufi Articulations of Civility, Globality, and Sovereignty." *Journal of Religious and Political Practice* 4, no. 2: 156–74.

———. 2019. "Secularity through a 'Soft Distinction' in the Islamic Ecumene? *Adab* as a Counterpoint to *Shari'a*." *Historical Social Research* 44, no. 2: 35–51.

Salvatore, Armando, Johann P. Arnason, Babak Rahimi, and Roberto Tottoli. 2018. "Introduction: The Formation and Transformations of the Islamic Ecumene." In *The Wiley-Blackwell History of Islam and Islamic Civilization*, edited by Armando Salvatore, Roberto Tottoli, and Babak Rahimi, 18–35. Oxford: Wiley-Blackwell.

Salvatore, Armando, Roberto Tottoli, and Babak Rahimi, eds. 2018. *The Wiley-Blackwell History of Islam and Islamic Civilization*. Oxford: Wiley-Blackwell.

Turner, Bryan S. 1976. "Conscience in the Construction of Religion: A Critique of Marshall G. S. Hodgson's *The Venture of Islam*." *Review of Middle East Studies* 2: 95–111.

Van Ess, Joseph. 2006. "Islam and the Axial Age." In *Islam in Process: Historical and Civilizational Perspectives*, vol. 7, *Yearbook of the Sociology of Islam*, edited by Johann P. Arnason, Armando Salvatore, and Georg Stauth, 220–37. Bielefeld: Transcript; New Brunswick, NJ: Transaction.

Weber, Max. 1920. *Gesammelte Aufsätze zur Religionssoziologie*, Vol. 1. Tübingen: Mohr.

Wittrock, Björn. 2001. "Social Theory and Global History: The Periods of Cultural Crystallization." *Thesis Eleven* 65: 27–50.

8

The Reception of Axial Age Legacies

Christianization and the Byzantinization of Russia

Yulia Prozorova

The Axial Age hypothesis initially articulated in Karl Jaspers's historical-philosophical study (Jaspers 2014) has evolved into an important research program for social-historical inquiry since its launch into the orbit of sociological reflection nearly forty years ago (Eisenstadt 1982). The revival of research interest in the Axial Age as a historical period of unique synchronism of sociocultural creativity in the Eurasian macroregion, concurred with—and in some respect impelled—the renaissance of a civilizational problematic in comparative-historical sociology.

The vibrant discussion and ongoing studies of the Axial Age conundrum raised important theoretical questions on cultural determinism and cultural autonomy, historical continuity and contingency, gave rise to new approaches to the Axial Age and "axiality," reconsidered the axial chronology as well as the overall chronological framework for historical sociological inquiry, expanded the number of case studies, and enriched the range of phenomena representing both a unity and a diversity of cultural traditions that emerged from—and are rooted in—the axial turn. The legacies of the Axial Age, its connection with later developments such as Christianity and Islam, and its relation to "late antiquity" and modernity constitute a formidable research agenda for contemporary historical sociology.

In this context, it is worthwhile to investigate the later transmission and effects of the cultural frameworks and religious-political patterns associated with the axial turn. The present essay is an attempt to introduce Russia's case, which has heretofore been underdeveloped in the analysis of the long-term and far-reaching consequences of Axial Age innovations. Medieval Russia was separated from the original Axial Age by centuries and it was Christianity that brought closer those distant historical epochs and cultural worlds and made Russia accessible to axial legacies. Christianity, as a major cultural constituent of Byzantine civilization, appeared to be a formative framework for medieval Russia as it became a new member of the "Byzantine Commonwealth" (Obolensky 2000). The multifaceted engagement with the Byzantine Empire resulted in the adoption of the Eastern Christianity and the Orthodox Byzantine political theology, which played a pivotal role in the formation of Russian political culture and cultural-institutional complexes.

The intention of the essay is to study distant axial repercussions entailed by Christianization, more specifically, to trace Russia's reception and effects of the Christian Byzantine politico-theological views on secular power and its relationship to the sacred dimension associated with the cultural innovations and imprints of the Axial Age—dichotomy between the mundane reality and the transmundane order and a distinct "religio-political nexus," the institutional and ideological intertwining of religion and politics. Later cultural engagements and intercivilizational encounters along with revisions of the original Byzantine paradigms gave rise to social imaginaries, which significantly affected the institutional configuration and cultural-political dynamics of Russia.

The Axial Age and Christianity

The relation of Christianity to the original epoch of the Axial Age (the middle of the first millennium BCE) is still a matter of debate. In his early works, Eisenstadt (1986a) introduced the notion of a "secondary breakthrough": even though Christianity falls chronologically ahead of the Axial Age, it retained a close affinity to its major innovations. He suggested that Christianity had developed within the framework of the first Axial Age civilizations: it can be viewed as a transformation of the originally Jewish religious orientations and as an effect of the opposition between, on the one hand, the ruling "orthodoxies" and coalitions of new cultural elites and, on the other hand, the sectarian movements and heterodoxies that developed within them (Eisenstadt 1986a).

Although our knowledge of the Axial Age is incomplete, and the current state of the debate lacks uncontested agreement with respect to its defining features, this period is distinguished by "the formation of culturally entrenched structuring principles for macro-institutions" (Wittrock 2005, 64). There is convincing evidence that a "religio-political nexus," an intimate and dynamic relationship between the cultural-religious orientations and political structures, was integral to Axial transformations and should be seen as a meta-institutional framework (Arnason 2014a, 2014b).[1] The connection between religion and politics is a central aspect of the civilizational dimension of human societies, most emphatically articulated in the axial civilizations, but not irrelevant or totally absent in historically preceding (pre–Axial Age or early civilizations) or structurally different societies (e.g., stateless) (Eisenstadt 2000; Arnason 2014b). A full development and articulation of the distinct civilizational dimension and the rise of "ideological politics" occurred in the first place in the historical settings of the axial civilizations, whose ontological vision is characterized by the conception of a schism between the transcendental and mundane orders (Eisenstadt 1982). The emergence, conceptualization, and institutionalization of this basic tension[2] coalesced with a growing reflexivity, problematization, and reconstitution of a this-worldly order, for which the higher realm provides normative models and regulations. Axial Age transformations entailed a redefinition of the relationship between religion and politics; the new cultural orientations suggested a new understanding of sovereignty. The ideologies that drew on axial interpretations of the world, provided resources for legitimation or protest against power structures (Eisenstadt 1993; Arnason 2014a). Religious visions and reorientation correlated with a variety of political outcomes and projects. The Axial Age brought onto the scene a new historical ontology of the political as a concretization of cultural visions of power that shaped the later history of civilizations.

The close association of king and god emerged in the pre-axial history, when the homology between the sociopolitical reality and the religious realm was unbroken, underwent complex transformation in the axial period (Bellah 2011). The relationship between the religious and the political, the divine transcendental and the secular authority arose as a key ontological problematic for which the Israelite resolution is of crucial importance. The monotheism of ancient Israel substantially reconsidered the theocratic vision of sacred kingship—the divinity of secular rulers was negated as the transcendent god could not be embodied by a profane ruler, and the realms of the divine and the political were categorically separated. This development was accompanied by a redefinition of religion in many respects, as it became an autonomous sphere endowed with superior authority and normativity (Assmann 2005). The Judaic reformulation of the religio-political nexus was "radical and unequivocal": the sovereignty was transferred from this-worldly sacral rulers to the sole divine creator and legislator, and salvation became his sole property and responsibility (Assmann 2009; Arnason 2014a, 195). The secular rule was seen as dependent and conditional on divine will. Christianity and Islam evolved from the radical Judaic "breakthrough" and, in Bellah's words, both "are historically intelligible only as developments of Israel's axial breakthrough" (Bellah, 2005, 72). However, it was not until the fourth to sixth centuries that Christianity emerged as a "world" religion closely associated with imperial political visions and order (Wittrock 2005, 69). Christianity draw on the Israelite sources and played its distinct changes on the theme of transcendental and secular ruler by assimilating the old royal epithet of the king as Son of God to proclaim the reign of Christ the King. As Bellah claims, although the pre-axial unity of god and king, political and religious power, was broken albeit not totally abandoned, it was paradoxically reaffirmed in the new axial formulations (Bellah 2011, 266–67). Whenever monotheism established itself as the ruling order, its political theology easily shifted to legitimation of the state, and despite the monotheistic distinction between the religious and the political, an ambivalent union of political power and religion emerged in early Jewish, Christian, and Islamic versions of monotheism in the religio-political forms of theocracy, Byzantine caesaropapism, or domination of spiritual leaders over secular rulers (Assmann 2009, 48).

The concept of a "secondary breakthrough" initially appeared as "an attempt to clarify the relationship between late antiquity and its axial ancestors" (Arnason et al. 2005b, 287). One of the crucial advantages of Christianity in the religious competition of late antiquity was the combination of strong outworldly or otherworldly orientations and activities and the inherent this-worldly vision of reconstruction of the mundane world as relevant to salvation (Eisenstadt 1986a). The Christianization of the Roman Empire, the emergence of the Byzantine state as its major successor, "a continuation of the old *imperium romanum*" (Ostrogorski 1969, 28), and the triumph of universal monotheistic religions became conspicuous characteristics of what is now regarded as a distinct historical period: late antiquity. The rediscovery of this epoch of original and wide-ranging transformations shed new light on its developments and their connection with the Axial Age.

Proponents of the "secondary breakthrough" were criticized for labeling such unprecedented elaborations of the axial legacies as "secondary," for this designation implied their subordinate status in relation to the original axial developments. The overall inadequacy of the "secondary breakthrough" framework led scholars to search for another theoretical solution. Eisenstadt suggested that the emergence of two monotheistic world religions, Christianity and Islam, can be interpreted as a new "axial" turn posterior to the Axial Age, thus subsuming these developments to a general category of "axiality." A new ontological vision and institutionalization of the fundamental disjunction between the transcendental and mundane orders was claimed to be a common typological criteria of "axiality" (Arnason 2014a).[3]

The typological model resolves the "hierarchical" issue of the "primary" versus "secondary" breakthroughs, which, however, downgraded originality and the significance of the transformations that took place during late antiquity. In contrast to the "secondary breakthrough" framework, which inferred a long-lasting connection between the later developments with the chronological Axial Age, the typological model renders this connection open: it suggests that axial patterns can emerge in different historical and geographical settings. Moreover, a "generalized axial model is conducive to cultural determinism of the kind that civilizational analysis has, in principle, striven to avoid: the common denominator of axial civilizations can be seen as a cultural programme" (Arnason 2014a, 180).

The abstract typological model proved vulnerable to criticism for decontextualization and ahistorical account of axial and postaxial transformations. Contrary to this perspective, Johann Arnason upholds the significance of "bringing history back in" to "historicize" the Axial Age as a distinct epoch comparable to other notably innovative periods (such as late antiquity with its expansion of monotheistic religions) (Arnason 2012; Arnason 2014a). These two approaches, the typological and historical-phenomenological, provide diverse analytical visions of a complex ontology of Eurasian transformations characterized by cultural continuities and structural affinities, on the one hand, and radical abrupt changes and original reinterpretations, on the other. The "historicizing" and "contextualizing" analysis does not negate that "the *longue durée* of Eurasian civilizations is marked by successive adaptations and reinterpretations of axial legacies" (Arnason et al. 2005a, 4) but provides an account more sensitive to diversity, changes, and later mutations highlighting creativity of the postaxial developments emerging into a new historical contexts of intercivilizational encounters and cultural contacts. This perspective seems more promising and relevant to the current essay aiming at a preliminary survey of the reception of the Byzantine Orthodox–political conception and its axial components in Russia.

Christianity evolved as a development of the Judaic axial tradition, and it inherited its paradigmatic vision of the relationship between this-worldly rulers and a divine sovereign perceived as a source of normative models, ethical principles of being in the world, salvation, and the ultimate power over the mundane order. This legacy predisposed civilizations crystallized around Christianity to inherit the religio-political nexus as meta-instituting framework and the crucial problematic intrinsic to the axial patterns. The Christian's "constant ambivalence toward political power" (Stroumsa 2005, 305) never impeded the Christian tradition and its religious elite from being an integral institutional part of the state edifice playing a formative role in the development of particular state-society relationships, political culture, and power patterns. The monotheistic universalism of Christianity was conducive to its "symbiotic relationship with imperial power" in late antiquity," which made it a "defining part of imperial rule" (Arnason et al. 2005b, 289–90). The expansion of monotheistic religions along the imperial contours marked a cardinal change in identity conception, when universalizing religious identity overshadowed the other. Christianization became the main cultural vehicle of distribution of these innovations and the transference of its axial constituents.

Christianization and Byzantinization of Russia

Karl Jaspers (2014) portrayed Russia as a successor of the Byzantine Empire, which, in turn, is a progeny of the Axial Age. Christianization and Byzantization are two fundamental coalescent processes that had a profound impact on the spirituality and cultural patterns, economic ethics, political structures, and power imaginaries in Russia. Christianization was a form of initiation to enter the Byzantine civilizational orbit as a new member of the Byzantine Commonwealth and Orthodox Christendom. The role of the Byzantine legacy, as well as its continuity in the history of Russia are debatable (Arnason 2000), however, Christianization and the diverse contacts with Byzantium and the reception of Byzantine law, political theology, literature, art, etc. provided a crucial formative impact on Russia's historical trajectory.

The Christian tradition in its Eastern Orthodox version developed within the framework of the Axial Age constituted the basic cultural premises of the Byzantine civilization. In the Byzantine Empire, the ontological vision of schism played a role of a paradigmatic cultural framework that configured the societal concepts and imaginaries. The major cultural orientations, which the Byzantine Empire shared with "all Christian civilizations" were characterized by the conception of tension between the transcendental and the mundane realm, a close relationships between this- and other-worldly orientations of salvation and a commitment to the maintenance of the social roles related to such conception of salvation. The conception of tension between the transcendental and the mundane order is associated with an outworldly attitude and a vision of a distinct higher world not fully embedded in the mundane (Eisenstadt 1986b).

Christian orientations are immanent to the Byzantine political visions and conception of the rulership. The Byzantine Empire regarded itself to be coterminous to the Christian *oikoumene* centered at Constantinople and claimed control of all lands that belonged to Roman *orbis*. The "unique" role of the imperial capital inherited from antiquity (Kazhdan and Cutler 1982, 469) and imperial institution exemplify a remarkable civilizational alternative to the Western model of urban autonomy. The Byzantine political theology saw the religious and the political, the priesthood (*sacerdotium)* and the emperor (*imperium*), as interdependent legitimate sources of power constitutive for this-worldly imperial reality and the state edifice. Christianity and imperial order were intrinsic and inseparable components of the universal Christian Empire designed as an earthly copy of the divine realm, the Kingdom of Heaven, and ruled by the emperor as incarnate law and viceroy of God but accountable to higher regulations and the law (Runciman 2004). The religious definition of power and the emphasis placed on the sacred character of imperial authority, justified in terms of the Christian theological framework, along with the image of the emperor as a representative of God, are crucial constituents of the Byzantine religious-political framework. This cultural-ideological complex imprints the axial problematic and the religious-political connection, for which the relation between the church and the state became the focal theoretical and practical issue. The conception of a Christian empire made the church and the clerical elite a part of the state polity. The church functioned as a relatively autonomous institution involved in the political process, and the relationship between the secular and ecclesiastic authorities were of an interdependent character, they could not exist without each other as the two pillars of the Christian Empire.

"The most salient characteristic" of Byzantium was its "consistently high level of differentiation": between the transcendental and the mundane realms, between the church and the state, between different elites (emperor, bureaucratic, military, and clerical), and between social groups (aristocracy, peasantry, and urban groups) capable of relatively autonomous actions and interests (Arnason 2000, 44). These forms of differentiation, tensions and, protests on the cultural/ideological, institutional, and social levels reflect the distant effects of the Axial Age.

Christianization of Kievan Rus in the late tenth century is undoubtedly an epochal event and a turning point for the Russian history, which entailed a profound reformulation of the cultural meanings and sociopolitical relations according to the new religious ideals. Christianity once being, as Stroumsa (2005) puts it, a religion "in search of a culture" encountered a culture in search of a religion. Christianization introduced new cultural visions specifying the foundations of authority and justice, and "the place of different institutional arenas in the overall conception of man and cosmos" (Eisenstadt 1986b, 313). Christian monotheistic tradition brought a new conception of tension between the transcendental and the mundane orders, a new cultural ontology representing far-reaching repercussions of the Axial Age cultural innovations (Eisenstadt 1982). The former was regarded as an autonomous higher moral realm, with God being a source of normative frameworks and regulations for the latter. This ontology contrasted with the pagan "homologue" conception of relations between these realms, perceived mainly in terms of their parallelism or "mutual embedment," in which the "schism" or "sharp disjunction" is not recognized and articulated (Eisenstadt 1981; Eisenstadt 1982). The Christian vision of disjuncture posed the problem of salvation. A relatively close interweaving of this- and otherworldly orientations of salvation is characteristic of Christian civilizations (Eisenstadt 1986b, 302). The search for ways to bridge the ontological abyss made a political order the main arena of its resolution. The reconstruction of mundane reality in accordance with principles of Christian ethics was associated with salvation. The Christian doctrine assumes a heteronomy of societies, their submission to a higher otherworldly authority as the divine extrasocial source of societal principles of existence.

Eisenstadt's analysis indicates that the institutionalization of such cultural ontology is accompanied by complex cultural and structural transformations. The adoption of the Eastern Orthodox framework induced considerable reconfiguration of the receptive Russian society and was conducive to the emergence of the civilizational patterns centered on cultural interpretations of power. Institutionalization of these cultural visions is concomitant with the creation of an autonomous religious cultural elite (Eisenstadt 1981; Eisenstadt 1982). Christianization instituted a distinct cultural-religious domain, and the church represented an alternative center of symbolic authority and cultural production with a new group of religious professionals, the carrier of a conception of social and political order embedded into the Christian doctrine. The ecclesiastic community was the legitimate carrier of the religious ideology that claimed monopoly on the matters of faith and the divine transcendental. The clerics played the roles of the interpreters of the esoteric knowledge of the transcendental and salvation, and acted as spiritual specialists, missionary promoters of believers, intellectuals, and religious educators. The political realm gained importance as an arena for implementation of religious principles, symbols, and imaginaries turning into organizational premises of social life and collective identity.

At the very early stage of the Russian state, the Byzantine political theology and political ideas were selectively adopted and assimilated in the medieval Kievan Rus' since "to a considerable extent the East Slavic ruling elites were beholden to the Byzantine model in the matter of political concept" (Ševčenko 1984, 294). To a significant degree, such transfer became possible through the textual media, translations and adaptations of sacred and legal texts, commentaries, and hermeneutical writings. Religious and political ideas arrived with the Byzantine canon literature translated from Greek into Slavonic and were brought into scholarship and introduced into politico-cultural practice by monks and clerics who frequently advised the princes and constituted the first Russian cultural and intellectual elite. The juridical foundation of all new Christianized Slavic States—including Russia, Great Moravia, Bulgaria, Serbia—was built on the *Ecloga*, a Byzantine law (Dvornik 1956, 77). One of the oldest Slavic legal texts, *The Zakon Sudnyi Liudem* ("Law for Judging the People"), contains several adapted chapters from the *Ecloga,* which is thought to have been introduced to Russia in the tenth century soon after the conversion. This old legal source was later incorporated into the main collection of the Russian canon law *Kormcaja knjiga* ("The Pilot's Book"), and since the thirteenth century it has remained a constituent part of the Russian canon jurisprudence (Dvornik 1956).

The Russian canon law incorporated imperial *Novellae* and parts of legislation, which was a source of the Byzantine conception of kingship and this-worldly authority. The Rus' political and intellectual elites of the tenth and eleventh centuries encountered the Byzantine model of autocracy and assimilated the conception of *symphonia* of secular and sacral authorities, that is, "the Byzantine emphasis on an intimate church and state relationship" (Nielsen 1989, 510) that constituted the early Russian vision of the relationship between the state and the church, and the role of a ruler in a Christian community. The founding ideas of the relationship between the priesthood and the secular ruler came from the imperial decrees of Byzantine *Nomocanon,* especially the famous *Novella* VI of Justinian and are expressed, sometimes repeatedly, in different translated sources and collections (Dvornik 1956; Chichurov 1990). It is worthwhile to mention these ideas as they contrast with the later reformulation in a ceasaropapist conception. The following presents a short synopsis of the Byzantine religious/political perspective on the constitution of this-wordly power in accordance with the transcendental order. Two distinct authorities of higher divine origin, the *sacerdotium* and the *imperium* (*basileia*), are instituted by God to serve divine matters and control over human interests respectively. The secular and sacral powers are supposed to collaborate, and it is an emperor's duty to establish and maintain consensual relations between the spiritual and temporal powers and to oversee the church's ecclesiastical matters such as ordination of bishops and clergy, their rights, and hierarchy. The Byzantine conception of *symphonia* between the priesthood and the imperial dignity suggested "the internal cohesion and unity of purpose of a single human society" (Buss 2003, 107). The harmonious relationships between the *imperium* and the *sacerdotium* would, as it is said in the *Epanagoge*, "bring to the subjects spiritual and material peace and prosperity" (Dvornik 1956, 102). The mutual definitions of power of the patriarch and the emperor marked a crucial "transformation in the self-consciousness of the State" and "the new mentality of the Empire" (Schmemann 1954, 119). Thus, church and state, despite being entities autonomous and different by nature, constituted an "alliance," the "single body," "unity," "organic inherent fusion," the "symphony," which, as some scholars define it, marks "the final stage of Byzantine theocracy"—"the organic link between the State and its religion, the religious basis of the State itself, which is the common character of all the States of antiquity" (Schmemann 1954, 113, 119; Runciman 2004). The secular ruler, the emperor, is appointed by God as the creator of the universe, he represents God in this-wordly reality and is obliged to care for earthly and sacral things (Ostrogorsky 1956; Runciman 2004). The emperor exercises some priestly functions to secure and promote the interests of the church, supervises clergy, and defends the true Christian faith. The notion of a *good shepherd* reflects the Hellenistic idea of a ruler distinguished by justice, peace, and philanthropy (Dvornik 1956, 85–86).

According to the Byzantine sources, any form of legitimate authority and power is instituted by God and is sacral. Priesthood and monarchy collaborate to sustain the order in the ecclesiastic and secular domains respectively, however, it is the imperial ruler who entertains a privileged relationship with the divine and thus assumes a sublime position, as his sovereignty comes from God, he represents God and is his living image. God instituted a union of twofold ecclesiastic and imperial authority, within which the latter supervises and harmonizes the entire order. The Orthodox Byzantine conception of the world order constituted by two distinct but interdependent sources of power, secular and ecclesiastic, embodies an intertwining of political and religious dimensions. The sacralized Byzantine imperial rulership was a religious/political institution based on the Empire/Church "dogmatic unity."[4]

With the advent of Byzantine Christianity and with its emphasis on the notion that a prince's powers derive from above, not from below, the Nordic tradition of rulership in Kievan Rus' underwent considerable modification. Christianity instituted a better organized cult more sharply focused on the ruler's authority (Shepard 2007, 383). The nature of Rus' rulers was redefined in the vein of Judeo-Christian theocratic conception. It was not uncommon to express parallelisms of early Kievan princely power with the ancient Hebrew kings of the biblical tradition and conceptualize the nature of their authority in Christian terms (Hanak 2013). The secular rulers of Rus' were proclaimed anointed by God, and their authority was established by God to maintain the internal order within the state. The secular ruler was regarded as "the icon of Christ—an earthly replica of the prototype divine ruler" and presented as the shepherd of Christ's flock, the guardian of Orthodoxy, the teacher and the preceptor. The charismatic nature of a secular ruler was expressed in such epithets as "beloved of God," "guarded by God," "beloved of Christ," "pure of faith," "most pious," "orthodox" (Poppe 1991, 20–21). Russian writers of the Kievan period accepted the institution of monarchy but not absolute monarchy. Until the seventeenth century, no reference can be found to the Roman legal principle that "the ruler is not bound by the laws" (Valdenberg 1916). Christianity predisposed the subjugation of temporal power to the Christian moral laws, and that princely authority was therefore not unlimited (Valdenberg 1916; Vernadsky 1973, 287–88).

The original Kievan documents written in Slavonic support the fact of transmission and assimilation of the Byzantine political theology. The famous eleventh-century "Treatise on Law and Grace" by Ilarion, the Metropolitan of Kiev, illustrates the metropolitan's ideas on kingship and the image of an ideal ruler. It seems that "Ilarion was responsible, more than any other Russian writer, for the fact that Byzantine ideas on harmonious relationships between the Church and the State, and on the right of princes to watch over the purity and integrity of the Church and to care for the respect of the priests, became a guiding star for the political and religious evolution of Russia for many centuries" (Dvornik 1956, 106). The principle of a church-state unity remained pervasive even in the later period of political disintegration (Poppe 1991, 18–19).

The idea of unified autocratic power under the rule of one sovereign appeared in some of the early writings. Autocracy was considered one of the supportive foundations of Prince Vladimir's politics (Vladimir the Great [958–1015] Christianized Rus' in 988). At the beginning of the twelfth century a political ideal of a sole ruler who should represent national unity and protect the integrity of the church and purity of her doctrine was expressed for the first time. The Metropolitan of Kiev Nicephorus, in his address to the Grand Prince of Kiev Vladimir II Monomach (1053–1125), a grandson of the Emperor Constantine Monomachus, articulated two monarchic ideas—that the prince is chosen by God and is predestined to rule by the right of birth. The Greek prelates and their native disciples might have favored the autocratic regime and politics of unification of the "Lands of Rus' " because this could facilitate an introduction of the Byzantine political practices into the regulation of their principalities (Dvornik 1956, 110, 115–16). However, being significantly molded by Byzantine influences, the political thinking of the Kievan Rus was not identical to its Byzantine source but brought into being some differences in meaning, accentuations, and even reinterpretation induced by a genuine political culture, established political practices, and the historical context. For instance, in the Ilarion's text, the author highlights not the divine origin of power (although this idea was generally assimilated) but the transcendental source of the hereditary succession of power. Uncommon to the Byzantine views was an ideal image of the prince as a warrior that had emerged in the Russian medieval political representations as a reflection of the pre-Christian traditions and an exemplar of a distinct source of political imagination (Chichurov 1990, 148).

The Byzantine ideal of monarchic power was alien to Kievan Russia at the time of conversion. Christianization "did not implant the theory or practice of monarchy" (Shepard 2007, 409). The ingenious democratic traditions of the Kievan State, represented by *veches,* a collective institution of self-government and a practice of public assemblies that had authority in political, legal, and economic matters, coexisted for some period with the princely power and acquired greater importance in the period of weakening of the latter and political disorganization. *Demokratia,* on the contrary, was identified in the Byzantine sources with chaos and anarchy (Dvornik 1956, 94). Collective leadership of the princely clan dominated and rulership based on family principle of seniority prevailed. Kievan Rus' constituted an aristocratic state with no central government but a grand prince in Kiev being a *primus inter pares* (Ostrowski 2012). However, in the historical long run, it was the autocratic political imaginary that shaped the course of the political development, state formation, and empire building in Russia.

It can be concluded that some fundamental ideological elements of the Orthodox Byzantine political theology were adopted by the Russians and put into practice at the end of the tenth century and onward. Along with the Christian worldviews and a vision of distance between the mundane and the transcendental orders inherent to them, the most crucial innovations that Kievan Rus' had encountered were the autocratic monarchical and imperial political frameworks; theocratic vision and the conception of accountability and submissive role of secular power vis-à-vis higher God and Divine Law, the divine sanction of secular authority, legal/ethical views, the notions of sin and salvation that claimed to regulate the everyday life. The later ideological employment of Byzantine ancestry as a political imaginary maintained a continuous effect for centuries to follow.

Interpretations and Divergences

In lieu of a foreword to the following section, it is worthwhile to mention that the general presupposition about "Russia's affiliation to Byzantium seen as an unbroken and fundamental continuity of cultural patterns" has been legitimately problematized (Arnason 2000), and the focus on divergences of the trajectories and ruptures now seems a more promising approach to consider the peculiarities of both Orthodox empires. Such perspective, however, inevitably rediscovers persistence and recurrence of some Byzantine themes and structures that played a formative role and gave rise to original interpretations in Russian context.

Christianity infused the polytheistic popular culture of the Kievan period with more complex religious imaginaries, the notion of the transcendental realm as a source of normative societal models and ethical regulatory principles, and the sole God to whom the secular authority is accountable.

The engagement with the Orthodox Empire and assimilation of Byzantine political theology—the conception of the twofold foundation of the mundane order, monarchy and priesthood, and the Byzantine version of sacralized rulership incorporated into the ontological vision of distinction between the human and divine order—made the religio-political problematic constitutive for institutional structures and a subject of intellectual reflection. The religious definition of secular power, and the interplay between the God and the secular prince, the religious and political dimensions formed a societal meta-institututional framework. The following discussion focuses on the historical trajectories of the axial legacies in Russia, in particular, the transformation of the Byzantine religio-political patterns: reinterpretation of autocracy and the status of the ruler, changing configuration between the ecclesiastic and monarchic authorities, and the emergence of the imperial project.

The Mongol invasion and domination of Rus' for more than two centuries, and the rise and consolidation of power by Muscovy, induced mutations of the originally Byzantine frameworks and the political structures of early periods. The politics of the Grand Duchy of Moscow against the rival principalities resulted in a unification of lands and power around Muscovy as a nucleus of the Russian state and the precursor of the future empire. The first half of the fourteenth century marked "a sharp rift in institutional continuity" that "constituted a kind of 'punctuated equilibrium' in the evolutionary development of the Rus' political system," when Muscovite princes adopted the khanate's institutional models and practices to create their own administrative and military structures (Ostrowski 1990, 525).

It is possible to isolate several important processes that took place at the symbolic and imaginary levels. During the Mongol domination the title of *tsar*, previously attached to the Byzantine emperor as the highest hierarch in the universal Christian Empire, was referred to Tatar khan (exceptionally, to the khan of Chingizid dynasty) (Cherniavsky 1959). According to the Christian perspective, "tsar" the khan was perceived as instituted and ordained by God, which contradicted the image of the tsar as basileus of the Christian Empire who guides his peoples to salvation—the khan was a Muslim infidel.

> What did exist was yet another kind of tension, an atmosphere where the image of the khan overlapped that of the basileus, vaguely fused with the latter; exactly because it did not replace the latter, the image of the khan could borrow the attributes of

> the image of the basileus and could become identified in the popular and in the official mind with it. . . . [T]hrough the encounter of political reality and ideological tradition, the khan as "tsar" acquired, in the liturgy as in titulature, the attributes of the universal and unique emperor. (Cherniavsky 1959, 468)

This entailed conceptual ambiguities and tension between the tsar-basileus and the tsar-khan and also a necessity to approach and integrate both images of supreme rulership. The fall of Constantinople in 1453 and the declaration of independence from the Mongols by Ivan III (1440–1505) made the Russian rulers envisage the legacies of both empires that launched Russia into the orbit of intercivilizational encounters. Russia appeared to be a "civilizational crossroads" (Arnason 2000, 60) of diverse traditions and influences. It was crucial for Ivan III to revitalize the Byzantine imaginaries in order to solve the ideological "tsar"/khan dilemma and to establish the autonomy of Muscovite sovereignty. It could be achieved by reappropriation of the title and delegitimization of the Mongol authority. But even in the sixteenth century, "the title of 'tsar' was firmly connected with the image of the khan; more so than with that of the basileus" (Cherniavsky 1959, 473).

Both images of absolute power representing Byzantine and Mongol empires coexisted in the political imaginary and political practice of Muscovy. This situation, however, suggests not only an overlap and even a merger of images of power but also concurrency and entanglement in the same symbolic and ideological realm of the two models and visions of autocracy—the one of the Byzantine *basileus* as "a rule under the law," and the other of Mongol khans' absolute autocracy.

The conception of centralized autocratic power, which replaced the unstable archaic patrimonial federation based on kinship ties, originated during the rule of Ivan III and appeared along with a new concept of state—unification of all Russian lands under the autocratic sovereignty of the Grand Prince of Muscovy, with the ultimate submission of other princes. Since the liberation from Mongol rule, the Russian rulers proclaimed themselves as "*samoderzhets,*" which is the Russian word for the Greek "*autokrator.*" The new title was primarily introduced to emphasize the independence and autonomous sovereignty of the Russian ruler that emancipated his state from the foreign control.

The Russian monarch started to emerge as the God-instituted autocrat of all Russia, the Christian tsar, and claimed the Byzantine inheritance and primacy in the Christian Orthodox world. To legitimize these claims, it was needed to reinforce the imaginary of the Orthodox Empire and to reinstitute the conception and symbolic vision of the Christian ruler as the holy emperor, the source of orthodoxy and law, the living image of God on Earth, and the protector of the faith. This religious interpretation of political power and order, and the religion-induced image of Orthodox ruler remained invariant since the Kievan period. The conception of Moscow as "the Third Rome," a version of *translatio imperii,* was an ideological invention of the new political messianic project of a Russian tsar as the supreme sovereign of Christian nations and the protector of Orthodox Christianity. The Muscovite framework of autocracy integrated old Christian Byzantine concepts with new ideological interpretations.

The emerging doctrine of "theocratic absolutism" regarded the Russian ruler to be the only source of power claimed unlimited. Joseph Volotsky (1440–1515), "an early theorist of absolutism," claimed that the tsarist monarchy is a reflection of the heavenly monarchy on earth and that tsar is a "son" of God, who is human by nature but is equal to the Highest God by his dignity; he is God's representative and viceroy, the highest judge who is not subject to judgment by court and his judgment is without appeal on ecclesiastic or secular matters (Diakonov 1889, 99–103; Raeff 1949; Murvar 1968). The Josephite's conception contributed to the "societal monism," the unity of the church and the state and the institution of autocratic regime.

To fulfill the new role and embody the new ideal of the autocrat Ivan IV (1530–1584) (Halperin 2014), the ruler of Moscow, the "Grand Prince of Moscow and All Russia," acquired the title of Tsar, the "Orthodox and Universal Emperor," in 1547. His coronation entailed radical changes in the position of a ruling family, political institutions, domestic and international politics. The new title symbolized that Ivan IV acquired the status of a ruler chosen by God and received supreme authority over other princes and members of the court (Bogatyrev 2006). "Russian history of the fifteenth and sixteenth centuries is striking in the exclusive focus on the prince. One might say there was in the Russia of that time a myth of the ruler but not of the land, of the country and people as a whole" (Cherniavsky 1958, 620). As an autocrat, Ivan was meant to be an independent ruler, pious ruler, and unlimited ruler (Halperin 2014). Ivan's self-sacralizing mythology and the paradigm of legitimacy derived from the official ideology of sacred kingship was developed after 1547 by the Metropolitan Macarius (Hunt 1993). In comparison to the previous rulers, Ivan IV appropriated the symbolic status of tsar akin to the Byzantine *basileus* in the Orthodox world and claimed transcendental origins of his power, which was organic to the Byzantine political theology. However, the emergence of the conceptions of sacred kingship and the theory of almighty Godlike rulership signified a shift in the cultural vision of power.

Political aspirations of Russian rulers and their interpretation of the Byzantine conception of a universal Orthodox empire brought to the forefront imperial imaginaries coalescent with the messianic vision. The politics of unification of Russian lands correlated with the Byzantine conception of autocratic rule over all Orthodox lands, the Orthodox faith being coterminous with political boundaries, which corresponded to the idea of unity of the Russian Church promulgated by clerics. The Russian clergy and the church played an active role in the ideological justification of the politics of territorial and national consolidation, and the hegemony of Muscovy. The rise of the Tsardom of Moscow, the changing status of the Muscovite princes, and the gradually transforming nature of their sovereignty required ideological and theological explication, and the church "supplied the young Russian monarchy with a ready-made theory of divinely ordained royal absolutism borrowed from the Church of the Byzantine Empire" (Karpovich 1944, 13).

Although the Byzantine Orthodox religious/political conception of "dogmatic unity" of the ecclesiastic and the secular power remained referential, the rapidly evolving Russian autocracy and the progressing asymmetry in the church-state configuration eventually led to the transformations of the *symphonia* paradigm and the "diarchy" of the Basileus and the Patriarch to *caesaropapist* model.[5] The lack of distinction between the church and the state being the major problem for Byzantine theocracy (Runciman 2004, 4), now found a solution in the Russian model of subjugation of the *sacerdotium* to the *imperium*, alienation of priesthood, and limitation of ecclesiastic influence on the state matters. Although Russia received "a parental malady of Caesaropapism" from Byzantium (Toumanoff 1946, 232), the Russian version of caesaropapism apparently surpassed its prototype in the potential of the secular authority to dominate the church. Caesaropapism in Byzantium existed only in a restricted sense of imperial supremacy over the legal and organizational issues of the church, which, however, retained autonomy and independence in canonical and liturgical matters. In Russia, the tsar was seen as the head of the church and could intervene in ritual and dogmatic matters, sanction ecclesiastical legislation, convoke synods, designate clerical candidates, and at times judge clerical personnel. Russian tsars, especially after 1589, when the Metropolitan of Moscow was raised to the rank of Patriarch and recognized as an equal by the other Eastern Patriarchs, dominated both secular and ecclesiastic realms (Buss 2003, 114–15).

The abolition of the Patriarchate and the ecclesiastic court by Peter the Great in 1721 crystallized the caesaropapist pattern: "[T]he State-Church of Third Rome was now ruled by the autocrat alone through two channels: the *temporalia*, through the Governing Senate, and the *spiritualia*, through the Holy Governing Synod" (Toumanoff 1946, 242).

The Russian church did not evolve as an autonomous institution, as happened in the West. It developed as a heteronomous heterocephalous institution, with no economic self-rule, no independent bureaucratic organization or ideology, lacking theological and ethical rational systems (Murvar 1968). The distinction between the religious and political domains became formal and superficial. The growing autocratic and centralizing tendencies of the state came to a complete subordination of the church to the state. The church became, in Weber's words, "a branch of political administration" (Weber 1978, 1162), being integrated into the state apparatus in a role of a bureaucratic institution to be supervised by the state. The Russian clergy appeared to become spiritual bureaucrats for the ruler. The initial conception of the world order constituted by two interdependent powers of priesthood and monarchy was reformulated. The fusion of these entities into "societal monism" emerged in Russia as an ultimate case of caesaropapism. The modification of the Byzantine pattern of state-church relationship offered a much stronger religious sanctification and supernatural rationalization of the ruler's unlimited power. It was a new, more potent, and independently Russian interpretation of the universal monistic ideal of the identity and unity of all power, reflecting celestial unity and harmony (Murvar 1968, 5).

Petrine reformation and his rejection of Byzantine dualism of authority represented a new cultural/political program of secularization and rationalization, on the one hand, and building a strong absolutist empire, on the other. The paradigm of "service state" introduced under Mongol influence and reinforced by the Western doctrine of "regular state," now assumed a more pronounced rationalized form. It proclaimed unconstrained control of the state and its offices upon individuals and finally solidified the "monistic-patrimonial system" (Murvar 1971).

It was a state that did not see its purpose any more in the creation of the conditions for morality and religious salvation, but which saw in the interests of the state itself the ultimate standard for judging all actions; a state in which the emperor or tsar was considered to be above the laws (*princeps legibus solutus*) and which was not kept in check by anything resembling the modern tradition of thought that considers the State to be made up of autonomous individuals (Buss 2003, 116).

The Russian tsar was represented as a secular absolutist monarch and the "theocratic basileus," defined in terms of Muscovite theocracy (Kartashev 1996, 54). However, the eighteenth-century Russian political culture differed from the Byzantine prototype in its amplified sacralization of the ruler, as sacralization of the tsar became a crucial component of the new cultural-political framework centered on the autocratic sovereign (Zhivov and Uspenskii 1987).

The emergence of caesaropapist patrimonial state is associated with the spirit of Eastern Christianity and the Russian Orthodox tradition characterized by a contemplative-mystical attitude, the lack of the concept of "predestination," absence of the Western idea of a law-based relationship between the God and the human being, etc. (Buss 2003, 54–55). Weber points out that the caesaropapist formula "was most successful when religious qualifications still functioned as a mystical charisma of its bearers" (Weber 1978, 1161). The mystical attitude, however, is inconsistent with the "methodical organization of conduct" and the rational transformation of the mundane order: no inner-wordly success or achievements are significant with respect to salvation, which entails an "absolute minimization of all outer or inner activities" (Weber 1978, 545), and could not provide motivation for a rational and purposeful reorganization of political and economic life.[6] Weber argues that mysticism and contemplative features of an inner-wordly religion of salvation usually result in indifference toward the world and acceptance of a given social structure (Weber 1978, 550).

Since the establishment of caesaropapism and state bureaucracy in Russia, there had emerged a largely "unified culture" (Weber 1978, 1193) that lacked autonomous spiritual and institutional powers, which were able to resist and oppose the strong patrimonial state (Buss 2003, 57–58). Eastern Orthodoxy could not oppose the monistic pattern of the unity of all power spheres, but, on the contrary, it provided the supernatural rationalization of the absolute power of the ruler (Murvar 1971, 507–508).

Russian patrimonialism evolved from the consistent concentration of the political, religious, and economic power spheres into a monistic unity of the autocratic rulership. The trajectories of patrimonialism in Russia demonstrate its persistence throughout different historical epochs with diverse legitimation logics, rationales, and symbolic frameworks. The patriarchal/oligarchical environment of the Kievan State evolved into the Muscovite system of autocracy and patrimonialism that achieved its climax in imperial absolutism. Autocracy retained its formative impact in Soviet Russia and remains critically influential in the post-Soviet present.

Conclusion

The axial legacies—the ontological vision of a schism between the mundane and transcendental orders and the religio-political nexus as a meta-institutional framework, the problematic of the interplay between the religious and the political, and the relationship between the secular ruler and the divine—were transferred to Russia by virtue of Christianization and reception of Byzantine political theology and canon law, inducing transformations on symbolic/ideological and institutional levels. The religious foundation of the Russian vision of monarchical sovereignty contributed to the legitimation and institution of the Russian autocratic order and caesaropapism as political/religious phenomena.

The continuity of the Byzantine legacy in Russia is debatable. It is widely accepted that the Mongol impact was significant enough to modify the originally adopted models, although "the Russian strategies of subaltern adaptation made it very difficult to distinguish Byzantine disguises of Mongol imports from Mongol-inspired" (Arnason 2000, 41). The Mongol autocracy was effectively a mode of daily existence and a constituent part of the political environment for Russian princes, which could inspire the adoption of institutional elements of an absolutist-centralized state. However, even during the period of domination by "Mongol tsars" whose names were praised in liturgies and whose supreme rule was accepted as instituted by God (Cherniavsky 1959), the Mongol cultural ontology remained alien, the hermeneutical framework of Orthodox Christianity and Byzantine political theology never ceased to be referential and dominant. The autocratic ideology of Muscovite grand princes and the institution of a strong patrimonial state were developed on the basis of the Orthodox Byzantine paradigm. The tsar's authority was justified in terms of a Christian religious framework, and its symbolic legitimation and theological explication were rooted in the Byzantine conception of the sublime role of the imperial *Basileus Autokrator* as a viceroy of God. The "monistic" character of both Byzantine and Mongol cultural contexts facilitated the synthesis of the Mongol "theory and practice" of rulership with the Byzantine concept of sacred rulership and premises of autocracy. This promoted their integration into the Muscovite politico-religious perspective (Murvar 1971, 507).

The conception of Moscow as the Third Rome originated from the Byzantine doctrine of the universal Christian empire and the principle once articulated by the Constantinopolitan patriarch Anthony IV in his letter to Basil I, Grand Duke of Muscovy, in 1393: "It is impossible for Christians to have the Church, but not to have the Emperor" (Toumanoff 1946, 229). It suggested a new messianic image for the tsar as the ecumenical ruler. The new title of "tsar" and the elevation of the patriarchate signified not only rising autocracy, and national and ecclesiastic independence, but "a restoration of the Byzantine Empire" on the Russian ground (Uspensky 1998, 88). Byzantium reincarnated as a political imaginary still echoed in political discourse and practice.

The rise of Muscovy and the centralizing tendencies in the politics of Muscovite princes were conducive to the changing role and image of a ruler as the only sovereign and the sole owner of the Russian land. The concepts of autocracy as autonomous unlimited sovereignty and the idea of Russian messianism in the Orthodox world as a successor to the Byzantine Empire were ideological innovations and recurrent themes since the fifteenth century. The sixteenth century brought the conception of Russian tsardom and autocratic rule (with a renaissance of sacral kingship during the reign of Ivan IV).

The Byzantine ideas could hardly survive in the original articulation; the contextual redefinitions of the Byzantine sources created new orientations in the Russian political culture. Modernization of the eighteenth century was associated with visions of imperial absolutism and a rational "regular" state. In the spirit of these concepts, dualism of ecclesiastic and monarchical authority was rejected, and the church became an ordinary subdivision within the imperial bureaucratic architecture. The reinterpretation of the Byzantine paradigm of the dogmatic unity, alliance, and *symphonia* of the autonomous sacral and secular powers suggested an asymmetrical hierarchal model of unilateral control, submission of priesthood, rejection of the Church autonomy, and also uncovered the problem of the delimitation of state power.

The historical trajectory of Russia's development demonstrates a consistent strengthening of secular authority and state control—the role of *sacerdotium* shrank, whereas the potential of *imperium* advanced dramatically. As Arnason noted, the monotheistic mode of legitimation of imperial power entailed paradoxical and controversial implications—on the one hand, it accentuated the distance between the mundane and otherwordly matters and contrasted the corresponding domains of authority, while on the other hand, the conceptions of empire as a divine institution or the emperor as an image of God "brought the two worlds together again and provided a permanent incentive to imagine a more complete fusion" (Arnason 2000, 63). The vanished differentiation and assimilation of the sacral domain by the secular one produced a single source of power sanctioned by transcendental authority and embodied by the emperor, which preserved the sacral image of the viceroy of God. Russian history demonstrates an eventful path toward the "monistic unity" of authorities under the sovereignty of the ruler, who assumed not only unlimited political power but also sacral charisma.

Another difference of the Russian trajectory relates to the origins of the empire: in the Byzantine case, the Christian framework of legitimation was imposed on the Roman imperial legacy, while in Russia, the imperial project arose from a monotheistic Christian premise, Byzantine religious philosophy and the intention to revive the Christian Empire incarnated as the Third Rome. The development of autocracy as imaginary and institution coincided with territorial expansion and empire-building politics.

The Soviet state, although marked by aggressive atheism, retained a religious dimension. It evolved as a "sacral state" akin to an authoritarian theocratic state (Berdyaev 2012) but with secular religion, since communism replaced traditional religion. The communist totalitarian monistic state sacralized the politics and itself became a church that proselytized its "political religion" (Berdyaev 1955; Gentile 2006). The notion of schism between the mundane and the divine orders was replaced by the disjuncture between imperfection and injustice of now-worldly social reality and ideals of progress and then-worldly socialism. The communist doctrine was meant to resolve this tension—the socialist ideal could be approached and achieved through a revolutionary transformation that would lead to a creation of the "new man" and the "new world."[7] The post-soviet authoritarian model exemplifies continuity of the "patrimonial monistic" pattern organized around a personified source of power, albeit with a different legitimation framework. A democratic conception of "disembodiment" of power diffused among autonomous political bodies has never been fully institutionalized in Russia as well as democratic "civil religion." In contemporary Russia, the relationship between the ecclesiastical and state authorities cannot be reduced to the legal concept of "separation" but represents an ambiguous symbiosis of historical frameworks and practices of "symphony" and "political administration."

Notes

1. On revised understanding and application of the religio-political problematic see Arnason 2014b. See also Adams 2016.

2. The radical distinction between the transcendental and mundane orders was initially acknowledged in Jaspers's *The Origin and Goal of History* (2014) and later restated in Eisenstadt's programmatic article as a crucial innovation of the Axial Age (Eisenstadt 1982).

3. However, it is now clear that the disjunction between the transmundane and the mundane realities was not universal and formative to all Axial Age civilizations, see Wittrock 2005.

4. On the Byzantine theocracy, see Schmemann 1954; Runciman 2004.

5. In Max Weber's original definition, the ideal type of caesarorapism supposes "a complete subordination" of priesthood to secular power, when a secular ruler "exercises supreme authority in ecclesiastic matters by virtue of his autonomous legitimacy." However, the pure form of caesaropapism "can nowhere be found," since it usually exists as a combination of hierocratic elements. The power of secular rulers is limited by autonomous ecclesiastic charisma," which in the caesaropapist states secular authority tends to manage and appropriate (see Weber 1978, 1161–62). The term *ceasaropapism* is employed to define a broad spectrum of church-state configurations. In the case of Byzantium, this term "altogether exaggerates the degree of actual control of the church by the state" (Papadakis and Kazhdan 1991, 364–65), while in Russia the ruling autocrat was the head of the state and the church. For Byzantine and Russian versions of caesaropapism see Runciman 1957, 1–10, and Toumanoff 1946.

6. On Christian Orthodox orientations, sectarian movements and economic ethics in Russia see Nielsen 1989; Buss (1989a); Buss 1989b.

7. The well-known slogan of the Soviet period came from "The Internationale": "We will destroy this world of violence / Down to the foundations, and then/ We will build our new world . . ."

References

Adams, S. 2016. "On Johann Arnason and the Religio-Political Nexus: Some Preliminary Reflections." *Social Imaginaries* 2, no. 2: 121–36.

Arnason, J. P. 2000. "Approaching Byzantium: Identity, Predicament, and Afterlife." *Thesis Eleven* 62, no. 1: 39–69.

———. 2012. "Rehistoricizing the Axial Age." In *The Axial Age and Its Consequences*, edited by R. N. Bellah and H. Joas, 337–65. Cambridge, MA and London: Belknap Press of Harvard University Press.

———. 2014a. "Historicizing Axial Civilizations." In *Social Theory and Regional Studies in the Global Age,* edited by S. Arjomand, 179–201. Albany: State University of New York Press.

———. 2014b. "The Religio-political Nexus. Historical and Comparative Reflections." In *Religion and Politics: European and Global Perspectives*, edited by J. P. Arnason and I. P. Karolewski, 8–36. Edinburgh: Edinburgh University Press.

Arnason, J. P., S. N. Eisenstadt, and B. Wittrock. 2005a. "General Introduction." In *Axial Civilizations and World History*, edited by J. P. Arnason, S. N. Eisenstadt, and B. Wittrock, 1–14. Leiden: Brill.

Arnason, J. P., S. N. Eisenstadt, and B. Wittrock. 2005b. "Introduction: Late Antiquity as a Sequel and Counterpoint to the Axial Age." In *Axial Civilizations and World History*, edited by J. P. Arnason, S. N. Eisenstadt, and B. Wittrock, 287–98. Leiden: Brill.

Assmann, J. 2005. "Axial 'Breakthroughs' and Semantic 'Relocations' in Ancient Egypt and Israel." In *Axial Civilizations and World History*, edited by J. P. Arnason, S. N. Eisenstadt, and B. Wittrock, 133–56. Leiden: Brill.

———. 2009. *The Price of Monotheism*. Stanford: Stanford University Press.

Bellah, R. N. 2005. "What Is Axial about the Axial Age?" *Archives Européennes de Sociologie/European Journal of Sociology/Europäisches Archiv für Soziologie* 46, no. 1: 69–89.

———. 2011. *Religion in Human Evolution*. Cambridge: Harvard University Press.

Berdyaev, N. A. 1955. *Istoki i Smysl Russkogo Kommunizma*. Paris: YMCA-Press

———. 2012. Pis'mo deviatoe. O sotsializme. In "*Philosophy of Inequality*," edited by O. A. Platonov, 191–221. Moskva: Institut russkoy tsivilizatsii.

Bogatyrev, S. 2006. "Ivan IV (1533–1584)." *The Cambridge History of Russia*, 240–63. Cambridge: Cambridge University Press.

Buss, A. 1989a. "The Economic Ethics of Russian-Orthodox Christianity: Part I." *International Sociology* 4, no. 3: 235–58.

———. 1989b. "The Economic Ethics of Russian-Orthodox Christianity: Part II—Russian Old Believers and Sects." *International Sociology* 4, no. 4: 447–72.

———. 2003. *The Russian Orthodox Tradition and Modernity*: Leiden and Boston: Brill.

Cherniavsky, M. 1958. " 'Holy Russia' ": A Study in the History of an Idea." *The American Historical Review* 63, no. 3: 617–37.

———. 1959. "Khan or Basileus: An Aspect of Russian Mediaeval Political Theory." *Journal of the History of Ideas* 20, no. 4: 459–76.

Chichurov, I. 1990. *Politicheskaya ideologiya srednevekov'ya: Vizantiya i Rus.' K XVIII Mezhdunarodnomu kongressu vizantinistov*. Moskva: Nauka.

Diakonov, M. A. 1889. *Vlast' Moskovskikh gosudarei: Ocherki iz istorii politicheskikh idei drevnei Rusi do kontsa XVI veka*. St. Petersburg: Printing House of I. N. Skorokhodova.

Dvornik, F. 1956. "Byzantine Political Ideas in Kievan Russia." *Dumbarton Oaks Papers* 9/10: 73–121.

Eisenstadt, S. N. 1981. "Cultural Traditions and Political Dynamics: The Origins and Modes of Ideological Politics." Hobhouse Memorial Lecture. *The British journal of sociology* 32, no. 2: 155–81.

———. 1982. "The Axial Age: The Emergence of Transcendental Visions and the Rise of Clerics." *European Journal of Sociology/Archives Européennes de Sociologie* 23, no. 2: 294–314.

———. 1986a. "Introduction: The Secondary Breakthroughs in Ancient Israelite Civilization—The Second Commonwealth and Christianity." In *The Origins and Diversity of Axial Age Civilizations* edited by S. N. Eisenstadt, 227–40. Albany: State University of New York Press

———. 1986b. "Culture and Social Structure Revisited." *International Sociology* 1, no. 3: 297–320.

———. 1993. "Religion and the Civilizational Dimensions of Politics." In *The Political Dimensions of Religion edited by S. A. Arjomand,* 13–41. Albany: State University of New York Press.

———. 2000. "The Civilizational Dimension in Sociological Analysis." *Thesis Eleven* 62, no. 1: 1–21.

Gentile, E. 2006. *Politics as Religion*. Princeton: Princeton University Press

Halperin, C. J. 2014. "Ivan IV as Autocrat (*samoderzhets*)." *Cahiers du monde russe. Russie-Empire russe-Union soviétique et États indépendants* 55, no. 3–4: 197–213.

Hunt, P. 1993. "Ivan IV's Personal Mythology of Kingship." *Slavic Review* 52, no. 4: 769–809.

Jaspers, K. 2014. *The Origin and Goal of History (Routledge Revivals)*. London: Routledge.

Karpovich, M. 1944. "Church and State in Russian History." *Russian Review* 3, no. 2: 10–20.

Kartashev A. M. 1996. "Pravoslavie v ego otnoshenii k istoricheskomu protsessu." In *Tcerkov. Istoria Rossii. Stat'i i vistuplenia*, 44–60. Moskva: Probel.

Kazhdan, A., and A. Cutler. 1982. "Continuity and discontinuity in Byzantine history." *Byzantion* 52: 429–78.

Murvar, V. 1968. "Russian Religious Structures: A Study in Persistent Church Subservience." *Journal for the Scientific Study of Religion* 7, no. 1: 1–22.

———. 1971. "Patrimonial-Feudal Dichotomy and Political Structure in Pre-Revolutionary Russia: One Aspect of the Dialogue between the Ghost of Marx and Weber." *The Sociological Quarterly* 12, no. 4: 500–24.

Nielsen, D. A. 1989. "Sects, Churches, and Economic Transformations in Russia and Western Europe." *International Journal of Politics, Culture, and Society* 2: 493–522.

Obolensky, D. 1971. *The Byzantine Commonwealth: Eastern Europe, 500–1453*. New York: Praeger.

Ostrogorsky, G. 1956. "The Byzantine Emperor and the Hierarchical World Order." *The Slavonic and East European Review* 35, no. 84: 1–14.

———. 1969. *History of the Byzantine State*. New Brunswick: Rutgers University Press.

Ostrowski, D. 1990. "The Mongol Origins of Muscovite Political Institutions." *Slavic Review* 49, no. 4: 525–42.

———. 2012. "Systems of Succession in Rus' and Steppe Societies." *Ruthenica* 11: 29–58.

Papadakis, A., and A. P. Kazhdan. 1991. "Caesaropapism." In *The Oxford Dictionary of Byzantium*, edited by A. P. Kazhdan, 364–65. Oxford: Oxford University Press

Poppe, A. 1991. "Christianity and Ideological Change in Kievan Rus': The First Hundred Years." *Canadian-American Slavic Studies* 25, no. 1: 3–26.

Raeff, M. 1949. "An Early Theorist of Absolutism: Joseph of Volokolamsk." *The American Slavic and East European Review* 8, no. 2: 77–89.

Runciman, S. 1957. "Byzantium, Russia, and Caesaropapism." *Canadian Slavonic Papers* 2, no. 1: 1–10.

———. 2004. *The Byzantine Theocracy: The Weil Lectures, Cincinnati.* Cambridge: Cambridge University Press.

Schmemann, A. 1954. "Byzantine Theocracy and the Orthodox Church." *Cross-Currents* 4, no. 2: 109–23.

Ševčenko, I. 1984. "Byzantium and the Slavs." *Harvard Ukrainian Studies* 8, no. 3/4: 289–303.

Shepard, J. 2007. "Rus." In *Christianization and the Rise of the Christian Monarchy: Scandinavia, Central Europe and Rus'c. 900–1200,* edited by N. Berend, 369–416. Cambridge: Cambridge University Press.

Stroumsa, G. G. 2005. "Cultural Memory in Early Christianity: Clement of Alexandria and the History of Religions." *Axial civilizations and world history* edited by J. P. Arnason, S. N. Eisenstadt, and B. Wittrock, 295–317. Leiden: Brill.

Toumanoff, C. 1946. "Caesaropapism in Byzantium and Russia." *Theological Studies* 7, no. 2: 213–43.

Uspensky, B. 1998. *Tsar i patriarkh: Kharisma vlasti v Rossii: Vizantiiskaia model' i ee russkoe pereosmyslenie.* Moscow: Shkola: Iazyki russkŏ kul'tury.

Valdenberg, V. E. 1916. *Drevnerusskie ucheniia o predelakh tsarskoi vlasti: Ocherki russkoi politicheskoi literatury ot Vladimira Sviatogo do kontsa XVII veka.* Petrograd: A. Benke.

Vernadsky, G. 1973. *Kievan Russia.* New Haven: Yale University Press.

Weber, M. 1978. *Economy and Society: An Outline of Interpretive Sociology.* Berkeley: University of California Press.

Wittrock, B. 2005. "The Meaning of the Axial Age." In *Axial Civilizations and World History,* edited by J. P. Arnason, S. N. Eisenstadt, and B. Wittrock, 51–85. Leiden: Brill.

Zhivov, V. M., and B. A. Uspenskii. 1987. "Tsar'i Bog. Semioticheskie aspekty sakralizatsii monarkha v Rossii." In *Iazyki kul'tury i problemy perevodimosti,* edited by B. A. Uspenskii, 47–153. Moskva: Nauka.

9

The Forgotten Earth

Nature, World Religions, and Worldlessness in the Legacy of the Axial Age/Moral Revolution

EUGENE HALTON

Introduction: The Powers of Nature and the Myths of Mind

In 2014 my book *From the Axial Age to the Moral Revolution: John Stuart-Glennie, Karl Jaspers, and a New Understanding of the Idea* marked the rediscovery of the first fully articulated theory for the phenomena that became known three-quarters of a century later as the Axial Age (See Halton 2014a, 2017, 2019b). A philosopher, folklorist, historian, and founding sociologist, John Stuart-Glennie (1841–1910) first published his theory of what he termed *the moral revolution* in 1873. And he continued developing it in numerous subsequent writings to characterize the historical shifts roughly centered around 500–600 BCE in a variety of civilizations, most specifically ancient China, India, Judaism, and Greece (Stuart-Glennie 1873). There are many interesting parallels between Stuart-Glennie and Jaspers, though Jaspers did not know of Stuart-Glennie. In an 1876 work John Stuart-Glennie states tersely the transformation effected by the moral revolution in a way that goes to the heart of the differences between his and Jaspers's accounts: "[T] he Civilisations prior to the Sixth Century B.C. were chiefly determined by the Powers and Aspects of Nature, and those posterior thereto by the Activities and Myths of Mind" (Stuart-Glennie 1876, 479).

Egyptologist Jan Assmann, who has written extensively on the Axial Age, was awarded the peace prize of the German Booksellers Association in 2018, the same week his new book on the Axial Age was published. He devotes a whole chapter of the book to Stuart-Glennie and his philosophy of history, noting, "Had he not found his rediscoverer in the American sociologist Eugene Halton, he would undoubtedly have remained in oblivion, in which he disappeared soon after his death" (2018, 141; my translation). Assmann's book provides evidence that the history of the concept of the Axial Age has altered, and that Stuart-Glennie is now a key figure in that history. A number of other recent publications have now also acknowledged Stuart-Glennie's original contribution, thanks to my work. Here, I will begin by briefly discussing Stuart-Glennie's outlook in the context of his philosophy of history.

Stuart-Glennie also proposed a three-stage model of "Ages of Humanity" (see Figure 9.1), in which: (1) The First Age of Humanity, characterizing original precivilizational "folk culture" and early civilizations, originates

STUART-GLENNIE'S HISTORY OF RELIGION:

FIRST AGE OF HUMANITY
From Perceptive and Ritual Panzooinism
Through
Spectacular Rituals of Civilized State Relgions
To

SECOND AGE OF HUMANITY
(Centered Around 550–450 BCE)
The Moral Revolution
and
500 Year Dialectic Periods in the West
To

THIRD AGE OF HUMANITY
(Around the Year 2000)
Humanism

Figure 9.1. Stuart-Glennie's History of Religion.

out of nature relations, an outlook he termed *panzooinism*. He describes it as involving true intuitions of nature clothed in false conceptions. It is a relational consciousness of attunement to the powers inherent in the living and signifying habitat.

A common name for this relational consciousness is animism, though Stuart-Glennie showed in 1873, two years after E. B. Tylor coined the term *animism,* why Tylor had really described something that should be called "Spiritism," a power from without. Stuart-Glennie claimed that panzooinism more accurately got at how the powers of the natural environment itself, the power, for example, of a tree to clothe, heat, feed, etc., were active powers from within deserving spiritual significance. Stuart-Glennie's view seems to me to accord with recent theorizing on "the new animism," described by David Abram, Tim Ingold, Nurit Bird-David, Robin Wall Kimmerer, and myself.

(2) The Second Age of Humanity, growing out of civilizations and the progressive rise of supernaturalism, is the outbreak of the moral revolution, which figured positively as a transitional phase in the development of consciousness. It manifests across intellectual, sociopolitical, and religious domains and diverges in developmentally purposive ways from the previous phase, especially in involving a differentiation of subjective and objective. Religions move from custom to conscience, and, more so in the West, shift focus from the natural and immanent to the supernatural (of a transcendent divinity). Religions and philosophies develop a greater emphasis on reflectivity. In bringing about the differentiation of objective and subjective outlooks, it also marked a conflicted period of "progressively antagonistic and abstract conceptions of Natural Powers and Supernatural Agents" (1896, 519–20).

Stuart-Glennie drew attention to an interesting dialectic between the supernaturalism of the Judeo-Christian tradition and the naturalism of science, which he claimed was marked by five hundred–year cycles in the West. He described this antagonism as "incipient" in the first age of humanity, but as becoming central in the West with the fusion of Greek and Hebrew cultures in the development of Christianity.

Rational Greek philosophy and science, with its ideas of power immanent in nature, posed a conflict with Hebrew conceptions of a transcendent God above nature. In the later fusing of these traditions in Christianity there remained nevertheless an inherent clash, ultimately irreconcilable, and in Stuart-Glennie's view requiring a "new synthesis" for resolution through the triumph of the scientific outlook: the new Third Age of Humanity.

(3) In the Third Age of Humanity sociopolitical and religious outlooks find the means to realign with nature. The five hundred–year dialectical periods of tension between science and religion in the West resolve with the triumph of scientific humanism, which he projected to occur around the year 2000. He had some interesting insights in this prediction, but his belief in dialectical progress was overly optimistic in retrospect today. Still, an implication of Stuart-Glennie's schema is that human relations to nature not only were, but remain, elements of religious life: human religious life has roots in human nature and the perceptive relations to wild nature which shaped human nature, however those roots be denied or repressed. What Jaspers celebrated as the "heightening of the specifically human in man" may have come at the cost of the living primate animal that is humankind. "Heightening" may have been at the cost of depth, an elevation of an anthropocentrism that marked the development of civilized consciousness since its beginnings, a theme I shall return to later.

The differences in Jaspers's and Stuart-Glennie's understandings of the enduring significance of religious ideas is illustrated in Figure 9.2. Prehistory

Enduring Significance of Religious Ideas from Different Ages

Ages	Jaspers	Stuart-Glennie
Prehistory	Insignificant	Significant • "panzooinism" • "true intuitions of nature"
Civilization	Minor "islands of light"	Transition from supernal to supernatural
Moral Revolution / Axial Age	Pivotal • "Man, as we know him today, came into being."	Transitional Dialectic • Supernaturalism • Differentiation of subjective and objective • Conflict of Greek Naturalism and Christianity
Modern	Insignificant	Significant As Humanism • Through Science true intuitions clothed in true conceptions

Figure 9.2. Enduring Significance of Religious Ideas from Different Ages.

is insignificant for Jaspers, and significant for Stuart-Glennie as involving true intuitions into laws and patterns of nature, the age he termed panzooinism, an outlook he also called at times "Naturianism." Early civilizations held some minor significance for Jaspers ("islands of light"), though nothing in comparison with the pivotal nature of the Axial Age. Stuart-Glennie noted the rise of transition from more earthly "supernal" beings in religious consciousness to supernatural deities with early civilizations, and the moral revolution initiated in the West a conflict between Greek naturalism in science and the supernaturalism of Christianity, marked by the five hundred–year periods.

The modern era for Jaspers is notable for the rise of science and technology and their potential positive and negative consequences. But it does not carry the enduring significance of the Axial Age. Stuart-Glennie, by contrast, sees it as bringing about the culmination of the conflict between naturalism and supernaturalism, which would be resolved in favor of naturalism and a scientific humanism that would manifest in intellectual life as "relationalism," in sociopolitical life as socialism, and in religious life as humanism.

In retrospect, Stuart-Glennie's schematic resolution for the modern Third Age of Humanity was naively overoptimistic. Jaspers's warnings about the dark side of science and technology provide a corrective to that view. In my view, Lewis Mumford's critical theory of civilization as Megamachine provides a broader view than either Stuart-Glennie or Jaspers could provide. Mumford saw technology as a means, not an end, requiring being bounded toward broader human purposes, and human purposes in turn being bounded by yet broader ecological requirements. He traced how modern megatechnics are not novel, but rather a kind of replay with a twist of the original "megamachine," the bureaucracies and powers characterizing early civilizations and their pyramids, mass militaries, scribal accounting, engineering, etc. (Mumford 1967, 1970).

I have developed a three-part perspective toward human development and history as a paradoxical contraction of mind, involving genuine progress in precision, paradoxically counteracted by a regression in mind, which falsely neglects or excludes real aspects of the human relation to the earth (see Figure 9.3). In my view, humans evolved into being highly attuned to the animate Earth through a relational consciousness very different from the divergence brought about with agriculture and civilization. I call this long-term evolutionary attunement *animate mind* (see Figure 9.3 on page 214). With agriculturally based civilization the human mind contracts to *anthropocentric mind*, redefining the world through a narrower human filter. In this process there is genuine progress in precision counteracted by a regression of mind.

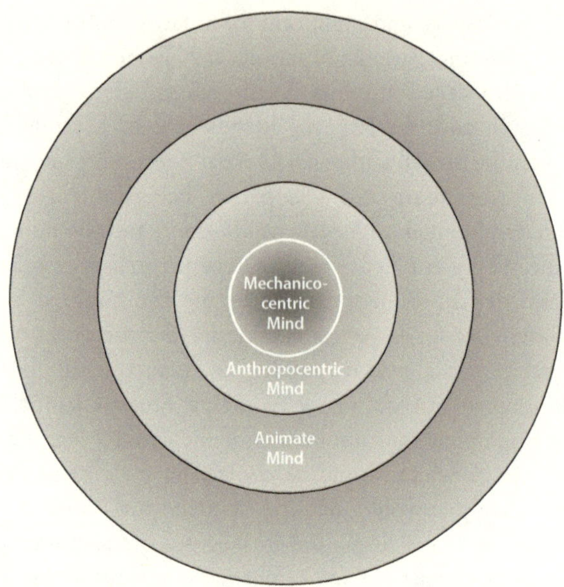

Figure 9.3. The Contractions of Mind.

Worldviews become myopically absorbed with the human perspective and the expansion of human power, excluding the wild earth and its laws, on which humans ultimately depend for long-term sustainability. The moral revolution/Axial Age seems to provide an alternative to this early civilizational Megamachine. But it tends to remain in the anthropocentric orbit, ultimately becoming absorbed by the very civilizational structures it arose in opposition to. In the modern era stemming from medieval Europe, mind contracts further to *mechanico-centric mind*, wherein the machine is taken as the ultimate metaphor defining existence, providing the objectivist filter through which the world is to be understood and made to fit.

Clearly, there were genuine advances in rational and mechanical practices from early civilization through modern life, in architecture, science, and technology, etc. Yet simultaneously the contractions of mind progressively devalued or excluded irreducible realities, such as qualitative and subjective experience, spontaneously alive to the present, imaginative projection and poetic wonder, and the palpable touch of organic life as experienced subjectively rather than abstracted through objectivism. In my view, the animate earth remains the touchstone, an evolutionary legacy indelibly embedded in human nature and its animate mind; not eradicated by the developments of civilization, the moral revolution/Axial Age, or modern life, but a latent capacity holding possibilities for what I have termed elsewhere, "sustainable wisdom" (Halton 2013, 2019a).

From A Vast Primal Morality to an Archimedean Ethics

> Upon the vast, incomprehensible pattern of some primal morality greater than ever the human mind can grasp, is drawn the little, pathetic pattern of man's moral life and struggle, pathetic, almost ridiculous.
>
> —D. H. Lawrence

When you consider the great moral teachers, capable of imparting wisdom to live by, who or what comes to mind? Do you see your personal morality, or the morality of your community or religion, as a human domain or as continuous with the morality of the community of life? Do you have animals or plants that you take as great teachers imparting wisdom to be learned? How many of you believe trees and forests to be sacred beings and communities worthy of religious or philosophic reverence?

We are all earthlings, bodied forth from the living earth. Yet most humans living today, whether religious or secularist, seem to consider themselves as something other than earthlings, primally bound in our human condition to the living earth. We seem to think that we are something transcendent, whether religiously or technologically.

Perhaps we are the people of Galileo's telescope. Philosopher Hannah Arendt saw Galileo's telescope, which demonstrated that the earth revolves around the sun, as one of the decisive events heralding the modern era, along with the discovery of America and ensuing global exploration, and the Reformation. Galileo's telescope seemed to provide the "Archimedean point" from which to move the world, to establish a universally valid scientific perspective. Archimedes had said that, with a sufficiently long lever, "Give me a place to stand on, and I will move the Earth."

What seemed a great achievement for science and human progress was yet problematic for Arendt. The human condition involved being "still bound to the earth," and yet the march of modern science and technology fostered ways of becoming untethered from it:

> [I]t is as if Galileo's discovery proved in demonstrable fact that both the worst fear and the most presumptuous hope of human speculation, the ancient fear that our senses, our very organs for

> the reception of reality, might betray us, and the Archimedean wish for a point outside the earth from which to unhinge the world, could only come true together, as though the wish would be granted only provided that we lost reality and the fear was to be consummated only if compensated by the acquisition of supramundane powers. . . . For whatever we do today in physics . . . we always handle nature from a point in the universe outside the earth. Without actually standing where Archimedes wished to stand . . . still bound to the earth through the human condition, we have found a way to act on the earth and within terrestrial nature as though we dispose of it from the outside, from the Archimedean point. And even at the risk of endangering the natural life process we expose the earth to universal, cosmic forces alien to nature's household. (1958, 262)

The universalist perspective came at the loss of the place of our senses for perceiving reality: no sunrise or sunset in the heliocentric universe, only the earth revolving around the sun. Arendt got at the costs of scientific objectivism in the modern world for the loss of qualitative, perceptive, direct human experience. But what if that Archimedean point goes back farther?

A number of commentators have noted how the rise of world religions out of the moral revolution/Axial Age has been marked by heightened ideas of transcendence. With the moral revolution/Axial Age also comes the possibility of transcendence of the world per se, whether in Buddhist Nirvana, or in religions of the Abrahamic tradition. As Robert Bellah said of ancient Judaism, "A God who is finally outside of society and the world provides the point of reference from which all existing presuppositions can be questioned, a basic criterion for the axial transition" (2011, 322). That "point of reference" by "a God who is finally outside of society and the world" signifies a kind of Archimedean ethics. Does it also potentially involve a similar diminution of perceptive experience, displaced in this case by a book? What is the place of perceptive experience in religion?

It is ironic that the world itself, in the literal sense of the actual Earth, took on a diminished role as a central element of religious sensibility in the world religions, admittedly more so in the Abrahamic religions of the West. In the East, Stuart-Glennie argued that panzooinism, rooted in the powers of nature, remained more prominent, and we can take, for example, Daoism or Buddhism. Given the issues today of unsustainability in ecological and other domains, including massive die-offs of wildlife and continuing ever-increasing global human population and consumption, the legacies of those world religions face the question I consider here: Can religion transcend the earth in the long run?

For aboriginal hunter-gatherer peoples of the past as well as today, as evident in ethnographic and archaeological records, the wild habitat is a common focus of reverential as well as practical attunement, a great teacher and source of wisdom, and central to religious life. Whereas the idea of participation in the community of life and practical balance with wild habitat have been central in informing aboriginal outlooks, elevation above it, and ultimately transcendence of it, mark many axial/moral revolution views.

With agriculture and civilization, the wild habitat begins to recede from a central place in religious belief, even as the domesticated environment and human interests become pronounced in state religions. In the place of the wild earth, sacred history comes to the fore, signaling locations of human activity deemed sacred or significant, often centered in cities and humans.

The moral revolution/Axial Age represented significant changes in civilization, to be sure, but it can also be taken, as I do, as a second phase in the radical shift to anthropocentric mind already begun with the advent of agriculturally based civilization. Bellah's celebration of the rise of theoretic culture in the Axial Age represents an idealization of cognitive mind and undervaluing of passional mind as a basis for practical life as well as religion. It also prevented him from fully appreciating the place of perceptive relations to wild habitat in the evolutionary origins of religion, despite his attempt to work out of an evolutionary perspective. He extolled Hans Joas's depiction of the rise of "the sacredness of the person" as an axial achievement: "[S]o the axial age certainly proclaimed the sacredness of the person" (Bellah 2013). But he ignored how the attunement to the livingness of all things, including humans, had earlier been the source of sacredness for precivilizational peoples, later "bottlenecked" to progressively human-centered forms and perspectives with civilization, state religions, and divine kingship. The costs of progressive loss of those perceptive relations are involved in the desacralization of the wild habitat in the heightening of anthropocentric mind.

From my perspective, Bellah did not really comprehend the watershed between the hunter-gatherer versus agriculturally based, civilized ways; a gulf that involved all facets of life, including religion and even physical stature. The supposed bounty produced by agriculture in fact systematically introduced nutritional deficiencies through dependencies on a limited variety of domesticated grains, causing people universally to become four to six inches shorter on average in Old World civilizations as well as New World ones (Mummert et al. 2011). Two of the three noncivilizational peoples Bellah discusses in his chapter on that theme were traditionally horticulturalists rather than hunter-gatherers, and he terms all three "tribal," which misses the fundamental distinctions between these ways of life. In a 2013 lecture, "The Modern Project in Light of Human Evolution," Bellah argued that the axial "theoretic attitude" only went off track in the past couple of hundred years, especially since the development of Watt's steam engine near the end of the eighteenth century (2013).

I asked Bellah during the question period after his lecture whether Axial Age cultures also came with hidden costs, Malthusian hidden costs of population expansion and wildlife population decimation; whether they continued the civilizational turn to the desacralization of the Wild Other, of the animals, plants, the living habitat, and the limits of nature that we have become distant from since living in cities began; and whether the "sacredness of the person" he had discussed may be a kind of endorsement in some ways of our human separateness from the sacredness of the habitat. He responded that though one reading of Genesis would support the idea that, "certainly there is a triumphalist notion that since we are human beings made in the image and likeness of God we are the rulers of the universe," still, figures such as St. Francis or religions such as Buddhism show the potential in axial cultures.

Yet Christians do not accept the wild hunger of the wolf that St. Francis tamed for local villagers as sacred. Similarly, Buddhists, though retaining a greater sense of panzooinism, of appreciation for living nonhuman beings as yet spiritual, still regard rebirth as an animal to be a lower kind of rebirth. Despite a greater Buddhist connection to nonhuman "sentient beings," as Bellah put it, Christians and Buddhists are focalized around human figures as sources of religious belief, not circumambient life.

In my opinion, Bellah missed the significance of the wild habitat as the chief source of physical and spiritual sustenance in the course of evolution; the means, through our close attunement to its varieties of life, of developmental passage to maturity. In the panzooinist outlook, the world itself is a sacred place, not a neutral place, or an evil place, or a place where only locations associated with human prophets or saviors are revered for spiritual significance. As author Daniel Quinn put it in an interview,

> Christianity . . . sees the world as just a neutral place, or actually if you read St. John, for example, as an evil place. But at best a neutral place where people live being tested for their true home,

> which is heaven. . . . In the Christian view not only is the world a neutral place, if it was a sacred place humans would not be fit for it. Humans are fallen, are sinners. And of course that's not a view any aboriginal people have. They don't see people as sinners or fallen or anything like that. They see humans as no different from anything else that lives, which is why they respect anything else that lives, they live in a respectful way in respect to the animals they live on. (Quinn 2015)

Humanity may have tasted of "the tree of the knowledge of good and evil" in the moral revolution/Axial Age (which also produced the biblical text of Genesis), generating new ways of knowing, new and valuable moral compasses. Yet that knowledge also blinded us to our continued dependence on ecological wisdom, which runs far deeper than knowledge or even humans, and includes that "primal morality greater than ever the human mind can grasp" to which D. H. Lawrence alluded. An emerging scientific consensus points to the potential sixth major period of extinctions we are entering, a human-caused "Anthropocene" era. In this sense, "the theoretic attitude" may not be a lasting achievement in the long run if the cost is mental blinders to the realities and requirements of the community of life on earth. As a basis for living it represents, rather, a contraction of mind from connection to the wild earth and a denial of our proper limited place in it and moral and spiritual responsibility to it.

The axial ideal of transcendence connects to a larger ideal, manifest not only in the legacies of the world religions but in contemporary science and technology, where transcendence of nature is brought about through progress. A less rosy description of such modes of transcendence is that of a philosophy of escape from the earth (Halton 2019a). Axial transcendence, celebrated by scholars such as Jaspers and Bellah, nevertheless involves an unacknowledged tragic cost, the forgetting of the earth and its lessons and limits as central to "sustainable wisdom."

To Put the Kabash on the Earth

Native American activist Vine Deloria described how the post-contact world for Native Americans meant that they were "wrenched from a free life where the natural order had to be understood and obeyed," and were "confined within a foreign educational system where memorization and recital substitute for learning and knowledge" (2006, xviii).

Indigenous Native American religions, centered on how "the natural order had to be understood and obeyed," were repressed by the European Christian tradition and its opposite view that nature had to be controlled, as though ordained by the transcendent divinity. This was a replay of the earlier transformation brought about through the moral revolution/Axial Age. The religions of the book shifted the focus of religious life from the natural to the supernatural, to a deity not immanent but transcendent, chiefly determined by "the Activities and Myths of Mind." (1876, 479). Stuart-Glennie described a movement from panzooinist conceptions of things as sentient powers and "homely" supernal beings, a latent antagonism, that, with the era begun with the moral revolution from 600 BCE on and its progressive differentiation of objective and subjective domains, develops into a latent antagonism between naturalism and supernaturalism. As described earlier, ultimately the latent antagonism would surface and be resolved in the Third Age, where science could reconcile with religion: through revealing the oneness of things, science would reconcile nature and humanity in a religion of humanism. Regarding the revolutionary developments of the moral revolution in the West, Stuart-Glennie again drew attention again to this shift in 1901:

> The new religions of Western Asia and of Europe,—Judaism, half a millennium later, Christianism, and, after another half millennium, Islamism,—were, on the contrary, for the first time supernatural religions, not in their popular forms only, but in their essential principle, the conception, not of a power immanent in, but of a creator independent of, nature. (1901, 457–58)

From the modern vantage point, hunter-gatherer religions and early civilizational polytheistic religions, with their spirits and deities, also seem supernatural. But it is important to realize that whatever is meant by "nature" today was far more broadly defined then. Stuart-Glennie's term *supernal* attempted to draw attention to conceptions of more earthy spirit beings in that period. Spirit beings and divinities were often personifications of nature, with the developments of polytheistic religions in civilization they began to grow into more "stately supernatural" beings. The turn toward monotheism in the Abrahamic religions marked a divestment of divinity and sacredness from wild nature. As Henri Frankfort stated in his book, *Gods and Kings*: "The Hebrew prophets rejected both the Egyptian and the Babylonian views. They insisted on the uniqueness and transcendence of God. For them all values were ultimately attributes of God; man and nature were devaluated, and every attempt to establish a harmony with nature was a futile dissipation of effort" (1948, 6).

A "futile dissipation of effort": such were the beliefs that entered into the prejudices against the earlier religions rooted in the wild habitat and later polytheistic religions. Paul Shepard put this in the context of the concept of history: "History is a collective memory of the past which denies the telluric [of the earth] dimension of place." Even the desert, which figured in biblical stories, was a symbol of emptiness rather than place: "Though important to the roots of Western spiritual life, the desert for the Hebrews was not valued as a place. It was a vacuum, idealized as a state of disengagement in alienation, a symbol of the condition of the human spirit" (2011, 58). The formless emptiness described at the beginning of Genesis, *tohu wabohu*, "without form," is a figurative use of the literal meaning of desert or wasteland. No desert aboriginal would describe the living desert in that way.

The detachment from wild habitat as object of religious focus marks this legacy. In Genesis 1.28 God calls for humankind to subdue the earth, and have dominion over its creatures: "And God blessed them, and God said unto them, Be fruitful, and multiply, and replenish the earth, and subdue it: and have dominion over the fish of the sea, and over the fowl of the air, and over every living thing that moveth upon the earth" (King James Version). The Hebrew word for subdue is *kabash,* meaning to subjugate, as one would do to an enemy. In contemporary slang, it is "to put the kabash on it." Again, Shepard: "However much seasonal festival and Mythic intuition the Jew and Christian clung to in their daily lives, the dominant thrust of the West was, at bottom, estrangement and abstraction" (2011, 58). From the point of view of the Earth, the celebrated achievements of the legacy of the moral revolution/Axial Age for the West, such as greater reflectiveness, the theoretical attitude, etc., are born out of the heavy costs of estrangement and abstraction, twin aspects of the forgetting of the Earth.

The Forgotten Conversations

> To be native to a place we must learn to speak its language.
>
> —Robin Wall Kimmerer, *Braiding Sweetgrass*

Religion runs deep in human nature, far deeper than the confines of human history, literacy, and the advent of civilization. In my view, it coevolved with human nature. Humans evolved from ongoing conversations of nature, conversations deeply rooted in the earth and in earth wisdom. Participation in those conversations through close attunement, wherein the wild others were treated as potential teachers, involved learning sophisticated levels of communication. As master tracker and naturalist Jon Young has shown in his book *What the Robin Knows*, songbird calls in the woods can act as a kind of radar, indicating movements of creatures a kilometer or two away. Emanated primarily by birds, concentric circles of calls radiating outward can be read for precise information on movement of creatures, with precision enough for likely location, size, and other features of the creature. This is information crucial to foragers, who, like soldiers in combat, need to know what is around them in their habitat and to be able to move silently enough to not set off the concentric circles alarms.

The calls are echoed out from the source area, like a stone thrown in a pond. Other species, such as deer and squirrels (Lilly et al. 2019), also understand these calls and respond to them. And hunter-gatherer humans do as well. These calls can indicate the location and approximate size of prey or a predator, and so are good for hunting as well as survival. A contemporary Special Forces soldier posting as T. A. L. Dozer, who was a fan of Young's book, noted in an Amazon online review how he learned the location calls for use in combat. Dozer titled his May 11, 2012 review, "Bird Language: the Tactical Advantage":

> What Jon Young has done is put this language in an easy to understand how-to format, essentially providing anybody the opportunity to learn this language if they so desire. I personally learned bird language a few years back to use operationally on combat operations. In doing so, I picked specific species of birds and animals to study and learn, that were common across my area of operation. I am by no means an expert at bird language but used it operationally successfully in locations specific to me in areas in Africa, Malaya and Borneo.

I also can take the same principles and with time apply them to my new operational areas as needed. This is because even though birds have different songs/calls, bird language is essentially the same the world over and is understood intuitively by many species of animals, which ultimately leads to the concentric rings that are made by disturbances to the baseline of the area you are operating in. The disturbances could be predators in the area or enemy personnel. I understand that this book is predominantly geared towards the naturalists, bird watchers and animal trackers, but I wanted to provide a review to show that bird language has application outside the intended realm and that military scouts, snipers and special forces operators, as well as hunters can apply this to the trade (2012, n.p.).

These songbird calls are not simply tools for survival, but are also beautiful. Songbirds produce the kinds of call and response timing as well as melodies of music, involving different species of birds. Participating in the conversation not only as a listener, but as a maker of calls through mimicry, can be a way to hunt birds and other species who pursue birds as prey.

This conversation has deeper implications as well, not only for music as an invention of birds, subsequently discovered from them by humans, but also as a potential source of human language as well. Songbirds have brains with analogues of the human Broca and Wernicke centers for language production and recognition, and produce "syntactic-like melodies." They may be closer precursors for syntactic communication than any of our primate relatives, as researchers have noted. Here is a brief excerpt from an article on birds and primates criticizing "primate-centrism" in the study of origins of language:

> Adding further complexity for understanding spoken language origins, recently the research focus has shifted towards species more distantly related to humans, such as certain groups of songbirds. This is in part because songbirds like humans and a few other species exhibit vocal learning and have what has been broadly classified as "syntactic-like" song production. . . . A summary of a consortium on the origins of human language syntax and its biological foundations encapsulates some of the current thinking.
>
> Another area of agreement might seem surprising in light of many current "primate-centric" studies of language evolution. . . . Most participants felt that there were no true precursors of syntax to be found among our nearest relatives. For anything like a syntactic precursor one had to go as far afield as songbirds. (Petkov and Jarvis 2012, 12)

The philosopher and Sanskritologist Frits Staal claimed to have found structural analogies between Hindu Vedic "Mantras and Bird Songs," in an article with that title. He held that mantras, though often using linguistic language, also have nonlinguistic ritual aspects he thought chronologically predated human language, and repetitions closely parallel to birdsong repetitions. He noted "analogies in structure, function and status between mantras and bird songs" (1985, 549).

Radar-like audio communications of movement in the surrounding habitat, music, and even language: if these indeed are the teachings we took from the birds and evolved with, one can better appreciate why the close practical and reverential sensing and attunement to bird conversations could play a central role in religious and ritual life. Whatever fantastic elaborations bodied forth in human ritual and religion, we see in this example how they could be rooted in learning relationships through perceptive sensings, experience, and practices of attunement to the wild habitat. Stuart-Glennie's idea of panzooinism as rooted in true intuitions of nature clothed in false conceptions can perhaps be better understood in this example as true intuitions of the forest symphonies and dramas played upon by the imaginative life: true art does not always equal false conceptions.

Consider the religious significance often accorded to trees by many hunter-gatherer peoples. We are only now in the beginning stages of rediscovering why trees and forests are far more sophisticated than what we have given them credit for. In his remarkable book, *The Hidden Life of Trees: What They Feel, How They Communicate—Discoveries from a Secret World*, Peter Wohlleben reveals recent findings of the communicative networks involving trees and mycorrhizal fungi, networks that forest ecology scientist Suzanne Simard characterized as the "wood wide web." Individual trees, forests, and fungi exhibit webs of complex interspecies communication and complexity. Individual "hub trees" or "mother" trees act not only as nodal points for the surrounding forest and its literal "underground economy," but they can also recognize their offspring and nourish them selectively. Coniferous fir trees trade nutrients, such as sugars, through the fungal web with deciduous birch trees, offsetting the energy deficits the different species have at different times of the year.

Here, the revering of trees and forests as teachers through entering the conversation of their lives, understanding, for example, the varying balances and imbalances between acorn and beechnut production over years as a strategy to keep wild boar and deer populations in check, can bring not only survival, but also a course of learning to become a mature participant in that ecological conversation of balance. Again, the immersion in the conversations of the wild habitat as a practical and religious source of earth wisdom was an ingredient in our evolutionary passage to becoming humans, and to becoming active citizens in the community of life. Wohlleben notes the stark contrast of wild plants and forests with agriculture:

> However, when we step into farm fields, the vegetation becomes very quiet. Thanks to selective breeding, our cultivated plants have, for the most part, lost the ability to communicate above or below ground—you could say they are deaf and dumb—and therefore they are easy prey for insect pests. That is one reason why modern agriculture uses so many pesticides. Perhaps farmers can learn from the forests and breed a little more wildness back into their grain and potatoes so that they'll be more talkative in the future. (Wohlleben 2016, 11–12)

Wohlleben shows how agricultural monoculture also acts as a form of communication repression, and a viable return to breeding smarter, wilder cultivated plants better capable of organic protective communication might even be possible within agriculture.

The biologist Lynn Margulis once said, "Life did not take over the globe by combat, but by networking" (1986, 15). In other words, evolution as Darwinian natural selection, propelled largely by chance mutation, is an incomplete understanding of evolution, overvaluing competition while undervaluing cooperation. Such "networking" Margulis called *symbiogenesis,* where symbiotic relations between individual organisms such as bacteria foster the development of composite forms. As she said in an interview, "Symbiogenesis recognizes that every visible life-form is a combination or community of bacteria" (2011, n.p.).

By analogy, nature can be seen as a vast networking on all levels, communities of conversations. Human evolution can be seen as involving a progressive development of prosocial capacities rooted in attunements to those conversations, both directly and in ritual and mimetic forms. Epigenetics has confirmed the means in which experience and culture can become genetically encoded in Lamarkian-like ways. I have attempted to frame epigenetic aspects of the evolution of humans as rooted in ritual and dramatic modes of interaction, including hunting and gathering per se, as *dramatic evolution.* As I put it elsewhere, dramatic evolution also

> involves a spontaneous element, live to the enactment of the situation. It involves what philosopher Charles Peirce called "energetic

> projaculation," the throwing forth in spontaneous creation, or "the putting of sundry thoughts into situations in which they are free to play." Peirce's claim for energetic projaculation, for a modality of spontaneous conduct capable of breaking the mold, so to speak, and of bodying forth new habits through experience allows creative conduct as a real capacity of the human creature. (Halton 2014b, 307)

Here, the hunting and gathering dramas of what Paul Shepard termed *the sacred game* play out in varieties of practical, ritual, and reverential conversations involving gestural, audio, musical, visualizing, and vocalizing "vocabularies."

The advent of agriculturally based civilization begins a diminution of the conversations of wild nature. Humans turn from being participants in conversations of the wild earth to voices and spectators in a progressive monologue. Relations to nature now become the one-sided conversation involving domesticates, animals, and plants, and polytheistic religions project these relationships and the forms of social organization developed out of them onto personified deities. Domesticated nature and human spectacle displace wild nature as a central feature in religious life. It is now the pharaoh, metaphorically speaking, at the top of the pyramid, who dictates the terms that must be obeyed. With the moral revolution/Axial Age, nature is further distanced as a source of religious attention, more so in the West than in the East, where, for example, Daoism and Buddhism retained a greater presence of nature.

When we left our two million–year trajectory of evolution as hunter-gatherers through agricultural settlement and eventually civilization, we stopped that primal conversation. We began to live in what Daniel Quinn calls *The Great Forgetting*. The Great Forgetting is a radically different conversation, one that progressively puts humans and human personifications at the center, while distancing from the wild Earth. The conversation with the earth transformed into a human monologue, that of ways of controlling the wild earth. The conversation contracted to the language of humans, speaking to each other and through their projected deities, their projections of their progressively anthropocentric and hierarchically ordered world, their state religions. Reality became redefined according to the contracted lens of anthropocentric mind.

With the rise of the moral revolution/Axial Age, the Abrahamic religions bodied forth a counterconversation involving greater human equality, while simultaneously radically increasing the monotheistic hierarchical gulf between humans and a transcendent deity. "The moral revolution" remained an anthropocentric monological conversation, between humans and "a God who is finally outside of society and the world," as Bellah put it, who must be obeyed, rather than a morality and conversation involving the natural order as something to be understood and obeyed. The wisdom of the earth was forgotten, even as dreams of transcending it through ever more control and progress took hold.

Later, the monological conversation becomes that of humans and the machine, which I view as a further contraction of mind to the mechanical worldview, to mechanico-centric mind. It begins with humans in conversation with the machine, or rather calling it into apparent conversation. From the humble origins of the mechanical clock in the Benedictine monastery to regularize prayer time, clockworks proliferated and, by the seventeenth century, came to symbolize the universe. Now the conversation shifts to conversations of *Deus-ex-Machina*, the crypto-religion of the machine: the conversations of technophilia. The objectivist clockwork universe, including its economic manifestation in globalizing capitalism, now progressively dictates the terms of the relationship. The early dreams of technical utopia eventually threaten to become the monologue of the rationalized machine dictating the lives of humans.

With the rise of postmedieval civilization, even humans began to be displaced as the new machine worldview emerged into centrality. Science and technology progressively shattered the enclosed premodern views, from the precision of the mechanical clock and its growth as a symbol that would eventually allow the universe to be understood as a clockwork, to the exploration of the globe, and, with Galileo's telescope, the displacement of Geocentrism.

The rise of science marked a return to nature as an object of learning, a positive turn. But the earth remained forgotten, eclipsed through its dissection into abstract quantitative parameters, or into a commodity to be exploited. Science claimed to provide the evidence to evict mind from nature, and God from the natural world. Religion was effectively rendered effete as far as the workings of nature were concerned. Nevertheless, a new crypto-religion was born, the *Deus-ex-Machina* crypto-religion. In this attitude a particular mechanico-centric understanding of science would be the measure of all things, capable of progressively taking complete control of the earth. The machine became model of the ultimate, the objectivist filter through which the world is to be understood and made to fit.

Unfortunately, the boundless enthusiasm for science and technology has come up against the bounds of the living earth in our time, a development already foreseen by Jaspers and Mumford. And even though technophiles still hold an uncritical faith in what Lewis Mumford termed, "the myth of the machine," believing that technical solutions alone can resolve the daunting and growing challenges of unsustainability, nevertheless the cries of the forgotten earth can be heard in the numerous accounts of ever-increasing species decline, atmospheric and oceanic pollution, climate change, and in the human displacements related to these.

D. H. Lawrence and the Tragic Excursus

Jaspers published a kind of follow-up to *The Origin and Goal of History* in 1957, excerpted from his larger book *The Great Philosophers* and titled *Socrates, Buddha, Confucius, Jesus*. There he reiterated his view that these exemplary figures from the Axial Age remain models for the present, though perhaps not completely: "What was essential in them will always be essential for philosophy" (1962, 95). His call for a humanistic ethos to confront problems of modern technology allows a continuing place for the axial outlook. Stuart-Glennie differed in holding that age as transitional rather than centrally pivotal or axial. It would give way to that future "third age of humanity," guided by science, shaped by the mutually determining relations of thought and things toward true conceptions, which would also bring about a religious humanitarianism. He believed that modern science would provide true intuitions of nature clothed in true conceptions, thereby allowing the oldest beliefs of humanity a partial legitimacy that could be refined through modern science. Jaspers, by contrast, saw no significance in aboriginal beliefs, and virtually none in the pre-axial religions.

Mumford shared Jaspers's critical attitude toward modern technology, and also the need for a revival of humanistic ideas. Yet he saw the axial age as but a partial ingredient in the longer "fibrous structure" of history and prehistory that should be brought to bear on transforming contemporary crises, including biocultural ways of thought. Mumford and Jaspers were far more critical of the idea that science should be the dominant force shaping the further developments of society, as Stuart-Glennie's optimism held, given their place as leading-edge thinkers of the nuclear era. Their criticisms remain even more valid today.

D. H. Lawrence presents a more critical view again of the moral revolution/Axial Age, though sharing with Stuart-Glennie and Mumford, in part perhaps, an acceptance of its role as somewhat of a transitional phase, or rather, as he puts it, an *excursus*. But it is an excursus toward nullity.

Unlike Jaspers's linear axial progressivism, even though tempered with a sober view of the dark tendencies released by modern technology, and Stuart-Glennie's more nuanced but naive progressivist optimism, Lawrence saw the consequences of the moral revolution as tragic, ultimately apocalyptic. He saw the rise of "mind," of reflective consciousness, not as a new and progressive activation of "axial" cognitive capacities, as Jaspers and more recently Robert Bellah did, but rather as an unsustainable cleaving from the cosmos. He proposed as an alternative a new balance involving a reactivation and institutionalization of what he termed *affirmative mind* as a counterbalance to the domination of reflective consciousness in modern life. He claimed that affirmative mind, the "primal way of consciousness," is a way of "being in touch" and being in wonder, an embodied human birthright and dormant key to a renewal of a potentially sustainable civilization. Without such a renewal, he foresaw the maximizing ideology of the machine, which dominates the modern worldview resulting in a suicidally unsustainable "nullity."

Lawrence's tragic view of the era he saw centered around 600 BCE marks a break with the many more positive views that dominate scholarship, and is worth serious consideration today. Compare his Buddha, Plato, and Jesus toward the end of the following quotation with Jaspers's view of Socrates, Buddha, Confucius, and Jesus given above. In the posthumously published essay on his last novel, *Lady Chatterley's Lover*, Lawrence hits on some of the key themes he also developed in his nonfiction book, *Apocalypse*, which was also published posthumously, in 1931.

> The last three thousand years of mankind have been an excursion into ideals, bodilessness, and tragedy, and now the excursion is over. . . . Today is already the day after the end of the tragic and idealist epoch. . . . Now we have to re-establish the great relationships which the grand idealists, with their underlying pessimism, their belief that life is nothing but futile conflict, to be avoided even unto death, destroyed for us. Buddha, Plato, Jesus, they were all three utter pessimists as regards life, teaching that the only happiness lay in abstracting oneself from life, the

> daily, yearly, seasonal life of birth and death and fruition, and in living in the "immutable" or eternal spirit. But now, after almost three thousand years, now that we are almost abstracted entirely from the rhythmic life of the seasons, birth and death and fruition, now we realise that such abstraction is neither bliss nor liberation, but nullity. It brings null inertia. And the great saviours and teachers only cut us off from life. It was the tragic *excursus*. (1968, 504, 501, 511)

Lawrence argued that the rhythmic relation to the living earth, the living cosmos, went to the depths of human nature, of the entire internalized and embodied human evolutionary heritage, and not simply the heights of the reflective turn of mind. And for this reason the divorce from that deeper relation to cosmos, manifesting in the movements begun around 600 BCE, was ultimately unsustainable. Here is one key statement of his view, illustrating his awareness of the revolution centered around 600 BCE, but also, why he believed that the shift to reflective mind involved a tragic loss rather than progress:

> Till now, till about 600 B.C., when the *real* change in the direction of man's consciousness definitely set in, the cosmos had consisted of Powers and Rulers. Now, it was to be proved subordinate and subject in itself to a greater rule. There was a new wild instinct on earth: to prove that all the great Rulers were subject to One Rule.

The phrase, "all the great Rulers were subject to One Rule," is a way of describing the moral revolution that could allow both the religious aspects, such as monotheism or Buddhist Nirvana, as well as Greek logos or the Dao. He continued:

> The rule of kings was over, in the consciousness of man. The immediate connection with the cosmos was broken. Man and the cosmos came out of touch, they became, in a sense, enemies. Man set himself to *find out* the cosmos, and at last to dominate it. . . . Henceforth it was the dominion of man over the cosmos, through the collective effort of Mind. Men must love one another, so that collectively Man could conquer the

> cosmos. And the conqueror was Mind. And Mind was One and indivisible. (1982a, 168)

Despite the dialectic between the supernaturalist religions of the moral revolution and the developing naturalist science of the Greeks that Stuart-Glennie drew attention to, which would continue in the rise of modern civilization, both sides shared a domination by mind, as Lawrence saw it. "Mind" in Lawrence's sense here includes processes of rationalization, such as Max Weber drew attention to, or "reflective thought." It also involves a quality usually ignored in discussions of the rise of modern civilization, namely idealization, the tendency to transform the expressive and incommutable passions involved in living into abstractions, so that people begin to live from the abstract ideal.

Lawrence directs critical attention to the elevation of "mind," the new increased valuation of reflective mind. But he contrasts mind in this sense to the primal way of consciousness, that of "affirmative" mind. The way of knowing, the relatively new critical consciousness, is a questioning consciousness, and a contrary to the older legacy of "the primal way of consciousness."

> If we can accept the *unquestioning* way of consciousness, the way of direct impression, which proceeds from affirmation to affirmation, we shall be much better able to understand the older form of the pagan consciousness. Long before Christ, the questioning method of consciousness had arisen, in India and Ionia particularly. But everywhere it had to struggle against the older form of consciousness, to which the question was obnoxious, or even impious, when applied to vital things or concepts. It was impious to question the gods. The feeling lasts to this day, and will always last, since the primitive consciousness, shall we say the primal way of consciousness in man is the unquestioning way of affirmation, and movement from affirmation to affirmation by way of image. (1982, 164)

Mind, as he is calling it, as the negating consciousness, is secondary to the affirming consciousness, the narrative or quasi-narrative flow of spontaneous image or quality. Think of being in a dramatic or musical performance, where negating or doubting would just break the flow. Something like

Lawrence's idea was given by W. E. H. Stanner in describing the Australian aboriginal idea of The Dreaming: "The separable elements I have mentioned are all present in the metaphysical heart of the idea of "person," but **the overruling mood is one of belief, not of inquiry or dissent.** So long as the belief in The Dreaming lasts, there can be no "momentary flash of Athenian questioning" to grow into a great movement of skeptical unbelief which destroys the given unities" (1956, n.p.).

Though primarily a novelist, Lawrence developed in the course of his travels and studies, especially his stays in the American Southwest and attendance at Native American ritual dances, a profound understanding of aboriginal mind, more detailed in ways than Stuart-Glennie's panzooinism, as well as the costs of civilizing. He saw clearly into the problematic development of anthropocentric mind, and argued that aboriginal mind, or "affirmative mind," actively participant in a living universe, remains an indelible reality of humankind, despite the overlay of civilized anthropocentrism. This was no false romanticizing of the "noble savage," but an acknowledgment of the evolutionary legacy of two million years of foraging, tempered into the human body-mind, repressed perhaps but not displaced by anthropocentric rationality. His description anticipates recent discussions of "the new animism" as a relational ontology (Bird-David 2000; Harvey 2005; Halton 2005, 2007; Ingold 2011).

Lawrence allowed hope for overcoming the domination by mind, or the "negating consciousness," by calling for a new outlook, a new understanding of human consciousness and human development, which could reconcile the still-resilient resources of the primal "affirmative consciousness," the capacities for mind as engaged, relational conduct, with the negating consciousness. Getting *in touch* with the dormant possibilities of the passions is key, and not only metaphorically.

Lawrence designates the cosmos as conscious, not in the human sense of "self-consciousness," but in the living quick of the consciousness of tigers and kangaroos, in the poetic wonder of variescent life, the being in touch with the animate earth:

> The cosmos is certainly conscious, but it is conscious with the consciousness of tigers and kangaroos, fishes, polyps, seaweed, dandelions, lilies, slugs, and men: to say nothing of the consciousness of water, rock, sun and stars. Real consciousness is touch. Thought is getting out of touch. The crux of the whole

> problem lies here, in the duality of man's consciousness. Touch, the being in touch, is the basis of all consciousness, and it is the basis of enduring happiness.

The being in touch, rooted in the haptic sense, is primal, and is the source of wonder, human sociality, and religious sensibility. He continues:

> *Thought is a secondary form of consciousness, Mind is a secondary form of existence, a getting out of touch, a standing clear, in order to come to a better adjustment in touch.*
>
> Man, poor man, has to learn to function in these two ways of consciousness. When a man is *in touch,* he is non-mental, his mind is quiescent, his bodily centres are active. When a man's *mind* is active in real mental activity, the bodily centres are quiescent, switched off, the man is out of touch. The animals remain always in touch. And man, poor modern man, with his worship of his own god, which is his own mind glorified, is permanently out of touch. (1982, 172–73; emphasis mine)

Thinking is "a getting out of touch." And why? Why, in order to get back in touch. But what happens when one starts living out there, in the "out of touch"? That, I submit, is our civilization, with its "theoretic attitude," its second-order thinking, its rationalization, its sense of transcendence of earthly bounds: out of touch. That is "our own mind glorified" civilization, so out of touch in delusions of religious and scientific/technical transcendence and escaping the earth. The ongoing devastation of the earth, the human destruction of the biosphere, is an apparent success for the philosophy of the escape from the earth, for the philosophy of getting out of touch permanently.

Exercising the contraries of primal bodily being in touch with the being of thinking mind as a means to "come to a better adjustment in touch," learning to "function in these two ways of consciousness," rather than either/or, is the way Lawrence saw of breaking the tragic overdependence on upper consciousness. Though he did not use the word *sustainability,* so prominent in contemporary ecological discussions, it is a key element to his call for a reconciliation with the longer human legacy, to getting back in touch with our earthly limits. He expressed this overturning of "the mechanical conquered universe of modern humanity," as a call for reconciliation: "[I]t will be [a] marriage set again in relationship to the rhythmic cosmos. The rhythm of the cosmos is something we cannot get away from, without bitterly impoverishing our lives" (1968, 509).

What Lawrence termed the philosophic-scientific age of modern life was for him a culture of alienation rather than progressive enlightenment. He suggested what the next state would be.

> The triumph of Mind over the cosmos progresses in small spasms: aeroplanes, radio, motor-traffic. . . . And alas, everything has gone wrong. The destruction of the world seems not very far off, but the happiness of mankind has never seemed so remote.
>
> Man has made an enormous mistake. Mind is not a Ruler, mind is only an instrument. . . . The cosmos is alive, but it is not God. Nevertheless, when we are in touch with it, it gives us life. It is forever the grand volute reality, Life itself, the great Ruler. We are part of it, when we partake in it. But when we want to dominate it with Mind, then we are enemies of the great Cosmos, and woe betide us . . .
>
> How they long for the destruction of the cosmos, secretly, these men of mind and spirit! How they work for its domination and final annihilation! But alas, they only succeed in spoiling the earth, spoiling life, and in the end destroying mankind, instead of the cosmos. . . . Man must inevitably destroy himself, in conflict with the cosmos. (1982, 171, 174)

Lawrence understood, as virtually every other commentator on the moral revolution/Axial Age has not, with the possible exception of Mumford, that the cleaving from cosmos that erupted 2,500 years ago was by no means sustainable progress in the long run, but a disastrous long-term mistake. When he wrote these words in 1929 during the "Century of Progress" they may have seemed outlandish, as perhaps they still are for many today, including more than four billion people who are believers in moral revolution/Axial Age religions, as well as the believers in scientific materialism. But in my view Lawrence understood the tragedy that is our time today, and the involvement of the changes that took place 2,500 years ago in it, as the world races toward cascading collapse. The dominant world religions, especially Christianity and Islam, which comprise together more than half the people on the earth, as well as science and technology, had lost the touch of the earth. What is usually depicted as the great contrast between religion and science in the modern world appears as only two sides of Mind seeking domination of the cosmos, not in a direction of a sustainable scientific humanism, as Stuart-Glennie proposed, but suicidally. Perhaps we should not forget that this is from Lawrence's last work, *Apocalypse*.

Lawrence raises the question Jaspers's treatment of Socrates, Buddha, Confucius, and Jesus evaded: Are the beliefs of the original figures of the Axial Age/moral revolution ultimately unsustainable in themselves, and not simply in how they might have been distorted or appropriated? Were the beliefs growing out of that period inadequate in not addressing our relation to wild habitat as a sacred source of learning, involving our relationship to the well-being of the community of life, the vast "primal morality" to which we remain morally and spiritually responsible? Were those axial ideals simply just too cerebral, too reflective, and insufficiently appreciative of the powers of passional mind, instinctively engaged?

Civilization began a long process of setting rational intelligence free, amplified in the moral revolution/Axial Age, maximized in the modern era. We have been discovering the mistake of maximizing that which should only be optimized. Rational mind is optimized for everyday living when bounded within the greater reasonableness of instinctive, emotional and spontaneous intelligence of passional mind, of Lawrence's affirmative mind, and what I term *animate mind*.

The rational-bureaucratic perfection of mechanico-centric mind in our time is the threat of the schizoid robot, calculating without compassion, colonizing everything, incapable of touching and being touched by the earth. It is on many levels the complete antithesis of Socrates, Buddha, Confucius, and Jesus and the humane visions they sought to body forth. But in my opinion, and Lawrence's as well, it is also not simply a distortion or perversion of the moral revolution/Axial Age, but rather a manifestation of the darkest consequences that could be set free by the elevation of anthropocentric reflective mind, unmoored from its passional roots. Regaining our own balance is key to human flourishing as it has been for most of human history. But a new balance is needed, one that reconnects what remains valid from the legacy of the moral revolution/Axial Age to the longer evolutionary past far beyond history, a legacy that remains tempered in us genetically, developmentally, and ontologically as human nature (Bowlby 1999; Shepard 2011).

For all of the genuine achievements in religion, philosophy, science, and technology that stem from the moral revolution/Axial Age, the dream of transcending life, whether through heavenly afterlife or Enlightenment, has continued the civilizational fantasy of escape from the wild earth. My call for reopening the forgotten resources of animate mind are not in opposition to the contractions of mechanico-centric mind and anthropocentric mind, but an acknowledgment that those resources remain indelibly within us.

Make no mistake: we are not rational creatures. We are passional creatures, with rationality as our newest and most unmatured capacity of brain and mind, who have recklessly set it free from its passional moorings, as though, with our moral revolution, we could live from the knowledge of good and evil, conveyed to us by human prophets. We decided to live from our image in the mirror that they provided, which celebrated the best of human virtues even while obscuring the wild others, forgetting them, forgetting our genetic inheritance tempered from eons of encounters with them, forgetting the earth, our mother. We lost the touch of the earth in the name of transcendence, the illusory transcendence of life.

References

Assmann, Jan. 2018. *Achsenzeit: Eine Archäologie Der Moderne*. Frankfurt: C. H. Beck.

Arendt, Hannah. 2013. *The Human Condition*. Chicago. University of Chicago Press.

Bellah, Robert. 2013. "The Modern Project in Light of Human Evolution." Lecture Presented at University of Notre Dame, March 19, Notre Dame.

———. 2011. *Religion in Human Evolution: From the Paleolithic to the Axial Age*. Cambridge: Belknap Press of Harvard University Press.

Bird-David, Nurit. 2000. "'Animism' Revisited: Personhood, Environment, and Relational Epistemology." *Current Anthropology* 41 (S1): 67–91.

Bowlby, John. 1999. *Attachment: Attachment and Loss, Volume One*. New York: Basic Books.

Deloria, Vine. 2006. *The World We Used to Live In: Remembering the Powers of the Medicine Men*. Golden, CO. Fulcrum.

Dozer, T. A. L. 2012. "Bird Language: The Tactical Advantage." [Product Review] *What-Robin-Knows-Secrets-Natural*. Retrieved June 18, 2016; www.amazon.com/What-Robin-Knows-Secrets-Natural/product-reviews/054400230X/ref=cm_cr_dp_d_show_all_btm?ie=UTF8&reviewerType=all_reviews.

Frankfort, Henri. 1948. *Kingship and the Gods: A Study of Ancient Near Eastern Religion as the Integration of Society and Nature*. Chicago: University of Chicago Press.

Halton, Eugene. 2005. "Peircean Animism and the End of Civilization." *Contemporary Pragmatism* 2, no. 1: 135–66.

———. 2007. "Eden Inverted: On the Wild Self and the Contraction of Consciousness." *The Trumpeter* 23, no. 3: 45–77.

———. 2013. "Planet of the Degenerate Monkeys." In *Planet of the Apes and Philosophy*, edited by John Huss, 279–92. Chicago: Open Court.

———. 2014a. *From the Axial Age to the Moral Revolution: John Stuart-Glennie, Karl Jaspers, and a New Understanding of the Idea*. New York: Palgrave MacMillan.

———. 2014b. "From the Emergent Drama of Interpretation to Enscreenment." In *Ancestral Landscapes in Human Evolution: Culture, Childrearing, and Social Wellbeing*, edited by Darcia Narvaez, Kristin Valentino, Agustin Fuentes, James McKenna, and Peter Gray, 307–30. Oxford: Oxford University Press.

———. 2017. "Sociology's Missed Opportunity: John Stuart-Glennie's Lost Theory of the Moral Revolution, also Known as the Axial Age." *Journal of Classical Sociology* 17, no. 3: 191–212.

———. 2018. "The Axial Age, The Moral Revolution, and the Polarization of Life and Spirit." *Existenz: An International Journal in Philosophy, Religion, Politics, and the Arts* 13, no. 2: 56–71.

———. 2019a. "Indigenous Bodies, Civilized Selves, and the Escape from the Earth." In *Indigenous Sustainable Wisdom: First-Nation Know-how for Global Flourishing*, edited by Darcia Narvaez, Four Arrows, Eugene Halton, Brian Collier, and Georges Enderle, 47–73. New York: Peter Lang.

———. 2019b. "John Stuart-Glennie's Lost Legacy." In *Forgotten Founders and Other Neglected Theorists*, edited by Christopher T. Conner, Nicholas Baxter, and David R. Dickens, 11–26. Lanham, MD: Lexington Books.

Harvey, Graham. 2005. *Animism: Respecting the Living World*. New York: Columbia University Press.

Ingold, Tim. 2011. *Being Alive: Essays on Movement, Knowledge, and Description*. New York: Routledge.

Jaspers, Karl. 1953. *The Origin and Goal of History*. New Haven: Yale University Press.

———. 1962 [1957]. *Socrates, Buddha, Confucius, Jesus*, New York: Harcourt, Brace and World.

Kimmerer, Robin Wall. 2013. *Braiding Sweetgrass: Indigenous Wisdom, Scientific Knowledge and the Teachings of Plants*. Minneapolis: Milkweed Editions.

Lawrence, David Herbert. 1936. *Phoenix: The Posthumous Papers of D. H. Lawrence*. New York: Viking.

———. 1968. *Phoenix II: Uncollected, Unpublished, and Other Prose Works*. New York: Viking.

———. (1982)[1931]. *Apocalypse*. New York: Viking.

Lilly, Marie V., Emma C. Lucore, and Keith A. Tarvin. 2019. "Eavesdropping Grey Squirrels Infer Safety from Bird Chatter." *Plos 1*, September 4, 2019. Retrieved September 5, 2019; https://doi.org/10.1371/journal.pone.0221279.

Margulis, Lynn, and Dorian Sagan. 1986. *Microcosmos*. New York: Summit.

Mumford, Lewis. 1967. *The Myth of the Machine: Vol. 1, Technics and Human Development*. New York: Harcourt Brace.

———. 1970. *The Myth of the Machine: Vol. 2, the Pentagon of Power*. New York: Harcourt Brace.

———. 1975. "Prologue to Our Time." *The New Yorker*. March 10. Retrieved September 28, 2016; https://www.newyorker.com/magazine/1975/03/10/prologue-to-our-time.

Mummert, Amanda, Emily Esche, Joshua Robinson et al. 2011. "Stature and Robusticity during the Agricultural Transition: Evidence from the Bioarchaeological Record." *Economics and Human Biology* 9, no. 3: 284–301.

Peirce, Charles Sanders. 1938. *The Collected Papers of Charles Sanders Peirce, Vols. 1 through 6*. Cambridge: Harvard University Press.

Petkov, Christopher I., and Erich D. Jarvis. 2012. "Birds, Primates, and Spoken Language Origins: Behavioral Phenotypes and Neurobiological Substrates." *Frontiers in Evolutionary Neuroscience*, August 16, 2012, 4: 12.

Pollan, Michael. 2013. "The Intelligent Plant: Scientists Debate a New Way of Understanding Flora." *The New Yorker*, Dec. 23. Retrieved September 28, 2016; www.newyorker.com/magazine/2013/12/23/the-intelligent-plant.

Quinn, Daniel. 2016. "Episode 50: Rewild Yourself." [Blog] *Inside the Mind of Daniel Quinn*. Retrieved September 28, 2016; http://www.danielvitalis.com/rewild-yourself-podcast/inside-the-mind-of-daniel-quinn.

Shepard, Paul. 2011. *Nature and Madness*. Athens: University of Georgia Press.

Simard, Suzanne. 2016. "How Trees Talk to Each Other." TED Talk, June. Retrieved April 27, 2018; https://www.ted.com/talks/suzanne_simard_how_trees_talk_to_each_other/transcript?language=en.

Staal, Frits. 1985. "Mantras and Bird Songs," *Journal of the American Oriental Society*. Indological Studies Dedicated to Daniel H. H. Ingalls. 105, no. 3: 549–58.

Stanner, W. E. H. 1956. "The Dreaming, an Australian World View." In *Australian Signpost: An Anthology*, edited by T. A. G. Hungerford, 51–65. Melbourne: F. W. Cheshire.

Stuart-Glennie, John. 1873. *In the Morningland: Or, the Law of the Origin and Transformation of Christianity—Vol. 1: The New Philosophy of History*. London: Longmans, Green.

———. 1876. *The Modern Revolution. Proemia 1: Pilgrim Memories*. London: Longmans, Green.

———. 1896. "The Survival of Paganism." In *Greek Folk Poesy: Volume 2, Folk Prose*, edited by Lucy M. J. Garnett, 519–20. London: David Nutt.

———. 1901. "The Law of Historical Intellectual Development." *The International Quarterly* 1901, no. 3: 457–58.

Teresi, Dick. 2011. "Discover Interview: Lynn Margulis Says She's Not Controversial, She's Right." *Discover*, June 17. Retrieved September 28, 2016; http://discovermagazine.com/2011/apr/16-interview-lynn-margulis-not-controversial-right.

Wohlleben, Peter. 2016. *The Hidden Life of Trees: What They Feel, How They Communicate—Discoveries from a Secret World*. Vancouver, BC: Greystone Books.

Conclusion

Saïd Amir Arjomand

Comprehensive statements on the axial civilizations debate by Arnason (2003) and Smith (2017) show the Jaspers-Eisenstadt thesis as the dominant paradigm in the field. S. N. Eisenstadt modified Karl Jaspers's idea of the emergence of universal values as a breakthrough in human history in what he called the Axial Age into that of axial civilizations as progenitors of multiple modernities. The Jaspers-Eisenstadt paradigm remains highly influential and has formed the basis for Jürgen Habermas's recent addition of "faith" to "knowledge" in his grand philosophical theory. Although his recent magnum opus (Habermas 2019) retains his earlier commitment to the Western project of Enlightenment modernity (Reason and Liberty, as in Habermas 2019, 2), Habermas now follows Jaspers and Eisenstadt by broadening its axial background via discussions of ancient Judaism, Buddhism, Confucianism, and Daoism (see chapter 1, by Wittrock, above).

We therefore took the Jaspers-Eisenstadt approach as our starting point. Several genealogies with roots in the nineteenth (see Halton) and eighteenth centuries (see Joas 2012) have been proposed for the idea, and our own discussion and contributions also suggested some modification of these genealogies as regards the intervening generation between Jaspers and Eisenstadt. A more crucial substantive result of our symposium has, however, been a return to Max Weber as the true originator of the paradigm for linking the world religions to axial civilization.

Our first four chapters accordingly discuss several aspects of Max Weber that have clear implications for this paradigm's theoretical presuppositions, while chapter 9 offers a radical critique of it. These chapters set the discussion of theoretical issues in a perspective that is considerably broader than that explicitly offered by Eisenstadt. Donald Levine (2004) had found the basic idea of axiality in the writings of the German sociologist of the classical period Georg Simmel. Other German contemporaries more commonly associated with this idea are discussed in chapter 1 by Wittrock. He highlights the importance of Ernst Troeltsch, as well as Jaspers, for an understanding of the historical context that called forth the view of axial shifts as major breakthroughs in human history. Above all, he singled out Max Weber's *Gesammelte Aufsätze zur Religionssoziologie*, the main sociological source of the idea of Axial Age *avant la lettre*. As we have also seen in chapter 1, Hans Joas (2013) draws on Troeltsch and Weber, as well as Jaspers's idea of transcendence, as the key feature of the Axial Age. Following on the volume he edited with the late Robert Bellah (Bellah and Joas 2012), Joas uses axiality as an analytical category to capture important tendencies in the contemporary world as well.

Within the broad framework of the history of ideas sketched by Wittrock, key issues in Weber's sociology of the world religions are examined by Kalberg, Motta, and Lidz. Kalberg, who earlier noted the ways in which the world religions for Weber introduced a rationalization of action anchored in values (Kalberg 1990; 2012, 13–93; 2021) turned here to the causal capacity of *both* "material and ideal interests" in Weber's comparative-historical sociology. The implicit aim of this reexamination of material and ideal interests as motives or causes of social action in Weber is to remedy what he sees as the unwillingness of the Eisenstadt approach to confront causal questions empirically. In this regard, Kalberg addressed in particular the routinization of charisma, the influence of social carriers, and the impact of "lay rationalism." Kalberg is not alone in complaining that the neglect of empirical proof of conjunctural causation is consonant with the pleas for historicizing the axial civilizations made by Arnason (2014) and Arjomand (2014).

In chapter 3, Roberto Motta analyzed the genealogy of Weber's first major contribution to the sociology of religion: his Protestant Ethic thesis. Motta's focus was exclusively on Max Weber. Utilizing likewise a broad framework in chapter 4, Victor Lidz compared Jaspers's view of axial founders as "paradigmatic individuals" to Weber's conception of prophets as charismatic leaders. Max Weber, in short, emerges as the initiating theorist of the civilizational impact of religion.

The remaining four chapters covered further new ground regarding the study of the world religion/axial civilization nexus. In chapter 5, Donald

Nielsen invoked Benjamin Nelson's idea of intercivilizational encounters, as did Yulia Prozorova in chapter 8, thereby suggesting a way forward for civilizational analysis. Nelson's (1980) idea of intercivilizational encounters, as discussed by Nielsen, is entirely compatible with the Jaspers/Eisenstadt paradigm, and offers suggestions for extending it. The term *civilizational analysis* is not found in our initial paradigm and is suggestive of its extension. Benjamin Nelson (d. 1977) was one of its founding members of the International Society for the Comparative Study of Civilizations (ISCSC), was elected president of the organization at its first American convention in Philadelphia in 1971, and remained its president until his death in 1977. The ISCSC gave currency to civilizational analysis in the 1970s. When Edward Tiryakian and I proposed *Rethinking Civilizational Analysis* (Arjomand and Tiryakian 2004), we characterized the encounter of civilizations as an intercivilizational process in contrast to the intracivilizational process that describes the internal dynamics of *each* world religion and its corresponding civilization.

In chapters 6 and 7 by Saïd Amir Arjomand and Armando Salvatore on the Islamicate civilization likewise broaden the parameters of the initial paradigm by bringing in yet another historical, macrosociological approach to the study of civilizations, preceding Eisenstadt's. A major figure in the civilizational analysis of the civilizational impact of Islam discussed by Arjomand and Salvatore extensively is Marshall Hodgson (d. 1968), who was a contributor to the University of Chicago project on the Comparative Social Anthropology of Civilizations led by Robert Redfield, a project that also made significant contributions to the comparative study of the Indian civilization (Arjomand 2010), which is, regrettably, not covered in this volume.

Nielsen's study of Western intercivilizational encounters in the Hellenistic era in chapter 5 is analytically interesting not only owing to the civilizational plurality of the epoch but also because it focuses on a single world region: the Mediterranean world. His chapter points to yet another promising avenue of advancement in civilizational analysis. The Mediterranean as a world region is a perfect example of a *Kulturwelt,* the term Max Weber chose over "civilization." A world region can indeed be fruitfully examined by reference to religio-civilizational encounters; one that may prove to stand at the cutting edge of the field.

The analysis of world regions as civilizational zones was pioneered by Peter Katzenstein (2010). He demonstrates that the coherence of a world region as civilizational zone rests primarily upon cultural factors and only secondarily upon geopolitical factors, as Huntington obsessively argued

(1996). The civilizational forms in different world regions need not be derived from religion (Smith 2010, 122). Long before Weber linked civilizations to world religions—that is, by the end of the eighteenth century—the growth of Orientalism had been responsible for a shift from unitary to pluralist conceptions of civilizations. The Sanskrit-based civilization of the "Hindus" and the Persian-based civilization, which was extended to pre-Islamic Iran with nineteenth-century archaeological discoveries, challenged the idea that Europe was *the* world civilization. For the emerging discipline of Orientalism, *language* rather than religion became the basic and decisive marker (Rudolph 2010, 144). Language is, if anything, the most obvious basis for the formation of a *Kulturwelt* or civilizational zone.

Likewise, Arjomand's study (2016) of the Persianate world brought out the critical significance of the Persian language, in interaction with Arabic, for the expression of Islam and the development of a Persianate variant of the Islamicate civilization. This study also highlighted the autonomy of a civilizational zone as a unit of analysis by noting how Islam's axial dynamics led to the dominance of a world religion in that zone. Following Hodgson's lead in identifying the Persianate phase of the Islamicate civilization, Arjomand founded the Association for the Study of Persianate Societies in 1996 and has edited its organ, the *Journal of Persianate Studies*, since 2008. This journal is devoted to the study of further intra- and intercivilizational dynamics in the Persianate world in an entirely empirical and often historical fashion without any paradigmatic presuppositions.

World regions, world cultures, and civilizational encounters are in fact intimately connected themes. They were jointly included among the six items Arnason (2003) placed on the agenda for civilizational analysis. On this occasion he discussed his treatment of civilizational regions, notably in regard to the civilizational background of Islam (2003, 317–18) and of communism, which he described as an alternative modernity (2003, 332–34). Civilizational zones, or regions, constitute the historical geography—or geopolitical and geocultural setting—of civilizations, and it is incorrect to reduce them to a single world religion. Arguably, nowhere is the confluence of world religions in a civilizational zone more important than in India.

This point is of great importance for the two world religions not covered in this volume, namely, Buddhism and Hinduism. In his volume addressing these world religions, published in English as *The Religion of India*, Weber offers important, albeit somewhat incidental, remarks on their joint civilizational impact as "Asian religions" (Weber 1958, ch. 10). He mainly focused on the multiple reasons for the absence of an indigenous development toward *modern* capitalism in India. In this regard, he emphasized the causal significance of the caste system. Louis Dumont's classic Durkheimian civilizational analysis *Homo Hierarchicus* (1966) likewise focused on castes.

However, neither Weber nor Dumont identified an axial civilization corresponding to Hinduism as a world religion. To do so, and to speak of the Indian civilization, requires consideration of the Indian subcontinent as a world region and, consequently, an analysis of the contributions of Buddhism and Islam to its historical development as a civilizational zone. Sheldon Pollock (1996, 1998) does assess the civilizational impact of Hinduism in reference to the emergence of the Sanskrit cosmopolis and its vernacular offshoots within the Weberian parameters, but the systematic civilizational impact of Buddhism in early India (Collins 1998, ch. 5), pioneered by Romila Thapar (1975; 2003, 164–73, 200–204, 270–79, 317–25), and of Persianate Islam for the later periods remains still to be undertaken. Richard Eaton's (2019) identification of a Persianate cosmopolis, which overlaps the Sanskrit cosmopolis for a millennium, constitutes a first step.

As for Buddhism, Tambiah's (1976) classic study of Theravada Buddhism as a world religion fails to address the issue of its civilizational impact as such. The formation and global impact of Buddhism, especially of Mahayana Buddhism, involves more than one civilizational zone and therefore requires the study of more than one axial civilization. In other words, it requires an approached that locates religious and civilizational encounters in a world region as pioneered by Nelson and as applied by Nielsen in his case study in this volume.

The study of intercivilizational encounters in world regions as civilizational zones can serve as the antipode to Huntington's (1996) geopolitical reification of civilizations as entities with bloody borders. His approach challenges the fundamental premises of the axial civilizations paradigm. This can be clearly demonstrated by studies on the Inner Asian civilizational complex, a region increasingly recognized as important by comparative historians (Arnason 2003, 176). Similar to the Persianate world more generally and the Mediterranean region covered by Nielsen, Inner Asia as a world region (*Kulturwelt*) is especially significant for religio-civilizational pluralism and for encounters across three major world religions: Buddhism, Manichaeism, and Islam. Although now extinct, Manichaeism was the first world religion so defined by its founder (Rudolph 1991); for centuries, it competed with Buddhism and Islam in the East and Christianity in the West. Its impact was transmitted through these world religions.

This brings us back to our title's last word. The "Beyond" recalls Eisenstadt's "multiple modernities" thesis. It raises immediately a puzzle: How can modernization in nonaxial civilizations be explained? Indeed, Eisenstadt's tight linkage of multiple modernities to axial civilizations rendered Japan—a nonaxial civilization and the first non-Western modernizer—an anomaly. He faced the challenge posed by Japan's modernization in *Japanese Civilization* (1996). Eisenstadt acknowledged that Japan never developed a cultural model with a transcendental claim to universal validity. Nonetheless, it proved highly amenable, he argued, to those Western axial civilizations that had given birth to modernity's universalistic civilization (Arnason 2003, 42, 175–76).

Doubtless, Eisenstadt threw considerable light on kingship symbolism's causal importance for the development of the structure of modern Japanese capitalism. Furthermore, he stressed the building of the Japanese modern state as a "family state" oriented to an emperor. Nevertheless, Peter Wagner's (2008) admonition—to avoid superimposing modernization theory upon the axial paradigm—must be heeded. Eisenstadt's *Japanese Civilization* remains too dependent on his roots in modernization theory (Knöbl 2017, 53–54). Alternative modes of civilizational analysis may be equally as or more fruitful with regard to Japan. Eiko Ikegami (1995), for instance, follows Elias's alternative paradigm; she points to state formation as embedded in "the civilizing process" and traces "the taming of the Samurai" back to the progressive sublimation of violence in this culture anchored in honor. It influenced distinctly the developmental path of the Japanese polity—a pattern Edward Tiryakian and Arjomand call an "intracivilizational process" (Arjomand and Tiryakian 2004). Also interesting in Ikegami's contrasting approach is the suggestion of an alternative power/culture nexus that opposes Eisenstadt's multiple modernities paradigm (Spohn 2014). The alternative power/culture nexus from the axial civilizational perspective brings into focus world religions and empires, while from the multiple modernities perspective it highlights the relevance of ancient democracy (Arnason, Raaflaub, and Wagner 2013). Ikegami's focus on power, furthermore, is parallel to Eric Voegelin's characterization of Jaspers's axial breakthrough in ancient Greece—as anthropocentric—emphasized this political dimension, which has been explored more recently for the Greco-Roman world by Raaflaub (2005) and Arnason and Raaflaub (2011).

Concluding with these few remarks on multiple modernities illuminates that which this volume's studies are investigating. All here have stressed the linkage looking backward of the axial civilizations to the world religions. It would be premature to close with any definitive assertions or conclusions concerning the forward linkage of axial civilizations to multiple modernities. As I have argued elsewhere (Arjomand 2013), the challenge of interlocking the idea of multiple modernities with comparative-historical sociology has not yet been met. It remains a task for further study.

References

Arjomand, S. A. 2013. "Multiple Modernities and the Promise of Comparative Sociology." In *Worlds of Difference*, edited by S. A. Arjomand and E. Reis, 15–39. London: Sage.

———. 2014. "Crystallization of Islam and Developmental Patterns in the Islamicate Civilization." In *Social Theory and Area Studies in the Global Age*, edited by S. A. Arjomand, 203–20. Albany: State University of New York Press.

———, and E. A. Tiryakian. 2004. "Introduction." In *Rethinking Civilizational Analysis*, 1–13. London: Sage.

Arnason, J. P. 2003. *Civilizations in Dispute: Historical Questions and Theoretical Traditions*. Leiden: Brill.

———. 2014. "Historicizing Axial Civilizations." In *Social Theory and Regional Studies in the Global Age*, edited by S. A. Arjomand, 179–202. Albany: State University of New York Press.

Arnason, J. P., and K. A. Raaflaub. 2011. *The Roman Empire in Context: Comparative and Historical Perspectives*. Oxford: Blackwell.

Arnason, J. P., K. A. Raaflaub, and P. Wagner, eds. 2013. *The Greek Polis and the Invention of Democracy*. Oxford: Blackwell.

Collins, R. 1998. *Sociology of Philosophies. A Global Theory of Intellectual Change*, Cambridge: Harvard University Press.

Dumont, L. 1966. *Homo hierarchicus: essai sur le système des castes*. Paris: Gallimard.

Eaton. R. M. 2019. "The Persian Cosmopolis (900–1900) and the Sanskrit Cosmopolis (400–1400)." In *The Persianate World: Rethinking a Shared Sphere*, edited by A. Amanat and A. Ashraf, 63–83. Leiden: Brill.

Eisenstadt, S. N. 1996. *Japanese Civilization: A Comparative View*. Chicago: University of Chicago Press.

———. 2002. *Comparative Civilizations and Modernity*. 2 vols. Leiden: Brill.

Elias, N. 1982. *The Civilizing Process, Vol. II: Power& Civility*. New York:

Habermas, J. 2019. *Auch eine Geschichte der Philosophie*: vol. 1: Die okzidentale Konstellation von Glauben und Wissen, vol.: Vernünftige Freiheit. Spuren des Diskurses über Glauben und Wissen. Berlin: Suhrkamp.

Halton, E. 2014. *From the Axial Age to the Moral Revolution: John Stuart-Glennie, Karl Jaspers, and a New Understanding of the Idea*. New York: Palgrave MacMillan.

Huntington, S. 1996. *The Clash of Civilizations and the Remaking of World Order*. New York: Simon and Schuster.

Ikegami, E. 1995. *The Taming of the Samurai: Honorific Individualism and the Making of Modern Japan*. Cambridge: Harvard University Press.

Joas, H. 2012. "The Axial Age Debate as Religious Discourse." In *The Axial Age and Its Consequences*, edited by Robert N. Bellah and Hans Joas, 9–29. Cambridge: The Belknap Press of Harvard University Press.

———. 2013. *The Sacredness of the Person: A New Genealogy of Human Rights*. Washington, DC: Georgetown University Press.

Kalberg, S. 1990 "The Rationalization of Action in Max Weber's Sociology of Religion." *Sociological Theory* 8, no. 1: 58–85.

———. 2012. *Max Weber's Comparative-Historical Sociology Today*. London: Routledge.

———. 2021. *Max Weber's Sociology of Civilizations: A Reconstruction*. London: Routledge.

Katzenstein, P. J., ed. 2010. *Civilizations in World Politics. Plural and Pluralistic Perspectives*. London and New York: Routledge.

Knöbl, W. 2017. "Confronting World/Global History with Eisenstadt's Civilizational Analysis." In *Dynamics of Continuity, Patterns of Change. Between World History and Comparative Historical Sociology*, edited by B. Z.Kedar, I. F. Silber, and A. Klin-Oron. Jerusalem: Israeli Academy of Science and Humanities.

Levine, D. N. 2004. "Note on the Concept of an Axial Turning in Human History." In *Rethinking Civilizational Analysis*, edited by S. A. Arjomand and E. A. Tiryakian, 67–70. London: Sage.

Murphy, P., and J. P. Arnason. 2001. *Agon, Logos, Polis: The Greek Achievement and Its Aftermath*. Stuttgart: Franz Steiner Verlag.

Nelson, B. 1980. *On the Roads to Modernity: Conscience, Science, and Civilizations. Selected Writings*. Totowa, NJ: Rowman and Littlefield.

Pollock, Sh. 1996. "The Sanskrit Cosmopolis, AD 300–1300: Transculturation, Vernacularization, and the Question of Identity." In *Ideology and Status of Sanskrit: Contributions to the History of the Sanskrit Language*, edited by J. E. M. Houben, 197–248. Leiden: Brill.

———. 1998. "India in the Vernacular Millennium: Literary Culture and Polity, 1000–1500." *Daedalus* 127, no. 3: 41–74.

Raaflaub, K. 2005. "'Polis,' 'the Political,' and Political Thought: New Departures in Ancient Greece, c. 800–500BCE." In *Axial Civilizations and World History*, edited by J. P. Arnason, S. N. Eisenstadt, and B.Wittrock. Leiden: Brill.

Rudolph, K. 1991. "Mani und der Iran." In *Manichaia Selecta. Studies Presented to Professor Julien Ries on Occasion of His Seventieth Birthday*, edited by A. van Tangerloo and S. Giversen. Louvain.

Rudolph, S. H. 2010. "Four Variants of Indian Civilization." In *Civilizations in World Politics. Plural and Pluralistic Perspectives*, edited by P. J. Katzenstein, 137–56. London and New York: Routledge.

Smith, J. C. A. 2010. "The Many Americas. Civilization and Modernity in the Atlantic World." *European Journal of Social Theory* 13, no. 1: 117–33.

———. 2017. *Debating Civilizations: Interrogating Civilizational Analysis in a Global Age*. Manchester: Manchester University Press.

Spohn, W. 2014. "Power: Nation-States, Civilizations, and Globalization—A Multiple Modernities Perspective." In *Social Theory and Regional Studies in the Global Age*, edited by S. A. Arjomand, 145–74. Albany: State University of New York Press.

Tambiah, S. 1976. *World Conqueror and World Renouncer*. Cambridge: Cambridge University Press.

Thapar, R. 1975. "Ethics, Religion, and Social Protest in the First Millennium B.C. in Northern India." *Daedalus* 104, no. 2: 119–32.

———. 2003. *The Penguin History of Early India from the Origins to 1300*. New Delhi: Penguin Books India.

Wagner, P. 2008. *Modernity as Experience and Interpretation*. Cambridge: Polity.

Weber, M. 1958. *The Religion of India* Edited and translated by H. H. Gerth and D. Martindale. New York: The Free Press.

Contributors

Saïd Amir Arjomand is the Distinguished Service Professor Emeritus of Sociology at the State University of New York at Stony Brook, and served as director of the Stony Brook Institute for Global Studies (2008–2017). He is the founder and president of the Association for the Study of Persianate Societies, and editor of its interdisciplinary organ, *Journal of Persianate Studies.* He has published extensively in the humanities and social science journals, and is the author of several books, including *The Shadow of God and the Hidden Imam: Religion, Political Organization and Societal Change in Shi'ite Iran from the Beginning to l890* (l984; new ed., 2010), *The Turban for the Crown. The Islamic Revolution in Iran* (1988), and *Rethinking Civilizational Analysis* (with Edward Tiryakian, 2004), and most recently, *After Khomeini. Iran under his Successors* (2009), *The Rule of Law, Islam and Constitutional Politics in Egypt and Iran* (with Nathan J. Brown, 2013), *Worlds of Difference* (with Elisa Reis, 2013), and *Social Theory and Regional Studies in the Global Age* (2014), *The Arab Revolution of 2011: A Comparative Perspective* (2015), *Sociology of Shi`ite Islam. Collected Essays* (2016), and *Revolution: Structure and Meaning in World History* (2019).

Eugene Halton is professor of sociology at The University of Notre Dame. He has written extensively on consumption and materialism, pragmatism, and the problematic nature of modern civilization. His recent works concern a new philosophy of history regarding the limitations of the civilizational mindset, and needed guideposts toward re-attuning contemporary civilization to what he has termed "sustainable wisdom." Halton is author of *From the Axial Age to the Moral Revolution: John Stuart-Glennie, Karl Jaspers, and a New Understanding of the Idea* (Macmillan, 2014), which rewrites the history of the Axial Age, bringing the unknown original theory of

John Stuart-Glennie to light, as well as another previously unknown and unexpected contributor, D. H. Lawrence. He is a coeditor of *Indigenous Sustainable Wisdom: First Nation Know-How for Global Flourishing* (Peter Lang, 2019). Earlier books include *The Great Brain Suck* (2008), *Bereft of Reason: On the Decline of Social Thought and Prospects for its Renewal* (1995) and *Meaning and Modernity* (1986), all with The University of Chicago Press. He is co-author, with Mihaly Csikszentmihalyi, of *The Meaning of Things: Domestic Symbols and the Self* (Cambridge University Press, 1981). This volume is now regarded as a keystone in material culture studies and has been translated into four languages.

Stephen Kalberg is Professor of Sociology Emeritus at Boston University. He is the author of *Max Weber's Comparative-Historical Sociology* (1994), translator of Max Weber's *The Protestant Ethic and the Spirit of Capitalism* (2001, 2011), and editor of *Max Weber: Readings and Commentary on Modernity* (2005) and *The Protestant Ethic and the Spirit of Capitalism with Other Writings on the Rise of the West* (2009). His introduction to Max Weber has been translated into German, Spanish, Italian, Portuguese, and Turkish. Kalberg is also the author of *Les Idees, les Valeurs et les Interets: Introduction a la Sociologie de Max Weber* (2010), *Max Weber's Comparative-Historical Sociology Today* (2012), *Searching for the Spirit of American Democracy: Max Weber's Analysis of a Unique Political Culture Past, Present, and Future* (2014), and *The Social Thought of Max Weber* (2017). His *Max Weber's Sociology of Civilizations: A Reconstruction* is forthcoming in 2021. In addition, Kalberg has authored numerous articles and book chapters that compare German and American societies.

Victor Lidz is Professor Emeritus in the department of psychiatry of the Drexel University College of Medicine, where he served as director of the Division of Substance Abuse Treatment and Research and administrative director of the Center City Clinic, a behavioral health service for HIV+ patients referred from the Drexel infectious disease clinic. As a graduate student, he studied with and was a research assistant for Talcott Parsons. Most of his publications over fifty-odd years have addressed problems in the theory of social action developed by Parsons. He has had long-standing interests in comparative civilizational analysis and in the post-Weberian understanding of the historical path of institutional developments in the modern West.

Roberto Motta, a native Brazilian, after studying philosophy and history in Brazil and abroad, earned a PhD degree in anthropology from Columbia University. His dissertation focused upon the Afro-Brazilian religion of Recife. Now semiretired from the department of sociology of the Universidade Federal de Pernambuco at Recife, Brazil, he has taught and researched elsewhere in Brazil and abroad (Paraíba, Paris, Lyon, Nice, Rome, Naples, Harvard, U.C.L.A.). He is a senior researcher at the National Research Council (CNPQ, Brazil). He has also been an associate foreign member of Groupe Sociétés, Religions, Laïcités, attached to the École Pratique des Hautes Études in Paris. He has published extensively in several languages on religion (including both the Afro-Brazilian and several papers on "the Weber thesis"), social and cultural theory, and race relations. His deep interest in the relationship between religion and society has led him to be increasingly concerned with religious enchantment, disenchantment, and plausibility in the Brazilian and world religions.

Donald A. Nielsen is Professor of Sociology Emeritus at the State University of New York at Oneonta, New York. He is the author, among other books, of *Three Faces of God: Society, Religion, and the Categories of Totality in the Philosophy of Emile Durkheim* (1999) and *Horrible Workers: Max Stirner, Arthur Rimbaud, Robert Johnson, and the Charles Manson Circle* (2005). He has written, as a comparative-historical sociologist, innumerable articles and book chapters, including "Rationalization, Transformations of Consciousness and Inter-Civilizational Encounters" (in *Re-thinking Civilizational Analysis*, edited by Saïd Amir Arjomand and Edward A. Tiryakian, 2004). He is presently examining the "intercivilizational encounters" central to the writings of Benjamin Nelson.

Yulia Prozorova was educated at St. Petersburg State University where she received training in sociology, history, and archaeology. She is currently a senior research fellow at the Sector of the History of Russian Sociology and Centre for Civilizational Analysis and Global History at the Sociological Institute, Federal Centre of Theoretical and Applied Sociology, Russian Academy of Sciences (St. Petersburg). Previously she worked as a curator at the St. Petersburg branch of the Archive of the Russian Academy of Sciences. Her research interests include microsociology of interaction rituals, development of civilizational analysis in historical sociology, Russia's civilizational dynamics and its path to modernity, and political discourse and post-Soviet transformations in Russia. Some of her works are interdisciplinary and cross the boundary between the social sciences and the humanities. Among her latest publications in English are "Civilizational Analysis, Political Discourse, and the Reception of Western Modernity in post-Soviet Russia" (*Comparative Civilizations Review* 77 [2017]); "Civilizational Analysis and Archaeology: Prospects for Collaboration" (*Anthropology and Civilizational Analysis: Eurasian Explorations*, edited. by Johann P. Arnason and Chris Hann. [SUNY Press, 2018]).

Armando Salvatore is the Barbara and Patrick Keenan Chair in Interfaith Studies and professor of global religious studies (Society and Politics) at McGill University. He is a scholar of comparative religion and a historical sociologist. He has taught and researched at Humboldt University Berlin, National University of Singapore, Leipzig University, and Australian National University, Canberra. He is the author of *The Sociology of Islam: Knowledge, Power and Civility* (Wiley Blackwell, 2016) and the chief editor of *The Wiley Blackwell History of Islam* (Wiley Blackwell, 2018) and of *The Oxford Handbook of the Sociology of the Middle East* (Oxford University Press, forthcoming).

Björn Wittrock is the founding director of the Swedish Collegium for Advanced Study and now a Permanent Fellow and a University Professor Emeritus at Uppsala University, He has been president of the International Institute of Sociology (2005–2013) and served on boards of some twenty institutes for advanced study. Wittrock is one of the founders of SIAS, a group of leading institutes for advanced study, and of NetIAS, a European group of such institutes. He is also a member and vice president of the Royal Swedish Academy of Sciences, Academia Europaea, and a member of the American Academy of Arts and Sciences. He is one of the five members of the Holberg Prize Committee. Wittrock has contributed in many publications to the sociology of ancient, medieval, and modern societies and to global history, including *The Cambridge World History*, Vols. IV and V (Cambridge University Press, 2015). He has published five monographs and fifteen edited books, including *Social Science at the Crossroads* (with Shalini Randeria; Brill, 2019), *Axial Civilizations and World History* (with J. P. Arnason and S. N. Eisenstadt; Brill, 2005); *The European and American University since 1800* (with S. Rothblatt; Cambridge University Press, 1993 and 2006). He has received honors from universities, the King of Sweden, and the president of Germany.

Index

A Study of History, 141
Abramowski, Günter, 106
Absolutism, caliphal, 143; theocratic (Orthodox), 198–99, 201, 203
Affirmative mind, 229, 231–32
Afro-Eurasian landmass/*oikoumene*, 7, 142, 162, 165–66, 169–70
Al-Azmeh, Aziz, 137–38
Allah, 137–38
Alexander the Great, 125, 139
Alexandria, 117–18, 121–24
Allgemeine Psychopathologie, 69
Almohads, 146
Almoravids, 146
Ammonius Saccus, 117, 124
Analects, 80
Ancient Judaism, 72
An Introduction to Islamic Law, 140
Andalusia, 152, 169
Animate earth, 213–14, 230, 232
Animate mind, 213–24, 235–36
Animism, 136, 211; new, 232
Anquetil-Duperron, 19
Anthropocene era, 219
Anthropocentric mind, 213–14, 232
Apocalypse, 229, 235
Apocrypha, 121–22
Aquinas, Thomas, 86, 149–50, 152
Aphrodite, 137
Arab Spring, 172
Arabia, 6, 136–39, 169
Arabic, 136, 141, 152
Archaic societies, 23, 29, 71, 87–90, 197
Archimedes, 215–16
Arendt, Hanna, 215–16
Aristotle, 120–21, 125
Aristotelianism, 30, 121, 149
Arnason, Johann P., 19, 33, 36, 161, 187, 203, 239–40
Arjomand, S. A., 6–7, 136, 152–55, 161, 240–41, 244
ʿasabiyya (group solidarity), 144, 149
Assmann, Jan, 26, 33, 210
Association for the Study of Persianate Societies, 242
Athens, 77, 80, 167, 174
Autocracy, 153, Byzantine, 191, Russian, 194, 196–203
Axial Age, 2, 71, 85–89, 183, 187. *See also* transcendence
Axial civilizations, 2–4; and Max Weber, 3; multiple modernities, 3; and world religions, 3; Asian, 7, 4l; Buddhist, 74; Byzantine, 7–8; Chinese, 34–38, 73, 141, 164–66, 209; Hellenic, 1, 19, 164, 171, 192; Indian, 1, 34–38, 73, 141, 149–50, 164–66, 209, 242–43; Hebrew, 164, 193, 209, 211, 221; Islamicate

Axial civilizations *(continued)* (Muslim), 6, 135–55, cities and nomads in, 6; the West (Western civilization), 1, 52, 74, 79–86, 141, 150–53, 162, 164–69, 175–76, 211–16, 220–26
Augustine, St., 75, 86, 91, 124
Axial Civilizations and World History, 33
Axiality, 2, 7, 34, 40–41, 71, 74, 85–88, 150, 161, 163, 183, 187, 240; multiple, 150
aʿyān-amir system, 143

Babylonia, 117, 220
Baghdad, 142, 170
Bandeirantes and Pioneers, 103
Basil I, 202
Basileus, 196–99, 201–202
Bastos, Aureliano Tavares, 95, 102, 105
Becker, C. H., 6, 135, 139–40
Bellah, Robert N., 3–4, 18–19, 26–30, 74–75, 174, 186, 217–19, 227–29, 240
Benares, 174
Bentham, Jeremy, 128
Berber empires, 6, 146, 152
Bird language, 222–23
Brague, Rémi, 174
Brahminism, 58, 150
Brazil, 5, 95–102, 105
Brazil and the Brazilians, 102
Breakthrough, to axiality, 161–63; anthropocentric and theocentric, 2; secondary, 2, 7, 34, 162–63, 184, 186–87; tertiary, 2, 7, 162–63, 166, 176–77; to modernity, 142, 165
Brown, Peter, 27, 178
Buddha, 4, 70, 74–76, 87–89, 228–29, 235
Buddhism, 2, 18, 23, 57, 84, 89, 150, 164–65, 216, 218, 226, 242–43; Hinayana, 81; Mahayana, 81, 164, 243
Burke, Edmund III, 167
Byzantinization, 188–95
Byzantium, 7–8, 188–90, 195, 203, 205

Caesaropapism, 7–8, 186, 199–202, 205
Caliphate, 139, 142, 153–55, 169, 174; Abbasid, 142; Omayyad, 169
Calvin, Jean, 75, 84, 86
Calvinism, 55, 74–75, 86, 101, 106
Canon Law, Russian, 7, 191, 202
Capitalism, 1, 4, 15, 18, 21, 25, 49, 72, 72, 147, 172, 227, 242; and Protestant Ethic, 95–112
Casanova, José, 28
Cassirer, Ernst, 24
Caste system, 57, 84, 149, 243
Catholic Nations and Protestant Nations: Compared in Their Threefold Relations to Wealth, Knowledge, and Morality, 97
Catholicism, 40, 55, 84, 96–105
Chabbi, Jacqueline, 137
Charisma, 5, 71–75; its routinization, 59–60, 74–75, 240
Charismatic leadership, 87–88, 154
Chelhod, Joseph, 2, 135–37
China, ancient, 23, 28, 50, 52, 57, 68, 70, 80, 164–66, 209
Christ the King, 186
Christendom, Latin/Western, 8, 17, 149, 162, 164, 171, 175; Orthodox, 188–201
Christian empire (Byzantine), 189–90, 194
Christianity, 14–17, 20, 79, 83, 86, 116, 147, 149, 162–63, 184–86,

211–13, 218, 220–34; early, 5, 117–18, 121–24; Eastern, 17; Byzantine, 6–7, 186–202; Nestorian, 165; Orthodox/Russian, 6, 183–204; Latin/Western, 7–8, 51–52, 73–74, 149, 167. *See also* Protestantism
Christianization, 186, 188–95, 202
Civic confraternities, Akhi/Futuwwa, 153
Civil society, 152, 175, 190, 194–95
Civilization, 1, 141, 144, 163–64; and empire, 7, 37, 139, 145, 168, 183–204; Christocentric view of 21–22, 162; clash of, 151, 241–43; direction/dynamics of, 5, 9, 30–35, 72, 74, 147, 230; Eurocentric view of, 22, 141, 148, 151, 162, 167, 171–73; in the plural, 1, 5, 242; Japanese, 32, 74, 244; of modernity, 3, 5, 7, 34, 36, 151–52, 174
Civilizational analysis, 7–8, 135–55, 161–77, 187, 241–44; and sociological theory, 6, 11–12, 239–43; black hole in, 7, 167, 170, 176
Civilizing process, 151
Clement of Alexandria, 117
Comparative[-Historical] sociology, 1–2, 6–8, 75, 89, 140, 146–48, 183, 240, 244
Comparative Sociology of Civilizations Chicago Project, 6, 141, 241
Confessions, 124
Confucianism, 2, 19, 23, 37, 57, 81, 84, 287–89
Confucius, 4, 70, 73–89, 228–29, 235
Constantine Monomachus, Emperor, 194
Constantinople, 8, 170, 189, 197
Cook, Michael, 166
Cosmopolitanism, 176–77
Crystallization, cultural, 35, 78, 169, 173, 175
Culture and power, 2, 149–51, 173, 188. *See also* Power-culture nexus
Consciousness and Society, 14

Daedalus, 28
Daoism, 19, 23, 37, 216, 226, 239
Day of Judgment, 83
De la Democratie en Amerique, 100
De l'Avenir des Peuples Catholiques (*Protestantism and Catholicism in Their Bearing*
upon the Liberty and Property of Nations), 97
Deloria, Vive, 219–20
Der Historismus und seine Uberwindung: Funf Vortrage von Ernst Troeltsch, 17
Der Islam, 139–40
Developmental path, 139–40, 148, 203
Die Macht des Heiligen (*The Power of the Sacred: An Alternative to the Narrative of Disenchantment*), 19, 39
Die Stellung des Christentums unter den Weltreligionen, 17
Digest of Justinian, 126
Disenchantment of the world, 39–40
Donald, Merlin, 26, 28, 30, 41
Dozer,T. A. L., 222
Dumont, Louis, 2, 27, 243
Durkheim, Émile, 1–2, 6, 40, 115, 136–38, 164, 173, 243
Durkheimian sociology, 2, 6, 135–38, 243

Eaton, Richard, 243
Ecloga, 191
Economy and Society, 140
Egalitarianism, 175–77

Egypt, 26, 33, 117, 136, 142–44, 153
Eisenstadt, S. N., 2–3, 7, 18, 26–37, 145, 148–51, 155, 161–63, 173, 184–87, 190, 239–40, 244
Elementary Forms of Religious Life, 136
Elias, Norbert, 151, 244
Elkana, Yehuda, 23
Emergence of Islam in Late Antiquity, 137
Enlightenment, 13, 79, 91, 162, 235, 239
Enneads, 124
Enoch, 122
Epanagoge, 192
Epicurianism, 121
Epigenetics, 225
Ethics, 50–54; Archimedean, 215–16
Euripides, 119–20
Ezra, 122

Ficinio, Marcello, 127
First Principles, 123
Fletcher, James Cooley, 102, 105
Forgotten earth, 209–35
Foucault, Michèl, 173
France, 5, 96–99, 104–105, 135–37
Francis, St., 73, 81, 218
Frankfort, Henri, 220
From the Axial Age to the Moral Revolution, 209
Fundamentalism, Islamic, 7, 146–55; Jacobin, 7, 151, 154
Fundamentalism, Sectarianism and Revolutions, 32

Gaius, 125–26
Galileo, 215, 227
Gellner, Ernest, 6, 144–47, 154–55
Genesis, 218, 221
German universities, 16–20, 22
Germany, 3, 22, 25, 97–99, 104, 135–40
Gesammelte Aufsatze zur Religionssoziologie (Collected Essays on the Sociology of Religion), 3, 18, 20, 240
Global Jihad, 155
Globalization, 151, 165
Gods and Kings, 220
Gospels, 79
Greece, ancient, 21, 25, 28, 37, 68, 70, 68, 115, 117, 125, 128, 209
Greek Philosophy, 2, 23, 85, 121, 123–26, 139–40, 211
Gunpowder empires, 144, 171

Habermas, Jürgen, 28, 35–38, 239
Halton, Eugene, 8, 85
Haram/hijr (sacred enclave), 137–38
Harnack, Adolf von, 16
Hegel, G. W. F., 23, 67–68, 96, 100–102, 105, 162
Heidelberg, 3, 22, 25, 32, 69, 91, 139
Hellenism, 19, 70, 116–24, 139, 241
Hellenistic-Roman era, 115–28
Heterodoxy, 149
Hierarchy, 83–84, 124, 149, 192
Hierocracy, 58, 148; Shiʿite, 148, 151, 154
Hinduism, 2, 18, 55–58, 63, 73–74, 84, 150, 242–43
Hijaz, 137, 169
Hodgson, Marshall G. S., 6–7, 135, 141–45, 161, 166–76, 241
Holanda, Sergio Buarque de, 103, 105–106
Homo Hierarchicus, 2, 243
Hughes, H. Stuart, 14
Hume, David, 37, 79, 91, 145
Huntington, Samuel, 162, 241–43
Hyacinthe, Abraham, 19

Ibn Khaldun, Abd al-Rahman, 6, 80, 144–47, 152, 154–55

Ikegami, Eiko, 244
Ilarion, Metropolitan of Kiev, 193–94
Imamate, 148, 174
India, 28, 50, 52, 57, 68
Indonesia, 147
Institutes of Gaius, 125
Institutes of Justinian, 125
Intellectualism, 8
Interests, ideal and material, 49, 59–62, 148
Intracivilizational processes, 128–29, 151, 241, 244
Intercivilizational encounters, 5, 7, 29, 115–29, 135, 150–51, 184–88, 197, 241–43
International Society for the Comparative Study of Civilizations (ISCSC), 241
Introduction to the Sociology of Islam, 136
Iqtāʿ, 143
Iran, 28, 68, 136, 146, 153–54
Isaiah 122, Deutero-Isaiah, 76
Ishtar, 137
Isidore of Seville, 127
ISIS, 172
Islam, 5–8, 74, 86, 135–55, 161–77, 196–97, 209, 220, 234, 241–43
Islamdom, 7, 168–72, 175
Islamic Revolution in Iran, 154, 172
Islamicization, 151
Islamstudien, 6
Israel, ancient, 68, 137–38
Ivan III, 197
Ivan IV, 198, 203

Jainism, 23.
James I of Aragon, 152
Janissaries, 145
Japan, 80
Japanese Civilization: A Comparative View, 32, 244
Jaspers, K., 2–6, 22, 24–37, 67–71, 75–85, 89, 135, 162, 188, 209–13, 228–29
Jerome, 118
Jerusalem, 32, 174
Jesus, 4, 8, 70, 67–89, 228–29, 235
Jihadists, 155
Joas, Hans, 19, 24, 28–29, 38–41, 240
Job, 122
John, St., 218
Journal of Persianate Studies, 242
Judaism, 5, 18, 37, 57, 63, 117–24, 128, 138, 162–63, 186, 209, 218, 220, 239
Jurisprudence, Islamic, 150–70, as jurists' law, 140; Roman, 124–27; Russian Canon Law, 191

Kabash, 221
Kalberg, Stephen, 4, 91, 105–106, 240
Kant, Immanuel, 37–38, 79, 91
Karma, 55
Katzenstein, Peter, 241–42
Khan, 196–97
Khatami, Mohammad, 154
Khomeini, Ayatollah, 154
Kiev, 194–95
Kingship, 150, 191, 194; sacral, 150, 185–86, 193, 198, 201–204, 217
Kinship and Marriage in Early Arabia, 136
Kormcaja knjiga, 191
Kuenen, Abraham, 15
Kulturwelt, 1, 241–43

Lady Chatterley's Lover, 229
Lao-Tse, 75, 91
Lasaulx, Ernst von, 19
Lāt, 137
Late antiquity, 37, 139, 162, 165–83, 186–88

Latin, 118, 127–68
Laws, 119
Lawrence, D. H., 228–35
Lévi-Strauss, Claude, 137
Levine, Donald N., 240
Laveleye, Émile de, 95, 98–99, 103, 105
Lectures on the Philosophy of History, 102
Lex talionis, 117–18
Lidz, Victor, 4–5, 240
Living earth, 8
Luther or the Advent of the Self, 100
Lutheranism, 51, 55

Macarius, Metropolitan, 198
Madrasa, 144, 153
Maghreb, 153
Maine, Henry Sumner, 128
Mamluk, 143–46, 149–51, 153–54
Man in the Modern Age, 80
Manāt, 137
Mandarins (Confucian *literati*), 73–74, 81, 83–84
Manichaeism, 124, 165, 243
Marabouts (Sufi saints), 6, 145–48
Marucs Aurelius, 125
Margulis, Lynn, 225
Maritain, Jacques, 100
Marx, Karl, 38, 128, 173
Maslaha, 150, 170
Mauss, Marcel, 1, 40, 115, 129, 164
McNeill, William, 141–42
Mecca, 137
Mechanico-centric mind, 214, 217, 227, 235–36
Medina, 137
Meineke, Friedrich, 21–22
Mencius, 81
Mesopotamia, 26, 33
Messianism, Russian, 198, 203; Shiʿite, 149
Metaphysics, 120
Meyer, Eduard, 33
Meyer, John, 36
Michalowsky, Piotr, 33
Middle Period (in Islamic history), 170–71
Military-patronage system, 143–44
Modernity, 31–34, 80, 85, 104, 141–42, 146, 151, 153–54, 163, 166; alternative, 154, 242; and tradition, 148, 154; early, 171; civilization of, 3, 7; European/Western, 1, 68–69, 166, 174, 239; and social sciences, 3
Modernities, Islamic, 166; multiple modernities, 2–3, 5–8, 32–36, 148, 151–54, 239, 243–44
Modernization theory, 1, 12, 148, 244
Mohammad, 74–77, 86–89, 135, 137–40, 156
Mohism, 23
Momigliano, Arnaldo, 27
Mongols, 8, 170–71, 196–97, 200, 202
Monotheism, 138, 185–86, 220, 230; and empire, 188, 190, 198, 200–201
Moog, Vianna, 103–105
Moore, George Foot, 19
Moral Revolution, 85, 89, 209–36
Moscow, 196, 198–99, 202
Moses, 123
Motta, Roberto, 5, 240–41
Mudéjar, 152
Münch, Paul, 98
Mughal empire, 144, 171
Multiverse. *See* Transcivilizational ecumene
Mumford, Lewis, 228–29
Municipal self-government; in Kiev, 194–95; in Islamdom, 153
Muscovy, 8, 196–99, 202–203
Muslim diaspora, 155

Muslim societies, 6–7, 144–49, 153, 169–70
Mysticism, 74, 201
Mythical thinking, 23–24, 28, 82

Naqshbandi order, 147
Nāser le-Din Allāh, ʿAbbasid Caliph, 142, 152–53
Nationalism, 146, 148
Native American religion, 219–20, 232
Naturalism (Naturianism), 211–23, 220, 231
Nicephorus, Metropolitan of Kiev, 194
Nef, John U., 141
Nelson, Benjamin, 116, 135, 152, 241
Neo-Platonism, 117, 124
Nielsen, Donald, 5–6, 241, 243
Nile to Oxus region, 142, 144, 170–72, 176–77
Nipperdey, Thomas, 99
Nomadic empires/kingdoms, 143
Nomadic pastoralism, 6, 144–47. *See also* Turko-Mongolian empires
Nomocanon, 192
Novella VI of Justinian, 192
Novellae, 191
Number-atomism, 120

Objectivism, 214, 216, 227
Occident, *see* Axial civilizations, the West
Old Testament, 70, 73–76, 79, 81, 91, 117, 121–24; Higher Criticism of, 136
Orientalism, 166–68, 171, 175–77
Origen, 117, 121, 123–24
Origins of the Muhammadan Jurisprudence, 140
Otto, Rudolph, 19
Ottoman empire, 144, 168, 170–71

Paleo-Islam, 138–39
Panzooinism, 210–12, 216, 218, 224, 232
Papal Revolution, 7
Paradigmatic individuals, 4–5, 71, 75–79, 81–82, 88–89, 135, 240; as charismatic leaders, 87–88
Parsons, Talcott, 12, 20–27, 31, 75, 90–91, 147
Patriarch Anthony IV, 202
Patriarch of Moscow, 199
Patriarchate, 199–200
Patrimonialism, 143, 145, 200–201
Peacock, James, 147
Peirce, Charles, 225
Pereira, Eduardo Carlos, 95, 98, 102–103
Persian, 136, 141–43, 242
Persian. *See* Iran
Peter the Great, 200
Petty, Richard, 128
Peyrefitte, Alain, 104, 106
Philo, 117, 121, 234–24
Phoenician Women, 119
Plato, 8, 78, 86, 89, 91, 119–27, 229
Platonism, 30, 37, 121, 123; Middle, 121, 123
Plotinus, 91, 117, 124
Pollock, Sheldon, 32, 243
Power-culture nexus, 144, 172–75, 244
Political religion, 140, 204
Political theology, 139, 184, 186–89, 191–99, 202
Politics, 152–53
Post-colonial critique, 167
Post-Traditional Societies, 148
Primal morality, 215, 219, 235
Princeps legibus solutus, 8, 200–201
Prolegomena to the History of Ancient Israel, 136
Prophets, 6, 53–54, 59, 61, 122, 218, 240; Hebrew, 2, 73, 164, 193, 220
Protestant Ethic Thesis, 4–5, 25, 49–50, 95–112, 147, 240

Provincializing Europe, 167
Prozorova, Yulia, 7–8, 241
Pseudepigrapha, 121–22
Putin, Vladimir, 8
Pythagoras, 120
Pythagorianism, 119–21, 127

Quinn, Daniel, 218, 226
Quraysh, 137

Radcliffe-Brown, A. R., 2
Rationalism, religious, 4, 50–56, 74–75; lay, 4, 55, 57, 60–61, 139–40, 240; Western, 80
Rationalization, 1, 4, 54–55, 74–75, 116, 122–23, 125, 129, 140, 240; theoretical, 116, 227
Rational Liberty. Traces of the Discourse on Faith and Knowledge, 36
Redfield, Robert, 6, 141, 241
Reflexivity, 23, 28–29, 185
Reformation, 7, 100, 106, 215; Petrine, 200
Relationalism, 213
Religionssoziologie, 72
Religion of China, 72
Religion of India, 72, 242
Religion as Human Evolution: From the Paleolithic to the Axial Age, 26, 28
Religio-political nexus, 7, 184–94
Republic, 119
Res publica christiana, 149–50, 170
Rethinking Civilizational Analysis, 151
Rethinking World History, 142
Robertson Smith, W., 136–38
Rome, ancient, 115, 124–25; Third, 8, 198, 200, 202
Roussel, Napoléon, 95, 97–101, 105
Rulership, 118–19, 150; Byzantine, 192–94, 197–98; Rus, Kievan, 7–8, 190–96. *See also* Kingship
Russia, 7–8, 75, 183–204; Canon Law of, 190–91, 202, post-Soviet, 8, 204

Sacredness of the person, 17, 41, 217–18
Safavid empire, 144, 171
Saintliness (*walaya*), 174
Salafiyya, 147, 155, 176
Salvation, 4, 50, 53–54, 189–90
Salvatore, Armando, 2, 7–8, 149, 241
Sanskrit, 31–32, 242–43
Sanskritic culture, 171–72
Sanskritization, 151
Schacht, Joseph, 140
Schluchter, Wolfgang, 18–19, 31–32, 75
Schwartz, Benjamin, 19, 23, 27
Scientific outlook, 13, 96, 211–12, 215–16, 231, 234–35; humanism, 212–13
Secondary-order thinking, 23, 233
Seedbed societies, 25, 116
Shadow of God and the Hidden Imam, 152
Shariʿa, 143, 170, 172
Shatibi, Abu Ishaq al-, 150
Shepard, Paul, 221, 226
Shiʿism, 148, 152, 154–55
Simmel, Georg, 79, 240
Singer, Milton, 141
Slavic states, 191
Slavonic, 191, 193
Smith, D. E., 147–48
Smith, Reuben W., 142
Social bearers/carriers (*Träger*), 57–59, 148–50, 154–55, 173, 201, 240
Societies: Evolutionary and Comparative Perspectives, 25
Sociology of Religion, 4, 14, 16, 18, 20, 25, 40–41, 50–62, 68, 135–36, 152, 155

Sociology of Islam, 148, 152
Sociology of Shi^cite Islam, 148, 152
Socrates, 4, 70, 75, 83, 228–29, 235
Sohravardi, Shaykh Abu Hafs ʿOmar, 142
Sophist, 125
Soteriology, 73, 75, 84–85
Soviet state, 201, 204
Stahl, Frits, 223
Stalin, Joseph, 8
Stanner, W. E. H., 232
Stoicism, 121
Stuart-Glennie, John, 8, 19, 85, 209–13, 220, 228
Sultanate, 144, 153
Sultanism, 143, 145
Sufism, 142–43, 154, 170–71, 177
Summa Contra Gentiles, 152
Supernaturalism, 211–13, 220
Symbiogenesis, 225
Symphonia paradigm (Orthodox diarchy), 8, 189–92, 199–200, 203
Syria, 142–44, 153, 155, 169

Tambiah, Stanley, 243
Taylor, Charles, 28
Taylor, Zachary C., 98–99, 105
Thaqif, 137
Thapar, Romila, 243
The Axial Age and Its Consequences, 28
The Cambridge World History, 166
The Creativity of Action, 37
The Future of the Catholic Peoples, 98
The Great Forgetting, 226
The Great Revolutions and the Civilizations of Modernity, 34
The Great Philosophers, 4, 70, 75, 82, 85–88, 228
The Hidden Life of Trees: What They Feel, How They Communicate—Discoveries from a Secret World, 224
The Natural History of Religion, 40
The Occidental Constellation of Faith and Knowledge, 36
The Origins and Diversity of Axial Age Civilizations, 31
The Origins and Goals of History (Vom Ursprung und Ziel der Geschichte), 20, 22, 24, 67, 69–70, 75, 80, 85, 90, 228
The Political Systems of Empires, 26
The Philosophy of Symbolic Forms, 24
The Protestant Ethic and the Spirit of Capitalism, 4, 72, 95, 100, 102; Brazilian view of, 101–105
The Religion of India, 243
The Religion of the Semites, 136
The Religious Problem of Latin America, 102–103
The Rise of the West, 141
The Sacredness of the Person: A New Genealogy of Human Rights, 39
The Venture of Islam. Conscience and History in a World Civilization, 6, 142
Theoretic thinking, 28–29, 217–19, 133
Theocracy, 148, 154, 186; Byzantine, 192–93, 199, 201
Theodicy, 52–56, 61–62, 84–85
Thrasyllus, 117
Timaeus, 127
Tiryakian, Edward A., 151, 244
Tocqueville, Alexis de, 5, 95–96, 99–103, 105
Toynbee, Arnold, 141
Tradition, Great and Little, 141, 151; and modernity, 148
Tragic excursus, 228–30
Transcendence, 2–3, 41, 190–91, 216–20, 233, 236, 240
Transcivilizational ecumene/formation, 7, 162–77

Transnationalization, 172
Troeltsch, Ernst, 3, 12–20, 39–41, 240
Tsar, 8, 196–201
Turko-Mongolian empires, 153–54; in Russia, 8, 196–97; tribal confederations, 164–65
Turner, Bryan S., 136, 152–55
Tylor, E. B., 211

Ulema, 145–46, 149–51, 154–55, 174, 177
Ulpian, 126
Unger, Roberto Mangabeira, 28
University of Chicago, 141
Upanishads, 23, 76
Utopia, 148–49
ʿUzzā, 137

Values, 4–5, 9, 50–54, 59–62
Veches, Kievan, 194–95
Villers, Charles de, 95, 97, 99–100, 105
Vladimir II Monomach, 194
Vladimir the Great, 194
Voegelin, Eric, 24
Vulgate, 118, 124

Wagner, Peter, 244
Was ist die Achsenzeit?, 19
Weber, Alfred, 1, 22, 24
Weber, Max, 1, 3–8, 13–24, 39, 49–62, 69–80, 95–112, 116, 135, 138–40, 143, 146–67, 154, 201, 231; and the Axial Age, 19; and axial civilizations, 3, 18–20, 239–43; and charisma, 69–75; and rationalization, 116; and world religions, 6–7, 13–21, 138–39; causal adequacy in, 139; ideas and interest in, 4, 49, 59–62; multicausality in, 4, 50, 57–62, 240
Weil, Eric, 27
Wellhausen, Julius, 136, 138–40
West. *See* Axial civilizations, the West
Westernization, 151
Westphalian order, 169, 172–74
What the Robin Knows, 222
Wisdom (*sofia*), 117, 121–22; in early-modern and modern Europe, 127–28; in medieval Europe, 127
Wisdom of Solomon, 116–18, 127
Wittrock, Björn, 3, 32–33, 161, 239–40
Wohlleben, Peter, 224–25
World History, 30–35, 39–41, 142–44, 155
World region, 241–43; Central Afro-Eurasia, 7, 165; Central Asia, 153, 165, 243; Eurasia, 144, 183, 187; India, 68–70, 231, 241–43; Inner Asia, 243; Irano-Semitic civilizational zone, 170–74, 176–77; the Mediterranean, 5, 31, 68, 115, 125, 168–69, 241, 243; Middle East and North Africa, 31, 76, 147, 151; North Atlantic, 12; the Persianate world, 141, 170–77, 242–43
World religions, 1–2; Abrahamic, 138, 140, 142, 216, 220, 226; and sociological theory, 6, 13–20. *See also* Buddhism, Christianity, Confucianism, Hinduism, Islam, Judaism, Manichaeism
Worldview (*Weltbild*), 50–54, 59, 61, 195, 214; modern, 227–29

Yemen, 137
Young, Jon, 222

Zeno of Elea, 120
Zakon Sudnyi Liudem, 191
Zoroaster, 68